VALUE AND UNDERSTANDING

Value and Understanding

Essays for Peter Winch

EDITED BY RAIMOND GAITA

ROUTLEDGE
LONDON AND NEW YORK

First published 1990
by Routledge
11 New Fetter Lane, London EC4P 4EE

Simultaneously published in the USA and Canada
by Routledge
a division of Routledge, Chapman and Hall, Inc.
29 West 35th Street,
New York, NY 10001

© 1990 Raimond Gaita

Typeset in 10/12 Baskerville by Laserscript, Mitcham, Surrey
Printed in Great Britain by TJ Press (Padstow) Ltd, Padstow, Cornwall

British Library Cataloguing in Publication Data
Value and understanding : essays for Peter Winch.
Gaita, Raimond II. Winch, Peter
100

Library of Congress Cataloging in Publication Data
Value and understanding: essays for Peter Winch/edited by Raimond
Gaita.
p. cm.
ISBN 0-415-04150-3
1. Philosophy. 2. Ethics. 3. Wittgenstein, Ludwig, 1889–1951. 4. Winch,
Peter. I. Winch, Peter. II. Gaita, Raimond, 1946–
B29.V324 1990
100–dc20   89–10362
                                                                                                      CIP

CONTENTS

CONTRIBUTORS

KARL-OTTO APEL, Professor of Philosophy, Johann Wolfgang
    Goethe-Universität
FRANK CIOFFI, Professor of Philosophy, University of Essex
CORA DIAMOND, Professor of Philosophy, University of Virginia
İLHAM DİLMAN, Professor of Philosophy, University College of
    Swansea
RAIMOND GAITA, Lecturer in Philosophy, University of London
    King's College
LARS HERTZBERG, Professor of Philosophy, Abo Academy
R. F. HOLLAND, formerly Professor of Philosophy, University of
    Leeds
ALASDAIR MACINTYRE, Professor of Philosophy, University of
    Notre Dame
NORMAN MALCOLM, Visiting Professor of Philosophy,
    University of London, King's College
GRAEME MARSHALL, Reader in Philosophy, The University of
    Melbourne
D. Z. PHILLIPS, Professor of Philosophy, University College of
    Swansea
DAN RASHID, Nuffield Research Fellow, Centre for the Study of
    Philosophy and Health Care, University College of Swansea
RUSH RHEES, late Honorary Professor of Philosophy, University
    College of Swansea

INTRODUCTION

Wittgenstein said that a philosopher who did not join in discussion is like a boxer who never went into the ring.[1] Most philosophers believe that discussion is important to philosophy but few would believe, and even fewer would have a conception of the subject which allowed them to believe, that discussion could have that kind and degree of importance. Wittgenstein would not have said the same about a philosopher who did not write (he is plainly thinking of verbal discussion) and since a boxer who avoids getting into the ring is hardly a boxer, so a philosopher who avoids discussion is (in Wittgenstein's eyes) hardly a philosopher. I will leave the internality suggested here between philosophy and discussion as weak and as ill-defined as that, but it is strong enough to reveal that Wittgenstein is one of the most Socratic of the great philosophers. He is one of the few great philosophers who judged discussion to be more than accidental to the character of philosophy. The idea that we need to discuss with others because of our contingently limited epistemic and logical powers is what I would call an *accidental* need of discussion with them.

Those who had frequent discussions with Peter Winch will see the point of Wittgenstein's simile. It is not, of course, that one must reveal what one is capable of in competitive discussion. Discussion with Winch reveals that (as Stanley Cavell puts it) '"not saying anything" is one way philosophers do not know what they mean. In this case it is not that they mean something *other* than they say, but that they do not see that they mean *nothing* (that *they* mean nothing, not that their statements mean nothing, are nonsense). The extent to which this is, or seems true, is astonishing.'[2] That, too, is not something that many philosophers will deny, but there are some who know it in their bones and there are others who would merely assent to its truth as a proposition. Winch knows it in his bones and those who discuss anything at length with him are likely to come to know it that way too; they are likely to think it amongst the deepest of their philosophical lessons. It matters that such discussion should be at length, for it matters that we be driven, like Hylas in Berkeley's *Dialogues*, into every spurious formulation of a point which we can devise only to find either that we have said nothing or that what we said is considerably less profound than we had believed it was. That does not come out in short discussion and it certainly does not come out in those discussions which condition part of the very character of the academic practice of the subject – those discussions, for an hour or so, which follow the delivery of a paper.

To repeatedly discover that we said nothing is to learn a dimension of philosophical depth and seriousness: that was Socrates' lesson and, in a different way, it was Wittgenstein's. Winch is one of the few contemporary philosophers who not only reveals that depth but who also reveals that reflection on it is itself vulnerable to exactly the same danger and that someone who does not realize it will mistake depth for one of its semblances. The nature of philosophical seriousness (as a practice) and the nature of what it is seriously to say or judge something are problematic in themselves and in their relation to one another, in ways that determine the character of philosophy's need to question itself.

It is therefore fitting that the first three essays in the volume critically discuss Winch's British Academy Lecture 'Ceasing to exist'. In this lecture Winch discusses a story by Isaac Bashevis Singer in which a shed is said to have disappeared in the sense of having simply 'ceased to exist'. Winch is interested in the question what would it be 'for me seriously to judge an object to have ceased to exist'? His interest is in the concept of 'seriously judging something to be possible' and the essay is an exploration of what it may amount to in such an example. But it obviously has a more general relevance and is to be found, in one form or another, in most of his work.

One way of seeing the importance of the concept of what it is seriously to judge something to be so or to be possible is by seeing how important it is in the formulation of philosophical scepticism. Towards the end of the *First Meditation* Descartes says 'I am forced to admit that there are none of the things I used to think were true which may not possibly be doubted; and not because of carelessness or frivolity but for sound and well considered reasons'. Here Descartes, or more accurately, the *persona* of the *Meditations,* is protesting the seriousness of his doubt, but he does not at any stage consider what conditions the concept of seriously judging that it is possible that, for example, he may be dreaming. He does not ask whether the human life which he thinks he may merely have dreamt conditioned the modal concepts with which he tries to express his earnest sense of the sobriety of his doubts. That is why he is able to conclude that the conditions of ordinary human life merely make it difficult for him to doubt what he professes seriously to doubt *qua* philosopher. Much the same is true of the mainstream of the philosophical tradition after Descartes.

Cavell says in *The Claim of Reason* that traditional epistemology is a 'denial of the human'. He means that the concepts in the light of which epistemological and logical questions have been raised and answered have been thought of as essentially unconditioned by the fact that they are concepts deployed by human beings. Much of philosophy is then conceived of as a struggle against the irrelevant human associations which attach themselves to such concepts and to the natural languages in which they are expressed. This can be an edifying conception: it goes with a conception of philosophical depth and purity, and philosophers are more vulnerable to its edifying resonances than they are aware of or are likely to admit. A sense of it marks Wittgenstein's *Tractatus* and accounts for much of its beauty. His struggle with it is recorded in *Culture and Value.*[3]

In his later philosophy, Wittgenstein revealed that much of what the philosophical tradition had judged to be superficial and peripheral to the concepts which particularly interest philosophers was essential to them. He revealed that the grammar of the very concepts necessary to any exploration of what is superficial and what is not – the concept of seriously judging something to be possible, for example – was conditioned by the quite concrete form which life took for those who reflected on such matters. Peter Winch's work is marked by his deep awareness of this, the most fundamental aspect of Wittgenstein's legacy – that we cannot purify our concepts of their embeddedness in human life and of their expression in natural languages without being left with only a shadow play of the grammar of serious judgment. That shadow play – sentences found on blackboards in many philosophy classrooms, or on the blackboard of the metaphysician's mind – has, at least since Descartes, been sustained and mistaken for something more substantial because of a mistaken conception of the relation between philosophy and ordinary human practices. Its contemporary form is in many uses of the contrast between truth and assertion conditions.

The human conditioning of what we can seriously find intelligible, of what we can seriously judge to be possible and impossible, the suspicion of an illusory transcendence – this theme and its variations unite the voices in this volume in different tones of sympathy and criticism. But it would be quite unlike Winch to assume that there is one way in which our concepts are embedded in a 'form of life', or that seriously judging something to be possible is going to be the same kind of thing across different subject matters. In this volume the issue is first raised in metaphysics and the philosophy of logic and is then pursued in ethics and the philosophy of the social sciences. Wittgenstein is the deepest influence in Winch's work: the volume therefore includes an essay discussing Winch on Wittgenstein.

Raimond Gaita
London, February, 1989

NOTES

1. M.O'C. Drury, *The Danger of Words* (London: Routledge & Kegan Paul, 1972,) p. vii.
2. S. Cavell, *The Claim of Reason* (Oxford: Oxford University Press, 1979) p. 210.
3. L. Wittgenstein, *Culture and Value*, trans. P. Winch (Cambridge: Blackwell, 1980).

Chapter One

ON 'CEASING TO EXIST'

NORMAN MALCOLM

In 1982 Professor Peter Winch gave a fascinating lecture to the British Academy.[1] The topic with which he began was Descartes's contention that 'finite substances depend on God's creative power not merely in respect of their origin, but equally in respect of their continuing existence'.[2] As Descartes puts it, 'in order to be conserved in each moment in which it endures, a substance has need of the same power and action as would be necessary to produce and create it anew'.[3] Winch interprets Descartes's view, rightly I believe, as implying that there is nothing in the nature of any finite being 'considered in itself which supports any presumption that it will continue to exist from one moment to the next'.[4] Descartes's 'contention is that there is nothing in the conception of a thing's existence at a given moment that implies anything at all about its existence at any other moment'.[5]

In considering Descartes's view Winch makes use of a story by Isaac Bashevis Singer. Zalman the glazier relates the following incident:

> Near Blonia there lived a man, Reb Zelig, the bailiff. He had a store and a shed where he kept kindling wood, flax, potatoes, old ropes. He had a sleigh there too. He got up one morning and the shed was gone. He could not believe his eyes. If during the night there had been a wind, a storm, a flood. But it happened after Pentecost – calm days, quiet nights. At first he thought he had lost his mind. He called his wife, his children. They ran out. 'Where is the shed?' There was no shed. Where it had been, everything was smooth – high grass, no beams, shingles, no sign of a foundation. Nothing.[6]

1

Everyone in the small town of Blonia knew Zelig the bailiff. When they went for a walk they usually passed the shed, and if it was raining they took shelter inside it. As the news passed around the whole town came running. 'People pinched their cheeks to make sure they were not dreaming.' They walked around the field and even dug in the earth where the shed had been, but found nothing. Two men drove for miles trying to locate the lost shed. 'They asked the peasants, but no one had heard or seen anything.' Zalman the glazier sums up the incident in these words: 'A heavy shed built of logs had burst like a bubble.'

We can enjoy this story as fantasy. Winch puts the difficult question of whether we could *understand* the story as a serious factual account of something that had happened. He links the temptation to think that we *could* with the conception that underlies Descartes's view:

> The existence of something or someone at one time, we think, is a totally distinct state of affairs from its existence at another time and is logically consistent with its non-existence at another time. So we can conjoin the judgement of the object's existence on Monday with the judgement of its non-existence on Tuesday with perfect consistency. Any further judgements we may or may not make about what happened between Monday and Tuesday are a completely different matter, having no bearing on the intelligibility of the conjunction . . .[7]

Winch says, rightly, that if someone who was trying to give a serious account of what happened to the shed, were to say 'It simply ceased to exist', or 'It just vanished', he would not be offering an *explanation* of what happened to the shed. Indeed, 'It simply ceased to exist' would come to the same as 'It ceased to exist without there being any explanation of its ceasing to exist'.

Winch asks us to reflect on the sentence: 'The shed existed on Monday and did not exist on Tuesday'. He remarks that 'our understanding' of this sentence 'is such as to presuppose that the shed was destroyed between Monday and Tuesday in *some* intelligible way. And what is an intelligible way is limited by our understanding of what a shed is.'[8]

According to Zalman's tale the shed was not destroyed in any

2

intelligible way. It was not torn down, or burned up, or blown to pieces in a tornado, or shattered by an earthquake or an explosion. A shed of heavy logs cannot 'melt away like ice' nor can it 'burst like a soap bubble'. It cannot even be said that the shed was 'destroyed'. To say that it was would imply that it was destroyed in some way or other. But the story makes it clear that there was *no way* in which the shed was *destroyed*. 'It was destroyed' is not a possible explanation of *what happened* to the shed.

Nor does the story provide us with any other possible explanation of what happened to the shed. No people moved it to another location. No cyclone picked it up and set it down elsewhere. It did not sink into the earth.

Can we say that the shed 'disappeared'? We can – but we won't be using that word as it is ordinarily used. A ship disappears over the horizon, a squirrel disappears in the tree top, a mouse disappears in its hole: but to say this does not imply that ship, squirrel, or mouse ceased to exist. Sometimes we do use the word 'disappeared' with that implication, as when we say that in two minutes after the ice cream was given to the children it had disappeared, or that the water in the saucer on the window sill disappeared. But here explanations are ready to hand: the ice cream was eaten up, the water evaporated. In Zalman's tale there is no explanation of what happened to the shed. If we speak of its 'disappearance', as I shall, this will mean no more and no less than its 'ceasing to exist'.

So far, I am in agreement with Peter Winch. The intention of Zalman's story is to deprive us of any description of what happened to the shed. To say 'It ceased to exist' is not to give a description of *what happened* to it. If someone who was fully aware of what did *not* happen to the shed were to say 'It simply ceased to exist', he would be using those words to imply that there is no description of what happened to it.

Let us consider again the conjunctive sentence, 'The shed existed on Monday and did not exist on Tuesday'. Winch says that our understanding of this sentence 'presupposes' that the shed was destroyed 'in some intelligible way'. I have just argued that it cannot be said that the shed was *destroyed*. Are we to conclude that this conjunctive sentence is not intelligible when applied to the incident of the shed? Is this 'a form of words to which, in these circumstances, we can attach no sense' – as Winch says in a similar connection?[9]

I think it depends on who *we* are. If we had never been in the vicinity of Blonia and knew none of its inhabitants, but had only read of this alleged incident, then, no doubt, we would respond with amused disbelief. We would think there was a prank at the bottom of it, or if not a prank then a strange delusion.

But if we were members of the Reb Zelig family our reaction would be radically different: a prank would be ruled out, since a heavy shed of logs could not be dismantled in the night without a disturbance which we would have heard. Furthermore, there would be evidence in the earth of where the shed had stood, instead of 'high grass' and 'no sign of a foundation'.

Could we believe that we were deluded by bizarre memory impressions of a shed? Surely not. We had gone to the shed every day for years to fetch kindling wood and potatoes. It was where we kept our tools: the children played there on rainy days: last summer we spent several days putting new shingles on the roof of the shed – and so on, and so on. The shed had figured in our lives in countless ways. We could not seriously entertain the thought that there had never been a shed there: for this would mean a complete dislocation of our thinking about *anything*. It would mean that we should no longer know *who* we are or *where* we are. As Wittgenstein says in a similar connection: 'the foundation of all judging would be taken away.'[10]

The inexplicable disappearance of the shed would be a tremendous shock. Zalman says of Reb Zelig: 'At first he thought he had lost his mind.' But would it not be easier for Reb Zelig and his family to come to terms with the belief that the shed had inexplicably ceased to exist, than with the conception that a long stretch of their lives – of daily perceptions, actions, work, worries, conversations – was pure delusion?

Peter Winch puts considerable emphasis on the fact that memory impressions, no matter how strong, do not have unimpeachable authority. As he says, memory claims are corrected or rejected on the ground of what *can* or *cannot* happen. If someone declared that he vividly remembers having disembarked in Madrid from an ocean liner, we would laugh and say, 'No. You *can't* have done that: It's a geographical impossibility.' Or I am exasperated by the disappearance of my pen: I 'distinctly remember' that it was on my desk only a moment ago; after much searching it turns up in the kitchen. I won't consider it to be a possibility that the pen travelled there by itself. I admit, reluctantly, that my memory impression was false.

Winch is certainly right in holding that when our understanding of the causal powers of objects collides with our confident memory impressions, this can force us to renounce the latter. Our thinking and judging *can*, and often does, take that direction. But whether this *will* happen depends on our particular situation. It is by no means a foregone conclusion that our understanding of the causal properties of physical things will take priority over our understanding of what our past has been.

Winch invokes the notion of 'the stream of life'. In elucidating it he stresses 'the interconnection between my present understanding of the situation I am in at this moment, what I can recollect about the antecedents of this situation, and my understanding of the causal properties of, and relations between, the objects in my environment'.[11] I do not disagree with that.

But Winch applies this notion in a way which seems to me to be too general. He says that to accept that something like a shed could just cease to exist from one moment to the next, is to remove both the object in question and oneself contemplating it from that 'stream'. But this removal is a cancellation of the conditions under which anything one says or thinks has sense: *including* the words 'It has ceased to exist'.[12]

I think this would not be true for *everyone* in *all* circumstances. If you were a member of the Zelig family, presented with this astonishing situation, wouldn't you *have* to say or think, 'The shed just ceased to exist'? This would be a staggering thought. But would it have *no sense*? Would it not be *given* sense by that very notion of 'the stream of life' to which Winch appeals? The Zelig family knew the shed as a centre of work and play, of storing, fetching, repairing. It was the object of countless perceptions, thoughts, concerns, intentions. Every year Reb Zelig's wife worked with him in the field digging potatoes which they then carried together to the shed. If all of this shed-related activity could be rejected as delusion, then Reb Zelig might ask himself, 'Who is this woman? Is she my wife? And who am I?' To believe that there had never been a shed, for the Zeligs would mean the destruction of the sense of their individual and collective lives. They would truly have been removed from 'the stream of life'. To avoid being plunged into chaos, to hold on to the framework within which they think and act, they would have to accept it as a fact that their shed had inexplicably ceased to exist.

It should not be supposed that I am supporting Descartes's view. I am not holding that there is nothing in the nature of a physical thing, such as a wooden shed, to support the presumption that it will continue to exist from one moment to the next. It is true that our understanding of the sentence 'The shed ceased to exist', presupposes that the shed was destroyed in some intelligible way. But it seems to me that it presupposes this only in the sense that we would immediately *assume* that there is a natural explanation of what happened to the shed. What I am arguing is that the life-situation of some people could be such that they would be *justified* in refusing, in a particular case, to cling to that assumption.

Towards the end of his lecture, Winch states his position rather cautiously. He says:

> I have not wanted to say in any absolute sense that purported reports of some physical thing's ceasing to exist can only have a sense when it is presupposed that we could, with sufficient knowledge, give some naturalistic account of what has happened. I have concentrated on the bewilderment that we – that is, you and I – are liable to feel at a claim about the bare cessation of existence of some physical thing where any sort of naturalistic explanation is ruled out. I have done so simply because the expectation of such explanations plays such a dominant role within the mode in which we are brought up to make sense of things. That is the prevailing direction in which the stream of our life goes.[13]

The Zelig family were indeed *bewildered* by the inexplicable disappearance of the shed, and so were the people of Blonia – just as you and I would be. What is the logical force of that bewilderment? Does it imply that the sudden vanishing of the shed was 'inconceivable' or 'conceptually impossible'?

In an acutely provocative essay Professor Roy Holland contends that 'the fact that something is conceptually impossible does not necessarily preclude its occurrence'; and he even maintains that 'something could be at one and the same time empirically certain and conceptually impossible. . . .'[14]

In speaking of an occurrence as being 'conceptually impossible' Holland does *not* mean that a description of the occurrence would be *self*-contradictory, as is the description 'a round square'. What he does mean, if I understand him, is that an occurrence is 'conceptually impossible' if it cannot be described by resorting to any of our concepts. Now this would be exactly the situation with the disappearance of Reb Zelig's shed, if we were to take seriously the tale of Zalman the glazier. Our understanding of the statement, 'The shed suddenly ceased to exist', does presuppose that the shed was destroyed – which means that one or another of our *concepts* of 'destruction', should be available for an account of what happened to that shed. None of them *are* available. That the shed suddenly ceased to exist is, therefore, a 'conceptual impossibility' in Holland's meaning of that phrase.

The Reb Zelig family would understand this logical point. They would realize that it could not be said that the shed was 'destroyed'. Their bewilderment was itself evidence of their awareness that there was no intelligible account of what happened to the shed. Would this awareness be inconsistent with their *being certain* that a shed, *their* shed, had suddenly ceased to exist?

Peter Winch appears to think so. Commenting on Holland's view he says that empirical certainty

'is an intentional notion, requiring an object': One is certain *of* something, or *that* something is so. Certain of what, or that what? The answer has to deploy concepts appropriate to the situation. But . . . we do not have the concepts which allow us to formulate an intelligible answer. We are reduced to uttering a form of words to which, in these circumstances, he can attach no sense. So no answer has been given to the question, 'What are we certain of?' . . . I do not at all want to deny that we may be confronted with circumstances which defeat our attempts to describe them coherently. What I am objecting to is the idea that, in such circumstances, the notion of empirical certainty can still be thought of as standing with rock-like firmness.[15]

In this passage Winch seems to be asserting that when a coherent description of presented circumstances is impossible, then any *certainty* about those circumstances is undermined.

Now it is true that the Reb Zelig family cannot describe coherently *what happened* to the shed. They cannot, therefore, intelligibly claim to be *certain* that such-and-such *happened* to it. Winch is entirely right on that point.

But is there not *something* of which the Reb Zelig family could be certain, and would be certain, namely, that their shed had suddenly ceased to exist? The *normal* presupposition of the statement, 'The shed suddenly ceased to exist', would be that the shed has been destroyed. But in the extraordinary circumstances described in the tale of Zalman the glazier, this normal presupposition would have to be dismissed. In particular, it would have to be dismissed by the Reb Zelig family, who could not accept it as a 'possibility' that they had never had a shed, and who knew that it was no longer present, nor had been transported elsewhere, nor had been destroyed. That family would be certain that something had occurred which, in Holland's phrase, is 'conceptually impossible'.

The following criticism will surely be voiced: 'I grant that the Zelig family would be *certain* that there was no natural explanation of their shed's disappearance. But *what* they were certain of would not, indeed *could not*, be *true*.'

Of course it often happens that people are certain of things that are not true. But in the story of the shed every intelligible explanation of its disappearance has been eliminated. It was there yesterday but not today. It was not dismantled, nor carried away by wind or flood, nor burned down, nor blown up – and so on.

The feeling that a shed *could not* cease to exist without any explanation, may be rooted in the assumption that nothing can occur without a *cause*. 'There *must* be a causal explanation.' This conviction is not justified by actual experience: often we do not *discover* the causes of occurrences. The conviction that there must be a cause of any happening is a priori.

There could, however, be circumstances in which the insistence, 'There *must* be a cause', would be an empty slogan. Wittgenstein imagines such a case:

Think of two different kinds of plant, A and B, both of which yield seeds: the seeds of both kinds look exactly the same and even after the most careful investigation we can find no difference between them. But the seeds of an A-plant always produce more A-plants, the seeds of a B-plant, more B-plants. In this situation we can predict what sort of plant will grow out of such a seed only if we know which plant it has come from. – Are we to be satisfied with this; or should we say: 'There *must* be a difference in the seeds themselves, otherwise they *couldn't* produce different plants; their previous histories on their own can't cause their further development unless their histories have left traces in the seeds themselves.'?

But now what if we don't discover any difference between the seeds? And the fact is: It wasn't from the peculiarities of either seed that we made the prediction but from its previous history. If I say: the history can't be the cause of the development, then this doesn't mean that I can't predict the development from the previous history, since that's what I do. It means rather that we don't call *that* a 'causal connection', that this isn't a case of predicting the effect from the cause.

And to protest: 'There must be a difference in the seeds, even if we don't discover it,' doesn't alter the facts, it only shows what a powerful urge we have to see everything in terms of cause and effect.[16]

This story differs from the story of the shed in that in the latter there is no basis for *prediction*. The resemblance between the stories is that in neither is there any *causal* explanation. The insistence that there *must* be a causal explanation would be pointless in both cases.

We do not have to depend on imagination for cases in which there is no apparent causal explanation. Not long ago I read an article by Oliver Sacks, whose studies of strange illnesses are well known. In this article Sacks recounted his observations over many years of two mentally retarded brothers. Although grown up they were quite helpless and had to be cared for like children. Among other things they were backward in the arithmetical operations of multiplication, division, addition. Yet they could determine quickly whether a large number is a *prime* number: Sacks would sit with a book of prime numbers in his lap. He would mention a number of six or more digits. After a brief silence the brothers would smile at one another, and then give the correct answer.

9

Sacks found this uncanny. How did they do it? The explanation that they achieved these results by *rapid mental calculation*, was ruled out by the fact that their ability to do simple arithmetical calculations was much below the normal ability of the average person. What would seem to be the only possible explanation was *not* a possible explanation. To speak of 'intuition' or of 'a feeling for numbers', would not be giving an explanation of their remarkable ability, but would only be giving another name to it. This is an example of an unusual power for which apparently there is no explanation of any kind, causal or otherwise.

I will mention now an ability which is not unusual but ordinary. I refer to *remembering* which can be remembering a past event, or a face, or the location of a house, or how to bake a cake, and so on. Philosophers and psychologists are generally of the opinion that remembering is not *intelligible* unless there are physiological memory traces. They postulate a *causal mechanism*. The idea is that when I witness an event, a representation of this event is deposited in my brain or central nervous system. Later this neural state or process is triggered by some stimulation, and the effect of this is the psychological occurrence of my remembering that event.

I have argued elsewhere that the notion of a physiological memory trace is not a coherent notion.[17] I won't go into that now. I will only say that postulating a causal mechanism is quite uncalled for, since it would not make remembering more intelligible than it already is. If I were describing some past occurrence in detail, you might be surprised at my ability to do this if you believed that I had not witnessed the occurrence. You then learn that I was there and saw it happen. You are no longer surprised – for you realize that I am describing something I *remember*.

If we were to conceive of my witnessing the past event as *causing* my subsequent ability to describe it (and if we didn't invoke a persisting physiological memory trace) this would look like 'action at a distance' – which many philosophers regard as a horrifying conception. Since this is the most familiar phenomenon in the world – *if* it is action at a distance then so be it!

I don't think, however, that we should conceive of the relation between witnessing an occurrence and the subsequent ability to remember the occurrence, as a 'causal connection'. It is rather more like Wittgenstein's example of the plants and seeds, where we are able to predict the plant solely from the history of the seed. We can predict a person's ability to remember an event solely from the history of the person. As Wittgenstein remarked about the seed example: if we say that 'the history can't be the cause of the development, then this doesn't mean that I can't predict the development from the previous history, since that's what I do. It means rather that we don't call *that* a "causal connection," that this isn't a case of predicting the effect from the cause.'

I have referred to the fictitious story of the seeds and plants, and to the true stories of the remarkable brothers and to the ordinary phenomena of remembering, in order to undermine the feeling that the inexplicable disappearance of a shed is unthinkable, since an event *must* have a *cause*. The aim of these examples is to show that the demand for *causal explanation* is not always an iron-clad principle of our thinking.

I do not believe that Peter Winch subscribes to such a principle of causation. What then is the disagreement between us? Winch rightly holds that there cannot be any understanding of what happened to the shed. I agree that in the context of the story there is no possible description of what happened to it: one cannot, therefore, rightly speak of *anything* as having *happened* to it. Winch seems to think that the Zelig family and their neighbours could not be *certain* of anything concerning the shed. But I think they could be certain that the shed had been there for a long time, that suddenly it was no longer there, *and* that there was no intelligible explanation of the change from its being there to its not being there. Of that much they could be certain. They would be bewildered, but this bewilderment would not necessarily undermine that certainty. Indeed, *that* bewilderment would arise from *that* certainty.

NOTES

1. P. Winch, 'Ceasing to exist', in *Annual Philosophical Lecture, Proceedings of The British Academy* (London: Oxford University Press, 1982) vol. 68.
2. ibid., p. 329.
3. *The Philosophical Works of Descartes,* translated by E.S. Haldane and

G. R. T. Ross (Cambridge: Cambridge University Press, 1979) vol. 1, p. 168.

4. Winch, op.cit., p. 329.

5. ibid., p. 330.

6. Isaac Bashevis Singer, 'Stories from behind the stove' in *A Friend of Kafka* (Harmondsworth: Penguin Books 1975).

7. Winch, op. cit., p. 345.

8. ibid., p. 335.

9. ibid., p. 343.

10. L. Wittgenstein, *On Certainty*, translated by D. Paul and G. E. M. Anscombe (Oxford: Blackwell, 1969) p. 614.

11. Winch, op. cit., p. 347.

12. ibid., p. 346.

13. ibid., p. 352.

14. R. F. Holland. 'The miraculous' in *Against Empiricism* (Oxford: Blackwell, 1980) p. 184.

15. Winch, op. cit., p. 343.

16. L. Wittgenstein, 'Cause and effect: intuitive awareness' in Rush Rhees (ed.) and Peter Winch (trans.) *Philosophia*, vol. 6, nos 3–4. September–December 1976, p. 410.

17. N. Malcolm, *Memory and Mind* (Ithaca and London: Cornell University Press, 1977) Part Two, Physical Mechanisms of Memory.

Chapter Two

INTELLIGIBILITY
AND THE IMAGINATION[1]

GRAEME MARSHALL

I

Peter Winch, in his lively British Academy lecture 'Ceasing to exist',[2] quotes Anscombe with approval to the effect that one should propose to one's imagination not the existence of some object but oneself *seriously judging* an object to have come into existence.[3] John Wisdom encourages us to 'imagine vividly the talkers and the occasions' when sentences of the sort we are interested in are used.[4] Norman Malcolm takes us through the fine detail of Wittgenstein's case of the tribe which uses 'pain' only for manifest injuries.[5] Behind all four, and of course so much more, is Wittgenstein's methodological practice of engaging with the actual use of words when they are put to work in real or well-imagined circumstances, with language games as played and with the rejection of the domination of the a priori. What dominates, on the contrary, is thought in the midst of life and projections from it. The responsible work of the imagination and the intelligibility of its products is constrained by how we understand ourselves as experienced agents.

This motivates much of Winch's writing about social science too.[6] One may be able to tell in advance of experience *that* a new tribe's language will be consistent, otherwise we should not be able to construe it as a language at all. But we cannot also thus determine what is to be regarded as consistent or not or what consistency for them means. For that we need to know their actual linguistic practices. We cannot merely project from the uses of our own words. There are limits to our understanding as confined by our experience so far, which can only be transcended

13

by further experience the content of which we cannot, prior to it, imagine.

Winch is quite right about that. If, for example, someone thought that the only proper objects of reference were spatio-temporal solid objects then sentences containing reference to events which shared the same space-time region would appear incoherent. To those who accept events, sentences containing reference to universals as being wholly present whenever they are present and able to be present in more than one place at the same time, would appear incoherent. That is, we need to know the identity criteria for the objects of reference in order to determine whether the referring terms are consistently used and the sentences containing them coherent. But such criteria are given only by the agreed use of terms in the language. Wittgenstein asks: 'Am I not getting closer and closer to saying that in the end logic cannot be described? You must look at the practice of language, then you will see it.'[7]

The same is true of witch-substance. Whether the natives proceed consistently with respect to it depends upon their practices for identifying it. These one might guess at but they cannot be decided a priori. Foreigners may consequently find it difficult to understand a primitive society and translations of the primitive language into their own may be hardly empirically adequate. But none of this suggests that they cannot do better. Their situation is no different from that of anyone else who has to learn something new. Radical relativism, for example, just does not follow.

A similar dominance of the actual is observable in 'Ceasing to exist', though there is a difference: here some limitations of experience apparently constitute limits that cannot be transcended. We seem to be able to play the game of imagining all sort of things different from those given in experience and we enjoy stories such as Singer's about a ploughman and a shed vanishing. But Winch's point is really in the quotation from Anscombe. For when we come to seriously judging such physical things going out of existence just like that, we must declare the supposition nonsense and the understanding we seemed to have at the beginning mere illusion. Anscombe takes the fun out of our imagining games by calling us to our senses, and Winch likewise has sadly to declare that if ploughmen and sheds are physical things then we just cannot understand the sentence 'they vanished', either as description or explanation.

After quoting from Singer's story Winch says:

> The conversation is presented in the form of an argument in which, by appealing to an example, Zalman apparently seeks to convince his audience that a certain kind of event, which they believe never happens, does sometimes happen. The effrontery of his arguments is of course intentionally comic. I apologise in advance to Mr Singer for spoiling the joke by subjecting them to rather solemn analysis. But as so often, a good joke conceals a deep philosophical point and I know no way of making that explicit without losing the joke. My own purpose at this stage of the lecture is not to argue either for or against the truth of Zalman's claim. I have a perhaps more fundamental worry. I am not sure that I understand the claim, what it means. That does not mean that I fail to understand Singer's story. I understand that in somewhat the way I understand Escher's drawings of impossible situations and objects. And to that extent I understand the sense of Zalman's claim 'People do vanish' too: I understand it as it occurs in Singer's story. But were I to be confronted with someone like Zalman who apparently tried to convince me in earnest that 'people do vanish', I do not think I should understand *what* he was trying to have me believe . . .[8]

There is something puzzling in these intriguing claims by Winch. First, he consistently and commendably adopts the same attitude to Zalman as he did to the Azande. There seems to be a good parity of reasoning argument concerning statements beginning 'In Zande . . .' and 'In a story by Singer . . .'. There is every reason to think that the context of use makes the world of difference to what is meant and our understanding of it. That is why there is no telling in advance of knowing their linguistic practices what the Azande think is consistent and hence coherent. Winch recognizes this in the passage quoted: he understands Zalman's claim *as it occurs in Singer's story*. But then, secondly, he proceeds to deal with the claim as if it did not occur in Singer's story but in real life, while leaving us in the dark about what it is to understand the remark in Singer's story or how we are to understand Escher's drawings. And thirdly, that raises the main question: if we do understand in some way the remarks in the story, the impossible drawings and the like, why is this understanding to be totally excluded from our understanding remarks such as 'it just vanished' in other contexts in real life? Or, if the sentence is nonsense in life, how can it make sense in the story? Or, why should modifiers such as 'In Zande' or 'In Singer's stories' change the identity of sentences within their scope? Winch concludes his lecture by appearing to draw back somewhat from the stronger position he earlier adopted by allowing that we may admit such circumstances as Singer describes to be a very *thin* context of utterance, but even so he says that 'the nature of the thought can hardly remain unaffected by such a drastic impoverishment of its surroundings'.[9] So the question remains of what is here left of the thought that occurs in rich contexts of utterance. Finally, there appear to be some disturbing consequences for the imagination. Winch's position, which may very well be the right one, seems to be that imagining unconstrained by the understanding produces only something unintelligible by the standards of real life (and what others are there?) but constrained by the understanding, it appears to deny itself. The paradox is that, on the one hand, imagining ought to be free of the constraints involved in serious judgment but it appears dependent upon them; on the other, fantasy would be no fun if we did not understand it at all and our airy castles no delight if we could not find our way around in them.

I want to tackle the main question by considering why it might be thought that in playing imagining games we do not really understand the possibilities we so freely imagine and think we understand, in the hope that some light might thereby be cast on the sort of understanding we do have of Singer's story, and so on the question of whether that understanding is continuous with what we understand in the rest of life.

But first, we need a prima facie case for the view that our understanding of what we imagine when we imagine things radically different from how we have so far experienced them as being, is not illusory. If it is not an illusion, then while it might not be enough for completely understanding remarks like Zalman's made in the normal course of life, it is enough for denying that we do not understand such remarks *at all*. The lemma is that context does not *totally* determine sense; but that surely need not be argued about. The sense of a word is its use in the language; there seems to be agreement from Frege through Wittgenstein to Davidson that there is a sense in which the whole language is the unit of meaning, even if some are a bit leery of talking of meaning here. Of course, it does not follow that there might not be some sentential contexts which produce meaninglessness, or at least demand interpretation, but we shall come to that.

II

So take Singer's story and Zalman's claims. Imagine a ploughman suddenly vanishing or a shed doing so. Now you see them, now you don't. We seem to be able to follow these instructions; we can run through a sequence of images, though that is not necessary for the success of our imagining; we seem to understand simply what we are supposed to do; nothing could be easier. We know the perfectly ordinary meanings of the words involved. It is the same with any other imagining game, and we seem to be able to imagine just about anything at all. That 'just about' is interesting, for if we could imagine *anything* at all, then anything goes, and so, as far as understanding is concerned, nothing does. There need to be some constraints which are sufficient for the beginnings of understanding and intelligibility.

The traditional constraint is contradiction: one cannot imagine what is contradictory. If one knows that something is contradictory then one knows that nothing one succeeds in imagining will be only describable by the contradiction in question. If one does not know that what one is trying to imagine is contradictory then though it is true that one will not succeed, one will not know that. Kant showed that this constraint is stronger than it might appear. Purely formal determinations of contradiction are not enough since contradictions so determined have no content. To set relevant limits to what we can imagine, the contradictions must use meaningful predicates. The question of what is and is not contradictory includes the question of whether the descriptions in question are intelligible.

17

Contradiction does not set limits to the intelligibly imaginable without presupposing those of intelligible experience. This could be put by saying that *possibly* p implies possibly *p*. The same thrust is behind Wittgenstein's concern with the *deployment* of a sense.

This does not mean that we cannot imagine anything that we have not in fact experienced; that would be absurd. All that is required is that we know the meanings of the words we put together in novel and imaginative ways. The old empiricists had an easy account of our ability to do this. If experience consisted of the getting of sensory impressions, the mind could put these impressions together in bizarre ways as well as in ways that are consonant with the regularity and temporal order of our sensory experience. Our habits in the formation of ideas could, with some effort perhaps and for purposes of entertainment rather than instruction, be undone. But we must abandon the atomism of the empiricists for the greater coherence of holism of a sort. The myth of the given gives way before the strong thesis that perception without conception is blind and the impossibility of precipitating out pure sense contents from our interpretative solutions. This goes to support Winch and Anscombe.

But if there would be no intelligible products of the imagination without some coherence between them and the rest of our relevant beliefs and practices, evidently we are not *concerned* in imagining with such coherence except in so far as it enables us to imagine what we will. Intelligible experience places us in a position to understand what we imagine and in that constraint lies our freedom to invent without falling into unintelligibility. So, to use a distinction Kant drew for another purpose, experience might be said to influence but not to determine our imaginings.

An illustration of how these constraints sometimes operate is provided by fictions. One cannot write a story about the very novel: too much novelty cannot be borne. It defeats memory, allusions are lacking, and, *ex hypothesi*, there is little for it to resonate with. It is not surprising, therefore, that Henry James, in *The Art of Fiction*, should have believed that 'the air of reality (solidity of specification) is the supreme virtue of a novel – the merit on which all its other merits . . . helplessly and submissively depend'. The writer Morris Lurie said to me about the very Singer story we have been concerned with that one of the things which is most palpably there is the sense of *something withheld* which the jokes gesture towards. None of this is conclusive, of course, but it inclines to the view that we do understand in no special way what we imagine and that while our understanding of it is not derived from the experience of it itself, nonetheless it is tied to reality in that our experience, objects unspecified, is sufficient for that ordinary understanding.

The prima facie case for this is strengthened by the obvious reflection that imagining is something we *do* and hence is constrained by the conditions for the exercise of the will. There are some peculiarities that imagining shares with most other mental acts: they are basic, not done by doing something else, their results are immediate and usually transparent, for example. But none of this casts doubt on imagining belonging to the category of acts though it removes some constraints, due in other cases to our actions having a course, such as those concerning means and ends. It is true that we sometimes just let our imaginings go, take their own course, leaving us apparently a mere interested spectator at a private picture show, musing along, which is more suggestive of relaxed passivity than activity; but the contrary is given by that 'let'. When we let things happen we are still as much in control as we ever are and on the alert for the wrong things happening. But that is how it usually is with our acts in the world.

Winch says: 'Suppose . . . that I am told to make the shed cease to exist – *not* by *any* means. In this case I have not been told to do something beyond my powers, I have not been told to do anything at all. What has been said to me merely apes the form of an order.'[10] But in the context of imagining, the order is genuine and success real. Here we know that we can exercise the will to make things vanish, spring into existence, recede, come close, without any process. This exercise of the will is of a piece with much of the rest of our mental activity. We think of a friend and dismiss the feeling of guilt, we summon Pythagoras' theorem and banish the thought of the sea-fight tomorrow. We can sometimes act as gods in the confines of our own minds. Of course, we can only *pretend* to be gods elsewhere, but pretence is altogether more knowing than talk of aping forms would suggest.

If imagining is something we do such that there is no question of our success at it then, first, we must know enough about what we imagine in particular cases prior to the event for us actually to imagine it successfully. So at least our understanding must be sufficient for that, which it would not be if it were totally illusory. But, secondly, action theory also tells us that what we do is determined by what, perhaps minimally, we want and that the world is such as to require us to order our wants. In our imaginings, however, we are not constrained by any reality principle so that our wants can be satisfied in fantasy worlds made to order. In imagining, our illusion, or better our delusion, is that we can make happen *whatever* we want. That might involve understanding something about what we imagine but it is obviously not an understanding conditioned by intelligible experience in this frustrating world.

The reply is, of course, that we are *imagining* things and our wants are strictly wishes and hopes; only pathologically do we confuse imagining and living in real life. In the normal course there is no delusion but, on the contrary, an understanding of the unreality of our wishes coming true hence an understanding of *them* that is entirely and sadly consonant with the conditions for intelligible experience, for all that sometimes we are surprised. Wishes are precisely what we *cannot* take seriously or imagine ourselves seriously judging anything about (unless it be with moral or psychological concern that we should be the sort of person who has such wishes).

This reply reveals a further realistic constraint on our imaginings. They are coherent, not, prima facie, under the category of empirical beliefs but under the category of desire. We put together or let come together what we want, what we fancy, and there is a coherence here which is not determined by logical implications alone but by sympathy of affective tone. This owes something to the logical relations between the beliefs involved in affecting fancies, beliefs about the appropriateness of various objects fancied, and, given that, the appropriateness of various responses to them, though 'belief' is much too weighty a word to use of these ephemera. But our feelings have to go together, too, and disagreeableness in match is usually sufficient for us to cease our imaginings, unless it is only superficial. William James writes: 'When any strong emotional state whatever is upon us, the tendency is for no images but such as are congruous with it to come up. If others by chance offer themselves they are instantly smothered and crowded out. If we be joyous, we cannot keep thinking of those uncertainties and risks of failure which abound upon our path; if lugubrious, we cannot think of new triumphs, travels, loves, and joys; nor if vengeful of our oppressor's community of nature with ourselves.'[11] The same is true of our fantasies. Clearly, Freud has much to tell us both about the ubiquity of wishes in this domain and the question of their coherence.

What occasions greater difficulty is imagining the beliefs and wishes actually going together. We might know what it would be to succeed at imagining being entirely enslaved by beauty – we might draw on Henry James's portrait of Gilbert Osmond; and we might know what it would be to succeed at imagining the more or less coherent beliefs that someone like Osmond has. But we might not be up to knowing that we have successfully imagined a coherent symbiosis of the two: a life for which beauty is the overriding *moral* value, for example. Uncertainty about what counts as success here is a genuine limit on the will. Or try to imagine someone accepting with equanimity Wittgenstein's remark, 'The only life that is happy is the life that can renounce the amenities of the world. To it the amenities of the world are so many graces of fate.'[12]

I conclude that it is reasonable to accept the claim that, by virtue of these constraints, we can and do properly understand what we imagine to be radically different from what we have so far experienced and that such understanding is dependent upon and influenced by intelligible experience, but not wholly determined by it nor answerable to it.

III

This is such a tame conclusion that it is a matter for wonder that it should be doubted, but philosophers may do so and with reason. There are at least five arguments, all variations on a theme, that must be confronted. The first is the Ramification Argument. It is that any change we imagine to the way we have experienced things affects so many of our other beliefs, attitudes, intentions and practices that we end up with so much put in question that we are no longer sure that we understand the change we initially proposed. Or, as Nietzsche believed, if you change anything, you change everything. A good example of this I mentioned at the beginning, Wittgenstein's case of the tribe that uses 'pain' only for manifest injuries. This seems a small change easily imagined but after following the ramifications of it even for a short distance we begin to wonder with Wittgenstein whether it is pain at all that they can be said to suffer. This is the point of much of his work with examples: to show the intricacies of how things stand so that if we were to change anything we should be in the position of, to use his memorable image, one, who has to mend a broken spider's web with his fingers.

It is clearly true that we do not know all the ramifications of any radical change we imagine. But it is an impossible requirement that we should before we are justified in committing ourselves to accepting let alone imagining, such a change. There would be nothing left to the notion of commitment if its justification required full knowledge of what we commit ourselves to. It would be a bad old mistake to set the requirements for serious judgment and commitment so high, and none of us would have a bar of it. But the claim is that radical imagining makes the opposite mistake of not taking any ramifications seriously. We hold enough fixed, as it were, to determine a subject and let everything else go free. But it is not only irresponsible to avoid thinking of what this commits us to, it also casts doubt on our understanding the subject we have apparently determined, since by a good principle, failure to understand the implications of a proposition leaves us with nothing to understand at all. We must avoid the paradox of analysis on the one hand and the aboulia of the imagination on the other.

But this is simply to deny imagining in order to make room for serious judgment. The mistake is to think that once we have given up the constraints of serious thought and judgment we are left with no constraints at all as a basis for understanding. But as we have seen this is not so; there are constraints enough. I am not accusing any particular philosopher of having made that mistake, though Hampshire and Anscombe may have come close to it. Hampshire says, for example: 'A man may try to imagine and to picture to himself various courses of action open to him without bringing words and careful characterization into the picturing. But he cannot in imagination alone, without some aid from conceptual thinking, *deliberate* upon alternatives: at most he can only rehearse them. He has not in imagination, as he has in conceptual thinking, the use of tightly controlled and directed comparisons with the past and an exact demarcation of the alternatives.'[15] This is doubtless not quite the mistake in question, but it is close. The point is that though a lot goes free in imagining, enough is held fixed to determine a subject. It is an interesting question, of course, what this includes. Kant might be represented, for example, as holding that there is something in common to whatever is ever held fixed, and Wittgenstein by saying that it depends on the game being played. Kripke might insist on the essential properties of the sort of thing in question; but that would be to assume falsely that a subject could be identified, determined, only by reference to its essential sortal properties. It is salutary to remember that De Gaulle had a long nose, in a famous example.

It is also not the case that there is no commitment in radical imagining; it is only that not all commitment is logical. Imagining commits as action commits: to not undoing what one has done if one's wishes don't change. One's thoughts cohere not under cognitive concepts but under wishes, some deep, some more or less idle. Desire is as necessarily excluded from the first as it is present in the second. Naturally conceptual thought is both presupposed and involved, but not exclusively. As to whether imagining is any *use* to us, or whether it matters if it is or is not, to that we shall return.

The second argument is the Interpretation Argument. It restates the first by claiming that radical imagining offends against any theory of interpretation governed by the principle of the maximization of true beliefs. We clearly have no choice about using such a principle in our interpretation of the verbal and non-verbal behaviour of other *persons* who we believe inhabit the *same world* as we do. The question is whether we can use it to understand the radical imagining sentences of another and whether others can understand our own uses of such sentences with it and crucially whether *we* can understand our own. While we do not need a theory of interpretation to understand our own idiolect, it is not clear that we don't when we depart from its realistic use, and such a theory governed by the above principle either makes our radical imagining sentences false, which is absurd, or us absurd, which is more so.

But the answer is obvious. Any theory of interpretation which is not able to distinguish between tales and assertions, dream reports and veridical memory claims, fantasies and serious judgments, is entirely useless for its purpose and would be quite unable to appreciate the significance of the differences in uptake and consequential behaviour, affective response and effective action. As for ourselves, if we do not know that we are departing from the constraints of reality in imagining, we are probably not making sense anyway.

The third argument is the Interaction Argument, alluding to Kant's principle that all substances are in mutual interaction. Winch uses a similar Kantian argument in his criticism of Descartes. The argument here is that there is no mere contingent connection between what a thing does, what it can do, what kind of thing it is, and what it is. But in radical imagining these connections are severed. One imagines that something which one identifies clearly as a thing of a certain sort does something that things of that sort cannot do: one imagines carnivorous cows, pigs flying, lions talking, tame tigers, and sheds vanishing. But this involves not a hidden but a manifest contradiction, given the identity criteria that must be used.

This is indeed a powerful argument but there are two considerations that reduce its force. First, our conceptual methodology must retain the open texture of our empirical beliefs which means, as Waismann put it,[14] that there is always a chance that something quite unforeseen may occur, either some totally new experience such as at present we cannot even imagine or some new discovery which would affect our whole interpretation of an entire class of phenomena. Now, it is important to emphasize that the radical imaginings we have been considering concern things *now being or becoming different* from how we have hitherto experienced them as being. We have not considered imagining *things having been* different nor our having experienced them differently. I cannot handle the epistemology of that and I know no one who can. Open texture is required by cases in which something which had been F is now determined to be G, where F and G are different kinds of predicates, leaving it as a further question whether that implies that the thing in question always was G unbeknownst, or that it has changed. If open texture must be provided for, so must the possibility of something being identified as an F now behaving in hitherto uncharacteristic G-type ways. Of course, how we should from now on seriously judge it is not thereby settled; we should have to wait and see what goes on. The point is that imagining something behaving in radically uncharacteristic ways cannot be a nonsense without closing the texture of empirical beliefs that we have to keep open.

It might be replied that open-texture is an epistemological matter, not something to do with intelligibility and meaning. It is salutary to keep in mind that we are not omniscient but it cannot be a regulative principle of reason that we never sufficiently master our own language. It is nonsense to suppose that if the sense of our words might radically change then we had better not rest with our present statement of that very possibility. The language which is the unit of meaning, unlike the scientific hypotheses open texture might require, is already one we sufficiently master and no sense can be given to the notion of *complete* mastery of it. So the open-texture of empirical beliefs cannot guarantee the intelligibility of any imagining that trades on it because open-texture requires the possibility that we go beyond whatever trading can here deliver. Only experience can disclose what open-texture provides for; the imagination is impotent to produce recalcitrance. The limits to our intelligible imaginings are provided rather by the language we already sufficiently master. And the ordinary use of that language eschews both Putnam's 'disastrous meta-induction' and the 'grue' problems, which is enough to reinstate the Interaction Argument.

But not so; the *a fortiori* argument remains. Open-texture requires that in conceiving of something that has hitherto characteristically and even exclusively behaved in F-type ways we still preserve our sense of that thing as grounding the permanent possibility of surprise. If so, then we do not lose our sense of that thing if we imagine it behaving in novel ways, conceptually familiar to speakers of a language, which fall well short of the kinds of surprise we cannot now imagine and for which we have no indications whatsoever.

The second consideration against the force of the Interaction Argument is that there is no requirement that in imagining a particular set of circumstances we must also imagine a physics adequate for a scientific explanation of it. In this we, as imaginative, imitate nature. Experience itself teaches us differences amidst our formulated similarities but does not disclose in the experiences in question the explanations of them. It is up to us to assimilate their novelty within our intelligibility scheme or to accommodate that to their recalcitrance. That takes conceptual work distinct from what is involved in just conceiving of the novel state of affairs. If our serious judgments usually do not go even as far as the beginnings of proper explanations, then, *a fortiori*, neither need our imaginings.

It may be replied that what is disquieting about imagining is not its falling short of explanation but rather its total unconcern with it and, in the case of imagining something vanishing, the rejection of it. In fairy stories magic rules, and the pleasure we take in them has much to do with fairy bricks both being bricks and doing no damage to the windows they pass through. The Interaction Argument says that that is nonsense. To reply that in fairy stories we are just playing different games with bricks is to dodge the issue. But emeroses are gred and that's all right: those predicate pairs are made for each other.[15] So fairy bricks only pass through fairy windows after all. That is, it is indeed true that if you change anything you change everything. The imagination does not make odd things happen in this world; it maps things in this world on to things in another world by means of the identificatory properties of the things in question; cross-world identity (but not rigidity) is necessary to its operation. This concedes the point of the Interaction Argument but not its use to restrict us to actual experience. If things vanish they had better do so in a world where that sort of thing can happen. It is the *mixture* of the real and the imaginary which is uncomfortable in Singer's story and in the possibility of someone trying to convince us in real life that an actual shed has vanished.[16]

The fourth is the Argument from Composition: there are clearly cases of impossible combinations of meaningful words. So even if our experience should have placed us in a position to know what we radically imagine by giving us the words to use there is no guarantee that the completed composition can be understood at all. The obvious example is Chomsky's 'Green ideas sleep furiously', where all the problems are semantic.

But within days of the publication of that Chomsky sentence there were poems written under its title. Serious judgments in literal prose do not exhaust the riches of the language, its history and manifold adaptability. The imagination can make sense out of sensible materials in its own way without that either being reduced to ordinary sense or rendered independent of it. Metaphor does not go without remainder into any literal translation but it is not therefore unintelligible. Figures of speech are figures of speech indeed and we do not always talk in simple sentences descriptively true or false. What Davidson says about metaphor is, I think, completely right: a metaphor means what the words in their most literal interpretation mean and what we attempt in paraphrasing it is to evoke what the metaphor brings to our attention, much of which is not propositional in character. 'A picture is not worth a thousand words or any other number. Words are the wrong currency to exchange for a picture.'[17]

The fifth argument is the Argument from Dreams. If it were doubted that radical imaginings much occur then the occurrence of dreams should dispel that doubt: they constitute a familiar range of examples. But the point about dreams is that they are often manifestly unintelligible; even the dreamer relating the dream may not know what it is about but only that it is, perhaps, inspiring, as Wittgenstein says. Dreams are manifestly not such stuff as we are made on.

For intelligent and curious creatures like us, however, not to go on and attempt to make some sense of a dream is as incomprehensible as it is to be totally bemused before what one imagines. Dreams appear unintelligible because they seem isolated from or out of joint with the rest of life and an interpretation makes the right connections that are lacking at the manifest level. In Wittgenstein's image, dream interpretation is literally an unfolding, the unfolding of a folded up picture, so that in the end there are new, revealing juxtapositions and a way between them. Here is sense and understanding restored.

Besides, all appearance of givenness to the contrary, we *make* our dreams and our activity is coherent under the category of wishes. We know what we are doing even if it sometimes takes time and circumstance to realize it. If dreams are radical imaginings they are splendid examples of what, *au fond*, we only too well understand. That we know what we are doing is shown by our commonly identifying changing subjects and objects in spite of the often bizarre changes in question. It is *agent's* knowledge that makes it plain beyond the raising of the question that it is we who, protean, interact with protean others and keep the threads. From an observer's point of view the flux could never secure the identities in its midst.

It might be argued that dreams often exhibit manifest contradictions – the same person in more than one place at the same time, for example – so that if dreams be instances of radical imagining the constraint of noncontradiction is flouted. But the contradictions exist only at the *manifest* level and dreams, qua imaginings, are not at the manifest level at all. The dream work is to muddy the waters and produce manifest obscurity. It is not surprising that contradiction should be so useful a means to this end and at the same time an indication that there is something noncontradictory to be understood.

IV

At the end of her lecture, *Dreaming*, Martha Kneale asks: 'What advantage has the dreaming creature over a possible non-dreaming creature? Simply this. In dreaming the connections set up in the pursuit of goals in daily life are broken and new connections randomly suggested. The dreaming creature is less at the mercy of conditioned reflex and mere habit. It is able to spot new connections, and in a word, to learn. It may be objected that the connections thrown up are so bizarre that they could not be of any practical use. This is obviously so of most of them, but it is notorious that nature is indefinitely wasteful and if one in a million of the connections thrown up in dreams should suggest a new insight or a new way of reaching a desired goal, the dreaming creature would still have an advantage over the one whose consciousness is restricted to those connections encountered in actual waking life.'[18]

Whether or not that is entirely right about dreaming, I should like to conclude something similar about radical imagining in general. Imagination without experience is impossible but experience without imagination is *quite* impossible. The significance and strength of a choice still depends on what is knowingly excluded and to be aware, within limits, of the possibilities one is rejecting in judging that *this* is the right way to go on, makes that judgment better, fitter, tauter. As critical discussion prevents dead dogmas, imagining the possibilities prevents rule-bondage: the felt constraint to go on in the same *old* way.

Our experience so far and the imaginative understanding of it in the light of possibilities of which we are aware, prepares us for the discovery of differences and gives us what we need to handle them. There is now no reason to think that our experience so far imposes untranscendable limits. If our understanding of the products of our radical imaginings is no illusion, then we can *trust* our imaginings to reveal understandable states of affairs. Since we can imagine things vanishing we can understand the sentence 'The shed vanished', though both Winch and I would think people *mad* if they tried to convince us that that sentence was true of a real shed. *But it is because I understand the sentence* that *I* would think them mad.

I understand the sentence in the way I understand any sentence, though when the sentence expresses my radical imaginings I know that I had better not confuse the circumstances in the imaginary world which provide occasions for its use with any set of circumstances in the real world as I have so far experienced it. There is no special way in which we understand Singer's stories and Escher's drawings. All that is needed is the imagination to make a world in which what we want comes coherently together.

According to his own lights, Winch should not allow that he understands Zalman's remarks even as they occur in the context of Singer's story. 'It vanished' is taken to be not an explanation but at most an expression of resignation or despair at not finding one. Neither must we suppose that it functions as a place-holder for a naturalistic explanation since were we to find such an explanation we would, he says, cease to call the case one of something's vanishing. But it is not allowed to be a description, either, since we have not been given enough to fix its meaning other than as an expression of resignation. We should reply to it by saying: 'Don't give up yet; there must be an explanation.' But, as Winch says, explanation of what? The obvious answer of course, is: of something's not being where we were entirely confident it would be, without the implication that there is no explanation. In this weak sense, 'it vanished' is a description and there is no problem. One understands the remark both in Singer's story and in real life in the same way. It is true that this is at least not the sense that it acquires as Singer's story develops; it does indeed become the rejection of the possibility of an explanation of the phenomenon in question. But what one may fail to understand then is not a sentence but an attitude: how could anyone accept that there is no explanation in this world or out of it of the phenomenon as weakly described? This is stronger than believing the phenomenon is miraculous which some have professed themselves able to understand, since the rejection of explanation includes the supernatural. But although one might not share or endorse such an attitude one can surely understand it both in a story and in real life and in the same way. It is perhaps easier to understand than the miraculous since it is none other than the acceptance of impenetrable mystery.

We should all agree that there is much much variety amongst the 'talkers and occasions' and serious judgment is not always in place. We run great risks, of course, in being cavalier, in not confining our wills within what we know. The world imposes limits on the will because the processes of the world are necessary to our successful manipulations of it. We can think those limits away in imagining no impediments to the exercise of our will, but the ghost of the Ramification Argument remains to haunt us down the corridors on the second floor. The question is whether we have so enlarged our volitional powers by dispensing with the constraints of knowledge that we no longer understand what we are conceiving.

What this may call into question is Descartes's theory of error which leaves the will free enough even to deny the deliverances of the natural light of reason. But while we may not accept Descartes's theory, it is not unintelligible. Neither, therefore, is the supposition of a will constrained only by recognized desire which may, inter alia, make sheds vanish. The pleasure in imagining is what would give way to surprise if its products occurred in fact and its delight is in putting known things together in novel ways to find whether and how they might hold. The real possibility of failure focuses the mind marvellously.

NOTES

1. I have profited much from discussing these matters, especially with Paul Fahey, Camo Jackson, and Raimond Gaita.

2. P. Winch, 'Ceasing to exist', in *Annual Philosophical Lecture, Proceedings of the British Academy*, (London: Oxford University Press, 1982) vol. 68.

3. ibid., p. 339.

4. 'Philosophy, anxiety, and novelty' in *Philosophy and Psychoanalysis* (Oxford: Blackwell, 1953) p. 118.

5. 'Wittgenstein and idealism' in G. Vesey (ed.) *Idealism Past and Present*, Royal Institute of Philosophy Lectures, vol. 13, (Cambridge: Cambridge University Press, 1982).

6. For example, 'Understanding a primitive society' in his *Ethics and Action* (London: Routledge & Kegan Paul, 1972).

7. L. Wittgenstein, *On Certainty* (Oxford: Blackwell, 1969) p. 501.

8. 'Ceasing to exist', op.cit., p. 331.

9. ibid., p. 353.

10. ibid., pp. 351–2.

11. William James, *Psychology: Briefer Course* (New York: Collier, 1962) p. 447.

12. L. Wittgenstein, *Notebooks 1914–16* (Oxford: Blackwell, 1961) p. 81.

13. S. Hampshire, *Thought and Action* (London: Chatto & Windus, 1959) p. 220.

14. F. Waismann, 'Verifiability' in A. G. N. Flew (ed.) *Logic and Language I* (Oxford: Blackwell, 1960) p. 124.

15. D. Davidson, *Essays on Actions and Events* (Oxford: Clarendon Press, 1980) p. 225.

16. David Lewis says: 'If worlds were like stories or story-tellers, there would indeed be room for worlds according to which contradictions are true. The sad truth about the prevarications of these worlds would not itself be contradictory. But worlds as I understand them are not stories or story-tellers. They are like this world; and this world is no story, not even a true story.' *On the Plurality of Worlds* (Oxford: Blackwell, 1986) p. 7 fn. Like Lewis, I have no use for impossible worlds; but the argument of this paper is that if stories are stories about them, I have no use for them either.

17. D. Davidson, 'What metaphors mean' in *Inquiries into Truth and Interpretation* (Oxford: Clarendon Press, 1984) p. 263.

18. M. Kneale, 'Dreaming' in *Knowledge and Necessity*, Royal Institute of Philosophy Lectures (London: Macmillan, 1970) p. 248.

Chapter Three

NATURALISM AND PRETERNATURAL CHANGE

R. F. HOLLAND

G. E. M. Anscombe's lump of phosphorus turning into a little bird or piece of bread (*Coll. Papers*, vol. 2, p.151; she called it a *lusus naturae*) is the kind of would-be phenomenon I have in mind when I speak of Preternatural Change. It is not the same idea as that of a miracle but has to be taken into account by anyone dealing with the topic of miracles.

Peter Winch's Academy Lecture on 'Ceasing to exist' is a discussion of preternatural change arranged round a story by Isaac Bashevis Singer. In Singer's story, someone tells the tale, as though it were true, of a shed that vanished without trace overnight. The question at issue is whether such a 'report' makes enough sense for us to be seriously able to imagine ourselves encountering the 'phenomenon'. Or can we only make the sort of sense of it that would permit us to follow a fairy tale?

Winch says, 'Our understanding of the conjunction: "The shed existed on Monday and did not exist on Tuesday" is such as to presuppose that the shed was destroyed between Monday and Tuesday in *some* intelligible way. And what is an intelligible way is limited by our understanding of what a shed is.' He places a very strong emphasis on that statement (p. 88).[1]

The general principle involved could be expressed in several ways. Here is one way: 'If something of a material nature, M, existed formerly, or was formerly in such-and-such a state, but is not in existence now, or is now in a different state, there must be an explanation, and the explanation must be one that fits in with our understanding of the kind of thing M is.' We could call this the Naturalistic Principle, taking it to cover the case where M has not existed previously but exists now.

Nobody in an important sense has ever rejected the Naturalistic Principle – I am thinking of a tacit acceptance, the nature of which I shall indicate in a moment – but there are at least four different ways in which the principle might be subscribed to. One way would be to regard it as, or behave as if it were, true by and large but subject to a number of on-going exceptions, all of them perhaps belonging to a single category. For instance, in Cornwall during the early medieval period when local saints were thick on the ground, the principle could have been regarded as inapplicable to the wonders wrought by the saints, while being counted on to operate in respect of the material changes brought about by ordinary labour.

There is no application for the idea of going to the extreme in the direction taken by those credulous old Cornish Christians. The reason for this is to be found in the fact that a very substantial degree of tacit regard has been paid to the Naturalistic Principle in all civilizations worthy of the name, as is shown by the development of their husbandry, pottery, architecture, met-allurgy, boat-building and so forth. However, there is certainly such a thing as going to the extreme in the opposite direction, and this happens at the intellectual level. It comes about as the result of an idealization, whereby the Naturalistic Principle's applicability is deemed to be subject to no restriction whatsoever. Arthur Danto begins his article on Naturalism for the Paul Edwards Encyclopaedia as follows: 'Naturalism, in recent usage, is a species of philosophical monism, according to which whatever exists or happens is *natural* in the sense of being susceptible to explanation through methods which, although paradigmatically exemplified in the natural sciences, are continuous from domain to domain of events. Hence, naturalism is polemically defined as repudiating the view that there exist or could exist any entities or events which lie, in principle, beyond the scope of scientific explanation.'

I shall not argue against either of the two positions thus far distinguished. I am interested only in what might be put in between; and half of the answer in outline can be readily stated. There is an attitude towards the Naturalistic Principle which could be called Tautological Naturalism – the fundamentally sensible form of Naturalism. All one has to do in order to make one's Naturalism tautological is to couple the Naturalistic

Principle with the idea that there are forms of understanding outside the natural sciences. It would be sheer rodomontade for a Monistic Naturalist of the kind described by Danto to claim his position were tautological on the ground that all other knowledge is reducible to, or representable as a structure of, for example, the knowledge physicists may one day come to have of fundamental particles. Our tenth-century Cornishman, on the other hand, qualifies for election to the club of Fundamentally Sensible Naturalists. However, the lax attitude towards natural explanation that I articulated on his behalf is alien to our modern minds.

So I turn to the second half of the problem: how to avoid Lax Naturalism without falling back into Scientism. And again there is a ready answer. The Tough-Minded Tautological Naturalism that presumably we all want is to be arrived at by pushing the Naturalistic Principle as far as it will go within its proper sphere, which is the sphere of material transformations. But down this road there is a branching of ways, at which Peter Winch and I part company.

In the passage from 'Ceasing to exist' which I quoted earlier, the Naturalistic Principle was functioning as a criterion both of the nature and existence of things. A case could be made out for denying that it has criterial power at all, but assuming we go along with what Peter Winch says in the quoted passage, we must not forget that there is another criterion-supplier in the running, with which we find the Naturalistic Principle agreeing, and we expect it always to do so. Yet this harmony between the two criteria is only given us by a kind of grace. We have no guarantee against a conflict's arising, and what is more, we have no knowledge that once in a while it does not. Were conflict to become part of the scene – and there is no guarantee against that either – scientific enquiries would be upset and craftsmanship hindered. But this would not be (or has not been) brought about by the conflict's arising once in a while.

The criterion which we expect to work in harmony with the Naturalistic Principle is animal awareness of existence. One of the most salient aspects of human life is that our understanding of what it is for something to exist and be present in our proximity finds expression in primitive reactions of a kind shared by all higher living creatures. For example, when something bulky comes speedily at us, we dodge out of the way. This preconceptual understanding of existence is both a phenomenon of perception, as in the case just mentioned, and equally of memory, as when we recoil from something that previously nauseated us: in the latter case of course it is a phenomenon of perception and memory combined. Only *some* judgments of perception and memory are expressed in animal reactions. Nevertheless it makes good sense to regard all such judgments as *extensions* of animal awareness.

What then would be the effect of a conflict between the two criteria of existence? Would it put us in a state of cognitive paralysis? That is one imaginable consequence, but not the only possible one: reactions could vary according to the nature of the person and the nature of the case. Another possibility would be that the person concerned might start entertaining thoughts of a philosophical character – although not necessarily derived from any formal study. He could delve into his stock of common understanding and come up with reflections like, 'I am more confident about these particular facts than I am about any theorizing', or 'I have been let down before through refusing to believe that my senses were deceiving me'. He might then choose to go by one criterion rather than the other, and the choice could go either way according to the nature of the reflections and the order he put them in. A third possibility is that, as can happen in a moral dilemma, he might find himself reacting in a particular way without being able to help it.

In a conflict between the Naturalistic Principle and perceptions, dealings, interactions of a kind that come very close to the instinctual, my guess is that, whether reflection were to intervene or not, Nature would prove too strong for the Naturalistic Principle. And the fact that the principle were not satisfied would no more mean that it had been destroyed and could henceforward be given up, than the (necessary) non-fulfilment of one of the constitutent obligations within a moral dilemma would show the status of the obligation to be less than that of a fully fledged moral necessity.

That a person could go against the Naturalistic Principle and be right is one way of characterizing the position I wish to defend on the subject of preternatural change. And when I say that he could be right, I mean that he could be right in relation to a reality that is not made what it is by his perspective or by any human history. However, I prefer not to speak of preternatural change as something that it makes sense for us to contemplate as a worldly possibility, because I want to avoid the implication that, for example, there would also be sense in our taking out insurance against it. There can be no sense in entertaining any expectations, positive or negative, in regard to preternatural change. It follows that the idea cannot be put to any ordinary practical use. Nevertheless, the person for whom it is a nullity thinks differently from the person for whom it is not. They take a different view of the world. Both persons should be credited with an impulse to cry Rubbish at the idea, but only the second has to stifle this impulse, so his is arguably the harder way to go. Descriptions of preternatural change can be made as absurd as you please. All must suffer from a deficiency of sense. But there does not have to be in all cases a *complete* loss of sense. I shall therefore introduce the expression 'sense gap' and say, for instance, that in the case of G. E. M. Anscombe's very short story of the lump of phosphorus changing into a little bird or a piece of bread, the sense-gap consists in the fact that the way the lump of phosphorus changes cannot be specified. The story can only speak of its changing *simpliciter.*

In my essay called '*Lusus Naturae*',[2] I sketched a case for regarding that attribution (in contrast, say, with the attribution of a change *simpliciter* to the weather) as incoherent. I said it would be like speaking of a hole in the road that was circular in the geometrical sense. But that strikes me on reflection as a needlessly pejorative interpretation, which represented the story as going further than it can go. For when someone speaks of a preternatural change, she can no more specify the change as being a pure one – she can no more go on to endow the subject with 'bare change' as a positive attribute – than she could specify the *how* of it. I also said in '*Lusus Naturae*' that a preternatural change would have to take place in (absolutely) no time. That too represented the story as running into a positive kind of nonsense which does not need to be attributed to it.

Would not preternatural change have to take place on a temporal knife-edge, so to speak, in order not to allow scope for observation and technical probing to come in? Very well; but then in the close examination of changes – the phenomena of combustion for example – scientific observation always comes up against limits, and preternatural change can be thought of as taking place at or outside those limits. We do not have to think of it as coinciding with one of Hume's nods and blinks. We do not need to adopt the Cartesian view of time which Winch objects to.

The sense-gap in descriptions of preternatural change is one that cannot rationally be closed. Unlike the logical space left by ordinary openness, it is a non-logical space. This does not make it impossible for a rational animal to jump or be carried across the space, but it does mean that he would be making a non-logical, non-intellectual move. If someone were to say for example, on the basis of judgments not far removed from the instinctual, 'This much I know[3] – that a minute ago there was a shed in this field, but now there is no trace of one', the relation between the two judgments in that statement would be non-logical. There would be no theoretical way of linking them, but that would not necessarily prevent them from being true so far as they go.

I must now return to Peter Winch's lecture, for his contention would be, or part of it would be, that even 'so far as they go' the two judgments fail to square with each other. In fact he would say, I believe, that they have already gone far enough to annul each other. If anyone asserted one and then the other, then no matter which order he asserted them in, the first one to be asserted would prevent the second from being a genuine judgment.

He moves towards this position by linking the Naturalistic Principle with Wittgenstein's idea of 'the stream of life, or stream of the world', and especially with the idea that verification needs to be carried out from a place within that stream. From these considerations he derives a test for the genuineness of (*inter alia*) memory impressions. And the outcome of this part of his argument is that, since memory impressions enter into the framing of observation reports about changes in situations, anyone who 'reports' a change that is disorderly – disorderly in the radical sense of not being in conformity with our understanding of the order of the world, not fitting in with the way the stream of life goes – will fail to do any genuine reporting. That is a very bald summary, but I want to get quickly to the focal point of disagreement. It is over the question as to which aspects of the stream of life or stream of the world should be treated as most fundamental in relation to an individual's capacity for observation and judgment.

Winch says that the main point to elucidate about 'the stream of life, or stream of the world' in our discussion is: 'the interconnection between my present understanding of the situation I am in at this moment, what I can recollect about the antecedents of this situation, and my understanding of the causal properties of, and relations between, the objects in my environment' (Winch 1987: 99). Then a little later: 'What I want to emphasise about all this is the extent to which expressions of recollection, reports of perception, quasi-causal inferences, are indiscriminately mixed together' (Winch 1987: 100). In between, he provides an example consisting of personal musings: 'I sit at my desk writing these words. It is about 9.30 a.m. on a cold September morning. I am a bit alarmed at how little time I have left to prepare this lecture to deliver to the British Academy, as I have agreed to do.' He comes close there to treating 'the stream of life, or stream of the world' as a stream of consciousness, although he is no Idealist; whereas I, who am no Materialist, offer as my receipt for relating the theme of order and disorder to the theme of the life-stream: Begin with the blood-stream. Then, are the reflexes OK? And so on.

Take, as a paradigm of order, someone who has not only passed all the medical tests, but proved himself in hosts of other ways, athletic and intellectual besides. Full of discernment, eye-on-the-ball and ready for anything, he conducts himself with detachment when all around behave as if they were in Bedlam. His name is Brearley-Constantine. Now if *per absurdum* Brearley-Constantine, while continuing to exhibit his customary acumen in general, were to testify to a preternatural change having taken place, nothing need have gone wrong with his relation to time (contrast sufferers from anxiety or the very senile); and although his testimony would mean that something had been removed from (or put into) the stream of the world, it would not mean that *he* had been removed from it.[4]

What I said just then was in the form of a conditional assertion based on an unfilled-out fantasy, and I must follow it with two disclaimers. It does not show that anyone would ever be justified in claiming that a preternatural change had taken place. And it was not meant as a demonstration that the claim even makes sense; but it undermines an important argument *against* that possibility. I add these disclaimers because I am aware that by presenting an example in which the supposed occurrence of a preternatural change is linked to the supposed testimony of a person of exemplary judgment, I may seem to have committed a fallacy, which I shall call The Fallacy of Incorporation. For an objector might say that all I did was take a story (the Brearley-Constantine story) and employ it in the role of an operator upon another story – a story which I did not bother to tell, though I indicated that it would be about a preternatural change, so it can be deemed to be the story of a vanishing shed (the one where Brearley-Constantine's club keeps its heavy roller). I then decked the whole thing out with a further story about my imaginary Brearley-Constantine's integrity of constitution when he observes successive states of affairs, however bizarre those affairs might be. In this way, the objector may say, I made it look as if what is recounted in the inmost story, the vanishing of the shed, is something that is in principle susceptible to verification, whereas in truth the would-be verification is only part of the story – a pseudo-verification which I incorporated into the larger fiction.

So I seem open to a charge of begging the question. But what question? In an article called 'Time, travel, parahistory and Hume',[5] Roy A. Sorensen says there are critics of Hume who 'maintain that well-attested miracles could take the form of annual levitations of key cathedrals around the world, pages of the Bible being written out as cloud formations in the sky, and so forth'. After proceeding to make some comparisons, he then says, 'The common flaw to these responses to Humean scepticism is that they are question-begging. In order to supply the requested description of evidence, they presuppose its existence as part of the content of the miracle...' (Sorensen 1987: 223). Sorensen emphasizes at the beginning of his article that the issue he is concerned to discuss is whether it is 'possible to justify a belief' in certain reports, especially reports of time travel.

Now justification has not been my aim at all in this essay and I have been careful not to speak of verification or of evidence – ideas that are connected with justification. My position on the topic of justification is actually that there can be *no* justification for anyone's believing, feeling sure, being in no doubt etc. that a preternatural change has occurred or that a miracle[6] has occurred. It is also part of my position that a person who has no justification for asserting something can nevertheless in certain circumstances assert it and be right (the converse is equally true: someone can be justified in what he asserts and yet be wrong).

My contention that a person can have no justification for believing that a miracle or preternatural change has occurred owes nothing to Humean reasoning about the balance of probabilities being always ranged against the truth of the testimony. For in my view there can be no probability at all in favour of a preternatural change's (or miracle's) occurrence. It is ruled out as a possibility by the Naturalistic Principle, and I am a subscriber to that principle. However, the Naturalistic Principle is not the only criterion-supplier in respect of the existence and non-existence of things. There is another criterion which could (I do not say necessarily always would) defeat it in the event of a clash – but we have been through all that.

With the justification issue out of the way, the charge of Incorporation can be seen to amount to this: that you cannot take a proposition, p which is senseless, and think to remedy its senselessness or mitigate its senselessness by operating on it with an epistemological operator like 'S is sure that', or 'S_1, S_2, S_3... are exemplary witnesses to the fact that'. We can also see that anyone who brings this charge will be begging the question himself, unless he or someone else has already established beyond doubt the senselessness of p. This has not been done in the present case, and I do not believe it *can* be done. No proofs are available either way; only suasions. My example of the cricketer was one of these, or more exactly it was a counter-suasion; also it was like a ladder to be thrown away, since I only needed a very ordinary instance of *mens sana in corpore sano,* and not an especially egregrious one, when I submitted that Brearley-Constantine would not lose his place in the stream of the world if he were to testify to the occurrence of a preternatural change. The testifying would consist in, or arise out of, a combination of reaction and expression; and he would be carried over the sense-gap, which I said was intellectually unclosable, by the only things capable of carrying anyone over it: flesh and blood.

NOTES

1. Peter Winch, 'Ceasing to exist' in *Trying to make sense* (Oxford and New York: Blackwell, 1987).

2. R. F. Holland, *'Lusus Naturae'* in D. Z. Phillips and Peter Winch (eds) Wittgenstein: *Attention to Particulars* (London: Macmillan, forthcoming).

3. This would be a perfectly proper use of 'know'. Anyone who said, 'No, you don't', would be wrongly suggesting otherwise, by bringing in, as though it were the only use, the Platonic use, according to which there is no knowledge without an account.

4. In *'Lusus Naturae'* I thought that the case for denying that there could be any disturbance to the life-stream of a witness might be strengthened by multiplying witnesses and splitting the testimony between two groups. I even added mechanical devices to the picture since it is possible for such devices to save our relying on memory. But these were needless diversions which only served to create confusion over what the example was intended to show.

5. Roy A. Sorensen, 'Time, travel, parahistory and Hume', *Philosophy* (1987).

6. I am not concerned here with the kind of background that would make the term 'miracle' the appropriate one to use.

Chapter Four

WITTGENSTEIN ON MAKING HOMEOPATHIC MAGIC CLEAR

FRANK CIOFFI

This paper is based on the J. R. Jones Memorial Lecture delivered at the University of Swansea in December 1984.

A member of a primitive culture is engaging in behaviour which involves mimicking or otherwise deliberately calling to mind a state of affairs which is of great moment to him – rainfall, spring, the hunting of prey, the destruction of an enemy. What is Wittgenstein's thesis with respect to these 'actions that bear a peculiar character and might be called ritualistic'?

Both commentators who are favourably disposed towards it and those who reject it, concur in attributing to Wittgenstein the view that, as it is put by John Cook, 'Wittgenstein was . . . offering a theory to the effect that the primitive magician, in the performance of his rites, no more intends to help his crops flourish or to harm his enemy than we intend to bring about some effect by kissing the picture of a loved one' (Cook 1983: 5). Howard Mounce too, assigns an expressive, anti-instrumental view of magic to Wittgenstein: 'The practice of destroying an effigy of one's enemy need not have a purpose in the sense of bringing something about, it is merely the expression of a wish' (Mounce 1978: 70). A. J. Ayer interprets Wittgenstein as maintaining that 'the stabbing of the picture (of an enemy) is a mere venting of the agent's spleen, a symbolic act, not seriously expected to have any practical effect' (Ayer 1980: 91). According to Brian McGuinness, Wittgenstein held that 'magical ways of thinking and acting' are not based on beliefs but are akin rather to acts 'like kissing the picture of a loved one or striking some inanimate

42

object when angry' (McGuinness 1981: 37). M. O. C. Drury puts the same construction on Wittgenstein: 'They were not mistaken beliefs that produced the rites but the need to express something' (Drury 1973: x). Still another anti-instrumental gloss on Wittgenstein runs: 'In Frazer's view the customs he describes are based upon opinions and interpretations of nature. For Wittgenstein, those customs are instinctual responses to an inner need for release and satisfaction, unconscious and with no other purpose' (Rudich and Stassen 1971: 86).

The view that Wittgenstein straightforwardly denied the instrumental character of magic is mistaken. What creates this impression is some hyperbolic remarks, particularly the oft-quoted:

> If I am furious about something, I often strike my stick on the ground or against a tree, etc., but I don't however believe that the earth is guilty or that the blows are of any use, 'I release my rage', and all rites are of this kind.
>
> (Wittgenstein 1979: 72)*

This is a dismally opinionated utterance and a profoundly un-Wittgensteinian one. All rites are not of 'this kind' nor of any other kind, and Wittgenstein himself knows that they are not since the statement that they are is contradicted by remarks he makes elsewhere as well as in the Frazer notes themselves.

What is most striking about Wittgenstein's attitude towards instrumental conceptions of magic is neither its penetration (Rhees, McGuinness, Drury, W. D. Hudson) nor its perversity (Rudich and Stassen, Ayer, Cook) but its incoherence. And this incoherence is striking because it is more than just a matter of Wittgenstein conceding on some occasion what he denies at others, but of himself providing the most persuasive arguments against his own anti-instrumental objections, so that what we have is more a matter of genuine ambivalence than simple inconsistency.

Now what is to be said for this exegetical thesis, since it goes against the unanimity of his commentators, both critical and laudatory, and against some of Wittgenstein's own explicit utterances?

---

* *My quotations are from an unpublished translation by Anthony Manser of the University of Southampton. Page references are to the corresponding passages in Berzelius's translation in Luckhart (1979).*

In Moore's notes, in contradicting Frazer's view that 'when primitive people stab an effigy of a particular person, they believe that they have hurt the person in question', Wittgenstein says only that 'primitive people do not *always* entertain this false scientific belief though in some cases they may' (Moore's emphasis – Moore 1966: 308–9). Wittgenstein is equally circumspect in Alice Ambrose's notes: 'People at one time thought it useful to kill a man, sacrifice him to the God of fertility, in order to produce good crops. But it is not true that something is always done because it is useful. At least this is not the sole reason' (Ambrose 1979: 33).

When we re-read Wittgenstein's remarks in the light of these statements their incompatibility with an unqualified anti-instrumentalist conception of magic emerges even more markedly.

Wittgenstein compromises his anti-instrumentalist thesis in those remarks in which he objects to Frazer's intellectualism and insists rather on the unratiocinated, spontaneous character of magical practices than on their lack of ulterior aims: 'Eating and drinking have their dangers . . . nothing more natural than wanting to protect oneself . . . and we could think out protective measures ourselves' (Wittgenstein 1979: 66).

In a remark that follows, Wittgenstein again concedes the correctness of the instrumental view of magic: 'In magical healing one indicates to an illness that it should leave the patient.' In his comment on this Wittgenstein implies that what is objectionable in Frazer is his ratiocinative, intellectualist view of magical practices. 'After the description of such magical cures we'd like to add: If the illness doesn't understand that, then I don't know how one ought to say it.' This is just the argument that R. R. Marett advances in attempting to enhance the plausibility and perspicuity of the instrumental conception of mimetic rites: 'How can nature refuse to follow man's lead when man points it out so clearly?' (Marett 1936: 29).

Though Wittgenstein does not explicitly generalize this argument it generalizes itself. If, as Wittgenstein says, the illness can't help but understand it is not welcome and thus quit the patient, why should any other portion of reality be more obtuse? Why should not the sky understand that it is to rain; the hemp that it is to grow; the witchety grubs that they are to flourish; the prey that it is to be killed (or rather, in such cases, the power that arranges these things, that the prey is to be caught; the enemy to sicken; the woman in labour to be safely delivered etc., etc.)? As Wittgenstein himself remarks, 'we could invent the protective measures ourselves'.

Another indication of Wittgenstein's undecidedness: at one point he distinguishes between an oversimplified notion of things and processes, ('a false picture, a picture that doesn't fit') as for example, when someone speaks of an illness as moving from one part of the body to another, and 'magical operations', by which he means the symbolic rites which Frazer mistakes for occult technology. Baptism is an example of a symbolic rite which, if it were construed as an attempt to exploit the occult consequential properties of water, would illustrate the mistaken imputation of 'a false oversimplified conception', in this case of guilt as something which could be washed away. But having made this distinction Wittgenstein then obliterates his own contrast by taking the very example he used to make it, that of the conception of illness entertained by 'uneducated people' as something which can move from one part of the body to another, and assimilating it to the principle on which protective magical practices are based (Wittgenstein 1979: 65–6).

One way of defeating the imputation of incoherence is by re-interpreting those remarks in which Wittgenstein has been taken to express an unqualified anti-instrumentalism. For example when Wittgenstein says that 'it is not characteristic of primitive man to act from opinions', we can let the emphasis fall on the word 'characteristic' and construe Wittgenstein as only denying the pre-eminence of the instrumental motive in generating those practices described by Frazer. (Similarly with 'It is nonsense to say that it is a characteristic feature of ritual actions that they spring from wrong ideas about the physics of things.')

On this view when Cook says '(Wittgenstein) is suggesting that the man who makes magic over his newly planted garden is not to be thought of as taking one more technological step after preparing his tubers and testing the soil but is to be thought of, rather, as expressing something in regard to his crop, the wish that it be abundant, the hope that it has not become infested, or whatever' (Cook 1983: 4), he is overstating Wittgenstein's anti-instrumentalism. Wittgenstein may be suggesting that the man who makes magic over his garden *need* not be thought of as taking a technological step rather than that he *must* not be so thought of and that he *may* rather than *must* be thought of as expressing his hopes and fears regarding it. Wittgenstein may be enlarging the range of options rather than foreclosing them in favour of the expressive conception.

On this view Wittgenstein is protesting at the exclusivity of Frazer's instrumental conception rather than advancing an exclusivist thesis of his own. But unfortunately for this reading, Wittgenstein's anti-instrumental utterances go further than this in both letter and spirit. How, for example, is the downrightness of the remark as to all rites being akin to spontaneous, self-sufficient gestures like striking the ground in anger, to be reconciled with a qualified anti-instrumentalism? Or the incredulity Wittgenstein expresses as to a primitive who is technically sophisticated enough to construct real weapons being at the same time naive enough to think he could effect ends by ritually mimicking employment of them?

Wittgenstein, then, has two apparently inconsistent views of instrumentalist conceptions of magic – that primitives are too sophisticated to hold views so absurd and that it is the most natural thing in the world that they should do so, not requiring any elaborate ratiocinative effort or theoretical justification on their part such as Frazer attributes to them. Which of these views best captures our relation to homeopathic magic? I believe that it is when he is advocating the intuitive compellingness of magic that Wittgenstein is at his most penetrating and that his unqualified anti-instrumentalism is partly hyperbole and partly misconstrued anti-intellectualism. But whether or not Wittgenstein qualifies his anti-instrumentalism in incoherent or incomprehensible ways, he certainly advances arguments against instrumentalist conceptions of magic. What are they and what are their merits? I shall deal only with the major ones – the arguments from implausible obtuseness and non-development and from the greater eligibility of the expressive.

Wittgenstein urges against the instrumental conception that primitives were bound to discover that magic has no influence on the events that Frazer thinks it is intended to bring about; all they need notice is that these occur in any case; furthermore, we see no changes in magical practices such as might be expected of an activity whose rationale was instrumental – 'magic has no principle of development'. But a great deal of our own instrumental life is conducted in darkness, from our criminal code and penal system to our therapeutic endeavours. If it takes the systematic monitoring of outcomes – a resolute attempt to discriminate our hits from our misses – before a practice can be considered instrumental then it is not just Frazer who is wrong about magic but it is we who are wrong as to a large part of what we have hitherto regarded as belonging to epistemic life. And though this is independently arguable it is not what Wittgenstein is asking us to credit. Wittgenstein's argument would render instrumentalist conceptions of herbalism, homeopathic medicine, astrology, and any other tradition-dominated, contemporary diagnostic and therapeutic practices equally untenable.

Wittgenstein's argument that the practitioners of instrumental magic would notice that the ends the ritual is meant to attain occur 'in any case' has no generality. It may always rain in any case, and the sun rise and the spring return in any case, but an enemy doesn't suddenly sicken 'in any case'. Furthermore, Wittgenstein's argument from implausible obtuseness only works against versions of Frazer's instrumentalism which treat the homeopathic ritual as a necessary condition of the occurrence of the desired event, but not against the belief that the representation of events, through mimicry, say, can influence rather than guarantee their occurrence. Why should not the pre-historic hunters described by Marett believe that their mimic slaying of prey influences the outcome of the hunt? The success of the hunt need not be related to the ritual in so straightforward a way as Wittgenstein's arguments demand. Its success need not be conceived as guaranteed by the performance of the ritual nor its failure by its omission. Since considerations identical to those Wittgenstein finds grossly credulous haven't kept our own contemporaries from believing that vitamin C plays a beneficent role in controlling the incidence and duration of head colds, why should it have weighed more with Frazer's primitives? And when the desired event is as indeterminate as that which Frazer often assigns his primitives – purification from evil, for example – it is hardly appropriate to speak either of the inevitability of the outcome or of its disappointment.

The problem is not why magic is retained but why it is abandoned. What counts in favour of Wittgenstein's emphasis on its non-experimental character is that when it does go it tends to go completely. There is no attempt to vary the conditions under which the practice has proved inefficacious or unreliable; no attempt to enquire, say, whether a more efficacious transaction with simulcra might not yet be discovered. People don't go from wax models to clay models or from a rite by the full moon to a rite by a gibbous moon.

But even if Wittgenstein had succeeded in establishing the implausibility of Frazer's instrumentalist view of magic, it would not serve to establish his own expressive view, for Wittgenstein systemically elides the possibility that a rite may have transcendental objectives and thus be non-empirical without being non-instrumental. Where this is so, its role in the lives of its practitioners will be quite distinct from the purely symbolic/expressive one which Wittgenstein assigns it. It matters that the priest who baptizes or absolves, or the bishop who ordains, should have the transcendental authority to do so, in a way that it doesn't matter that the foreign dignitaries, receiving a twenty-one-gun salute, are Oxford undergraduates in disguise. Pontius Pilate-like ablutionary practices remain impervious to discoveries as to the properties of water for reasons different from those for which baptismal rites remain similarly impervious. The one because they have no ulterior aims, the other because they have transcendental ones.

This brings us to Wittgenstein's second and more persuasive argument against Frazer's instrumental construals. They are gratuitous. The practices described by Frazer can be accounted for without such assumptions: they do not need to be explained because they can be 'explained', i.e. 'made clear', by being brought into connection with 'an inclination of our own' to 'express feelings not connected with beliefs'.

Shortly after contrasting the explaining which involves hypotheses with 'explaining', which is brought about by 'putting together in the right way what we already know' (which Rush Rhees felicitously renders 'making clear') Wittgenstein produces the following example of making a practice clear: 'burning in effigy, kissing the picture of a loved one. This is obviously not based on a belief that it will have a definite effect on the object which the picture represents. It aims at some satisfaction and achieves it' (Wittgenstein 1979: 64).

This remark has provoked much appreciative comment. What are the commentators appreciative of? What was their original relation to effigy burning and how was it improved by the reminder that we kiss pictures of our loved ones? What do they understand by 'making clear' and why do they think that Wittgenstein has succeeded in effecting it in this instance? This is how the matter is put in a work from another tradition: 'the task of making something understandable is to make us see how it could have happened by showing how akin it is to something we can already grasp' (Sabini and Silvers 1982: 87). Mounce writes of an aborigine's belief in the efficacy of a curse: 'This practice can be properly understood . . . only by comparing it with beliefs (which) rest on ideas which are absurd but which for all their absurdity, can nevertheless, in certain circumstances, affect us deeply', e.g. the belief that the loss of a wedding ring may have a baleful occult influence on a marriage. Mounce's remark suggests the general form of such issues: the question they raise is what we should have no difficulty understanding given what we already do understand.

As to the character of the satisfaction which Wittgenstein says we are seeking and which is not to be found in explanation, I think it epistemically akin to that to which Levi-Strauss refers in *The Savage Mind* : 'When an exotic custom fascinates us . . . it is generally because it presents us with a distorted reflection of a familiar image which we confusedly recognize as such without yet managing to identify it' (Levi-Strauss 1966: 238–9). 'Putting into order what we already know' facilitates identification of this obscurely familiar image.

Thus the most common objection to Wittgenstein's procedure, that he attempts to resolve empirical questions a priori, is misconceived; 'Making clear' is not non-empirical, intuitive explaining. 'Making clear' does not attempt to settle empirical questions a priori. It tries to take us from a state in which we find something 'difficult to understand' to a state in which we find it less so. For example: from finding it difficult to understand how people could burn effigies of enemies or of personified symbols of baleful forces just for the satisfaction it gave them, to not finding it difficult, in view of the fact that we thrash inanimate objects and kiss bits of paper for similar reasons. Or: from finding it difficult to understand that people would be sufficiently incensed about the failure to recover the bodies of their dead to take the lives of those they held responsible, as did those Athenians, who voted death for the Captains who conducted the battle of Arginousae, to not finding it difficult in view of our own multifarious manifestations of cadaveric piety.

The activity of making clear is often confounded with that of rendering an account plausible because the same considerations can be brought forward to effect either. When a practice is enigmatic, that is, when its rationale is unknown to us and we are attempting to render a conjectured rationale plausible, we adduce the same considerations as when the rationale of a practice is known to us but is found opaque and our aim is to render it more perspicuous. Cook, for example, says that John Beattie undertakes to render the primitive belief in occult connections plausible by 'suggesting how even one of us might think that his wishes had caused someone's death or injury' (Cook 1983: 6), and he quite reasonably observes that more than this is required to demonstrate the instrumental character of magic.

But the point of Beattie's invocation of our own irrational propensity to credit the occult influence of thoughts on events is not to provide additional grounds for the historicity or veridicality of his instrumental account of magic, but to facilitate its intelligibility, i.e., he is addressing the question (as Mounce poses it) 'How could they believe' in occult connections? The same is true of Wittgenstein. The point of the analogies which Wittgenstein provides is not to preclude instrumental accounts of ritual but to argue the intelligibility of ritual transactions with images without the necessity of invoking such accounts.

An argument isomorphic with Wittgenstein's on effigy-burning is G. K. Chesterton's as to the explanation of savage customs, and funerary practices in particular:

> misunderstanding of the real nature of ceremonial gives rise to the most awkward and dehumanised version of the conduct of men in rude lands or ages. The man of science, not realising that ceremonial is essentially a thing which is done without a reason, has to find a reason for every sort of ceremonial, and as might be supposed, the reason is generally a very absurd one – absurd because it originates not in the simple mind of the barbarian, but to the

sophisticated mind of the professor. The learned man will say, for instance, 'the natives of mumbo jumbo land believe that the dead man can eat, and will require food upon his journey to the other world. This is attested by the fact that they place food in the grave, and that any family not complying with this rite is the object of the anger of the priest of the tribe.' To anyone acquainted with humanity this way of talking is topsy-turvy. It is like saying, 'The English in the 20th century believed that a dead man could smell. This is attested by the fact that they always covered his grave with lilies, violets, or other flowers. Some priestly and tribal terrors were evidently attached to the neglect of this action, as we have records of several old ladies who were very much disturbed in mind because their wreaths had not arrived in time for the funeral'. It may be of course that savages put food with the dead man because they think that a dead man can eat, or weapons with a dead man because they think that a dead man can fight. But personally I do not believe they think anything of the kind. I believe they put food or weapons on the dead for the same reason that we put flowers, because it is an exceedingly natural and obvious thing to do.

(Chesterton 1905: 144–5)

Notice that Chesterton doesn't insist on the historicity of his account but only that it is 'natural and obvious'. Similarly with Wittgenstein. What he insists can be shown a priori is the perspicuity of a non-instrumental, expressive account, of effigy burning, say, not its correctness in particular cases.

When Alasdair MacIntyre asks of the Australian aborigine's belief in an external soul: 'Does the concept of carrying one's soul about in a stick make sense?' (MacIntyre 1970: 68), he is not expressing scepticism as to accounts of aboriginal behaviour which derive them from the belief in external souls; he is asking, not for more evidence that this is indeed their reason, but for it to be 'made clear', i.e., for the kind of thing which Wittgenstein attempts to do for effigy-burning by reminding us that we kiss the picture of loved ones and which Winch attempted to do for MacIntyre himself, when he compared the aborigine's dismay at losing his soul-stick with the feelings of a lover who lost the locket containing his loved one's hair (Winch 1972: 45). The activity of making clear which Wittgenstein recommends as the appropriate response to a certain class of perplexities is not at all peculiar to him and is indulged, when they think it is called for, by R. R. Marett, Jane Harrison, Lord Raglan, S. E. Brandon, Claude Levi-Strauss, John Beattie, and Frazer himself.

The necessity for making clear arises when either we have an account of a practice which comprises the rationale of the practitioners but this is opaque to us, or we are proposing an account of an enigmatic practice and are anticipating the objection that our account lacks perspicuity. In both these cases we put forward specimens of behaviour which we are accustomed to consider non-problematic and argue their analogy to the proffered rationale. This is what Wittgenstein is doing when he urges on behalf of his expressive conception of effigy-burning that we kiss the picture of loved ones.

Howard Mounce, for example, provides a specimen of making clear when he attempts to answer the question 'How is it possible for anyone to believe that a person's guilt can be established by administering poison to a fowl?', not by providing us with more information about those whose practice perplexes us but by calling our attention to our own relation to occult phenomena. The transition from the opacity to the transparency of a practice is accomplished via analogies and reminders. It might be helpful if some examples of making clear were laid out schematically:

PRACTICE: 'Putting a curse on someone by burning him in effigy, say'.
Analogy: dismay at a person's blindness following piercing the eyes in a representation of him (Mounce).

PRACTICE: cave drawing of transfixed prey or miming of a successful hunt.
Analogy: keeping a loved one's picture or her glove (Marett).

PRACTICE: The emperor remaining immobile to preserve the tranquillity of the empire.
Analogy: pressing one's lips together in a way which precludes laughing or talking when we wish someone else to desist from them (Wittgenstein).

PRACTICE: sprinkling water on ground to bring about rainfall; lighting of fires in mid-winter to assist sun.
Analogy: tendency of 'spectators of athletic or dramatic contest to assist action by some corresponding gesture' (Brandon).

PRACTICE: bringing food and drink to the graveside.
Analogy: our placing flowers on the grave (Chesterton).

PRACTICE: aborigine going through a ceremony appropriate to his having died because he has lost an object which contained his external soul.
Analogy: apologizing to loved one for having lost love token (Winch).

PRACTICE: Potlatch.
Analogy: extravagant expenditure on Christmas presents in Manhattan (Levi-Strauss).

PRACTICE: administering poison to a fowl to identify evil-doer.
Analogy: treating loss of wedding ring as an omen (Mounce).

PRACTICE: sympathetic magic in general.
Analogy: occasional absurd feeling that thought and speech can have occult influence (Beattie).

Two things about this list are obvious; that more of the examples are attempts to elucidate in cognitive/instrumental terms than in expressive ones and that they vary greatly in their degree of persuasiveness. But I postpone discussion of the general problems these raise until after the discussion of Wittgenstein's case for the expressive, non-instrumental construal of ritual activities.

Wittgenstein attempts to undermine Frazer's instrumentalism by reminding us of how often our transactions with images have no ulterior aim. We also engage in non-instrumental, symbolic transactions with images, though some of these are sufficiently nuanced to be misconstruable as evincing a belief in an occult connection between the image and its object ('the RC in his blindness/bows down to wood and stone').

Nuns who cover the crucifix before undressing don't really believe they have preserved Jesus from embarrassment and would even recognize the notion as heretical. The Catholic girl in Aldous Huxley's *After Many a Summer* who covers the statue of the Blessed Mother in her room before embracing her lover, did so for her sake and not the Virgin's. Napoleon, when he turned the portrait of the Prince of Rome away from the carnage of Borodino, did not think of himself as taking prophylactic measures (nor did Lord Blandower who deals similarly with his fiancée's portrait in J. Meade Falkner's *The Nebuly Coat).* If someone were to put any of these forward as specimens of occult instrumentalism the right procedure would be to remind him of the others – 'Human life is like that'.

In rejecting the necessity for imputing false conceptions of nature to account for primitive practices involving names, Wittgenstein asks rhetorically, 'Why should a man's own name not be sacred to him?' Let us see how the proposal to relate such practices to an inclination in ourselves works in the case of the sacredness of a man's name. What stands to practices suggesting that a man's name is sacred to him as does kissing the picture of a loved one to expressive effigy-burning? Kissing the name of a loved one, of course, but this involves another person's name and not our own. Is there anything closer?

In his autobiography Goethe provides an illustration of the peculiarly intimate relation in which we stand to our names. He tells us how annoyed he was at a verse of Herder's in which Herder took liberties with the name Goethe by punning on Goth:

> It was not in very good taste to take such jocular liberties with my name; for a person's name is not like a cloak which only hangs round him and may be pulled and tugged at, but a perfectly fitting garment grown over and around him like his very skin, which one cannot scrape and scratch at without hurting the man himself.

> (Goethe 1949: 112)

If someone knows this story and never found it odd or is told it and finds Goethe's reaction perfectly natural then calling his attention to this should do something to make clear why the name of a savage is sacred to him. Freud makes the same point as Goethe in *Totem and Taboo* : 'a man's name is one of the main constituents of his person and perhaps of his psyche'. This notion is dramatized in Athol Fugard's play *Siswe Banzi is Dead*. The eponymous hero displays a dismay at the prospect of parting with his name so that he can enjoy the amenities of someone else's pass book which is not accountable for in rational terms, and yet we are not at a loss to see why. Neither does the fact that an Algonquin Indian should, as Sapir tells us, refer to someone bearing the same name as 'another myself' strike us as particularly opaque or impenetrable.

Another area in which we seem to 'express feelings not connected with beliefs' is that of our relation to our dead. Fustel de Coulange thought the the execution of the Athenian captains for failing to retrieve the bodies of the fallen at the battle of Arginousae, was only explicable in terms of the conviction of the bereaved that the dead were thereby condemned to an anguished afterlife (Fustel de Coulange 1980: Chapter One). If we were ourselves unconvinced of this and wished to bring someone round to our point of view we would produce stories like that of the distress of those parents of the Moors murder victims whose bodies have never been found and therefore never properly buried; or of Lincoln's sentiments apropos the burial of his fiancée that he could not 'bear to think of her out there alone . . . . The rain and the storm shan't beat on her grave'.

Is the showing of respect for bodies of the dead where there is no distressing uptake for others unintelligible? For example, the convention observed in the dissecting rooms of American teaching hospitals of keeping the genital areas of the cadavers covered? Can such practices be exhaustively explained by invoking more and more subtle consequential considerations such as that first-year medical students are less upset if a certain decorum is observed? And what are the subtle consequential considerations in the case of the wish of lovers to be buried in a common grave? Are these not rather examples of what Wittgenstein calls attention to – 'feelings that need not be connected with a belief'?

In John Ford's *My Darling Clementine* Wyatt Earp goes to his murdered brother's graveside and fills him in on sundry matters. No one infers from this that he believes himself to have mediumistic powers nor thinks of the episode as an out-of-doors-seance. How much of what we do is an attempt to please our dead; and not just the 'passed over' Society for Psychical Research dead, nor the 'to be raised in the twinkling of an eye when the trumpet shall sound' dead, but the dead dead, the forever dead. Neither Wyatt Earp apostrophizing his brother through several feet of earth nor Dr Johnson standing in the rain at Uttoxeter Market on the anniversary of some unfilial act, need be assigned a theory of the after-life for their behaviour to be understood.

How does it follow from the fact that burning an effigy can be made clear by assimilating it to our kissing the picture of a loved one that effigies are not also burned in pursuit of some ulterior objective? Or, from our understanding that a man's name can be sacred to him in a way which dispenses with the necessity of deriving this from prudence based on occult conviction, that this isn't sometimes also the case as well? From the fact that we can make non-cognitive, expressive sense of Wyatt Earp's apostrophizing his dead brother it doesn't follow that all seances are really misunderstood memorial services. I think Wittgenstein's argument is meant to establish the gratuitousness rather than the erroneousness of Frazer's instrumentalism. But there are certain facts about our relation to Frazer's instrumentalist conception which make it necessary to modify even the charge that it is markedly strained or more difficult to fathom than an expressive one. (What is striking is that Wittgenstein is aware of these facts and himself calls our attention to them.)

The trouble with Wittgenstein's invocation of the potential perspicuity, the inventability, of rituals and practices in the service of an expressive construal of them is that it isn't only expressive rationales which can thus be related to inclinations of our own. Told that savages refuse to reveal their names because they fear they might come to harm we could be brought to understand why in the same way as those for whom non-instrumental effigy-burning was made clear by being reminded that they kiss pictures of loved ones.

Among the superstitious propensities which could be invoked to diminish our perplexity at the occult practices described by Frazer is the irrational dismay felt by the subjects of an ingenious *gedanken* experiment by Howard Mounce of Swansea. He asked his students to imagine that they had pierced the eyes in a drawing of their mothers and that they then discovered that she had gone blind. Would they think themselves responsible? A certain proportion did. This argument does not get its force from how large a proportion this was but from our relation to the response of those who felt rationally unaccountable remorse. (In fact Mounce's experiment is strictly otiose and we could just ask ourselves how we would feel under the imagined circumstances.) Why don't these feelings do for effigy burning and cognate practices when instrumentally construed, what Wittgenstein's picture-kissing does for them when expressively construed?

It might be objected on behalf of the superior eligibility of the expressive construal that what Mounce's experiment illustrated was not a conviction of occult influence but a momentary reaction. But is the transition from impulsive to institutionalized expressiveness any more easy to imagine than that from impulsive to institutionalized instrumentalism? Are the instrumental analogies any more remote from the magical practices they are meant to illuminate than the expressive ones that Wittgenstein reminds us of? Even those expressive magical practices which are most like striking the ground in anger aren't completely like them. Those who practise human sacrifice (or mimic it) to celebrate the harvest can't just agree to be angry at the appropriate time nor do they just find themselves growing more irritable as the days get longer. Even in the picture-kissing case there are disanalogies not to be neglected – effigies are not burned on impulse and pictures of loved ones are not kissed at calendrically determined intervals. There is thus a gap between the institutionalized practices and the impulsive inclination which Wittgenstein brings forward to illuminate them. So in either case, instrumental or expressive, a certain imaginative leap is necessary if an analogy from our own inclinations is to make an exotic practice clear.

Boswell told Johnson that since he had been happy for moments at a time he could imagine someone else to be so continuously. If we allow a related argument to be invoked on behalf of an expressive conception of effigy burning via picture-kissing and furniture-kicking why not on behalf of instrumental effigy burning via Mounce's *gedanken* experiment? It is not the fact of the practice which makes an exotic rite clear but the inclination it incites us to acknowledge, which we must then extrapolate to the problematic rite. We must, for example, traverse the ground from our inclination to do things analogous to pressing our lips together when we want someone to restrain himself, to the periodic immobility of the emperor as an expression of concern for the tranquillity of his empire. The distance from the inclination to the rite may be generally longer in the case of the rites instrumentally construed than when expressively construed but there is no difference in principle. And there are cases where the distance is not longer. It is difficult to see what expressive satisfaction could be derived from destroying the fingernails of an enemy, and in such a case thinking of our transactions with pictures of loved ones doesn't help. And it helps even less when the finger nails destroyed are one's own where the instrumental construal that it is a precautionary measure is markedly more eligible than the expressive. Does Wittgenstein pressing his lips together, or Jane Harrison making sympathetic pseudo-facilitory movements during a tennis-match, really make couvade, say, clearer than Frazer's occult homeopathic convictions make it? And in the case of the emperor's periodic immobility in connection with the tranquillity of his kingdom, Wittgenstein's expressive account is no more eligible than the instrumental one, because though we may find difficulty in crediting an instrumental rationale for the practice, we find as much difficulty in the notion that such effort would be expended in the interests of an expressive purpose alone. If someone kissed photographs of loved ones for hours at a time at fixed intervals, we would doubt the adequacy of a purely expressive account.

The real objection to Wittgenstein's pro-expressive argument from inclinations in ourselves is that it too often leaves us where we were before. Confronted by practices which are enigmatic and may be either instrumental or expressive, a more vivid sense of their connection with our own feelings and thoughts is as likely to confer perspicuity on an instrumental account as on an expressive one. I will support this claim with some instances.

Although there is no reason 'why a man's name should not be sacred to him' this does not preclude its also being a matter of occult concern to him. And there are cases where instrumentalist assumptions make as much sense as expressive ones. The assumption that a consequential rationale is required to make sense of the primitive's proscription on having a descendant named after him while he is still living, might well be felt gratuitous, but his keeping his name secret seems as intelligibly attributed to genuine apprehension as to a sense of dignity and may have as practical a rationale as an unlisted telephone number.

According to Guthrie, in the Athens of Plato and Aristotle a practice existed of writing the name of an enemy on a plate, transfixing it and then burying it in the expectation that this would injure or kill him (Guthrie 1950: 12–13). If we knew only what Wittgenstein calls 'the-external action' and not its rationale, would not rummaging among 'inclinations in ourselves' as readily provide us with an instrumental magical rationale as Wittgenstein's pro-expressive argument assumes it would an expressive one? (One of Pareto's residues is 'the mysterious linking of names and things'.)

Here is a contemporary instance of the practice described by Guthrie. It is from Nancy Mitford's *roman à clef, Love in a Cold Climate*:

> It was a favourite superstition of Uncle Matthew's that if you wrote somebody's name on a piece of paper and put it in a drawer, that person would die within the year. The drawers at Alconleigh were full of little slips bearing the names of those whom my uncle wanted out of the way, private hates of his and various public figures such as Bernard Shaw, de Valera, Gandhi, Lloyd George, and the Kaiser, while every single drawer in the whole house contained the name of Labby, Linda's old dog. The spell hardly ever seemed to work, even Labby having lived far beyond the age usual in Labradors, but he went hopefully on, and if one of the characters did happen to be carried off in the course of nature he would look pleased but guilty for a day or two.
>
> (Mitford 1949: 169–70)

Isn't there 'something in us too which speaks in favour' of this 'observance' of Uncle Matthew's?

When we go in search of inclinations in ourselves with which to make Frazer's examples of name magic clear (or attempt to bring to more explicit awareness those in virtue of which we already find them clear), we think of Rumpelstiltskin and are reassured that we are on the right track when we learn that Wittgenstein thought of him too. Fania Pascal tells us that Wittgenstein once read her the Grimm fairy tale about Rumpelstiltskin, the sorcerer dwarf, who agreed to relinquish his claim on the first born of the princess if she could tell him his name: 'I remember him picking up a volume of Grimm's fairy tales and reading out with awe in his voice: "*Ach, wie gut ist dass niemand weiss/ Dass ich Rumpelstilchen heiss.*" "Profound. Profound," he said. I understood that the strength of the dwarf lay in his name being unknown to humans' (Pascal 1981: 33).

Don't we find a peculiar appropriateness in the fact that it was Rumpelstiltskin's name that the princess had to divine rather than the number of hairs in his beard, say. And if the slips of paper which Uncle Matthew placed in drawers bore not the names, but the national insurance numbers of those he wished ill, would not his bizarrerie lose in intelligibility?

In the *Brown Book* Wittgenstein says: 'One could almost imagine that naming was done by a sacramental act and that this produced some magic relation between the name and the thing.' Isn't what 'one could almost imagine' one of the instruments with which making clear is accomplished? In a life of Hemingway we learn that he believed in what he called the 'spoken jinx', by which he meant the power of language to bring about misfortune merely by representing it, even inadvertently. Thus he was perturbed and angry when his publishers sent him the proofs of *Death in the Afternoon* with the identifying rubric, 'Hemingway's "Death"' at the head of each galley. Acquainting someone with facts like these might, as Wittgenstein says, make other facts like these appear 'more natural', but I don't think that this is the only, or even the main, rationale for their assemblage. I think that we are meant to feel an inwardness with the behaviour cited and this is why their historicity or veridicality is of little account. It doesn't really matter that no one may ever have kissed the name of a loved one.

Thus it is not the well-authenticated fact that men kiss pictures of loved ones which makes clear – thus depriving certain exotic practices of their opacity – but our relation to this fact. Its authenticity as custom does not guarantee its clarificatory power. Only our willingness to assimilate our expressive non-instrumental transactions with images and simulacra to that of the effigy burning and kindred activities of Frazer's primitives can do this. (Though the distinction between inwardness and mere familiarity is not one we will always be able to make with confidence and there are even instances where we will find, to our surprise, that though we do feel confident our confidence is not shared.)

It might be of no help in attempting to render perspicuous an expressive, non-Fustelian account of the execution of the victors of Arginouasae to point out that some among us have had the experience of trying to comfort cadavers for being dead and for the harm through which they came to be dead. Those to whom these facts are addressed may find them as opaque as the matters it was hoped to make clear by means of them. Someone may consider that Lincoln's response to the storm beating on Ann Rutledge's grave, rather than illuminating the vengefulness of the bereaved of the Arginousae's, merely shows that Lincoln was momentarily deranged and thus as beyond understanding as those his behaviour was meant to elucidate. But even where there is no denying our inwardness with the practice or inclination which has been introduced to clarify an exotic ritual it may be doubted whether it succeeds because of its remoteness. We can easily imagine someone who agreed that he would experience dismay at the absurd thought that he had harmed his mother in the circumstances described by Mounce, nevertheless protesting that the gap between his momentary dismay and the routine practice of homeopathic magic was too large.

There are several instances of making clear which seem to me to fail through the remoteness of the clear practice from the opaque one it is meant to naturalize. Brandon, like Jane Harrison, thinks that homeopathic magic is a natural extension of imitative action – 'the urge on the part of a spectator to assist action by some corresponding gesture' (Brandon 1973–4,vol. IV: 100). But is the analogy between the motion of our feet when watching a footballer (or the principle it illustrates) and 'lighting fires in midwinter to strenghten the weakening sun' good enough? And isn't there a gap, if not a gulf, between the girl Jane Harrison describes leaping among the growing hemp and the motoric overspill of a sympathetic observer watching someone attempting a high jump? The hemp unlike the athlete provides no incitement to vicarious participation. Marett's invocation of our custom of mitigating the absence of loved ones by carrying their pictures to support the naturalness of the view (which he thinks lies behind pre-historic cave paintings) that 'the vivid

61

suggestion of a desired event is a means to its realisation' (Marett 1927: 28), doesn't seem to me to draw the two practices close enough together.

On the other hand, when I think of the animated cartoon convention in which Tom or Jerry, or whoever, finding himself chased up a cul-de-sac, draws a door on a solid surface through which he then proceeds to escape, the notion that the cave paintings of speared and dying prey are examples of occult intrumentality, gains in intelligibility and plausibility. Of course in this case we can't even say that what the animated cartoon episode puts us in mind of are 'inclinations of our own'; they are more our deliria and phantasmagoria and, if Hallpike's Piagetan speculations about early childhood are right, our archaic reminiscences (Hallpike 1984). Some of us find ourselves wanting to say of the animated cartoon device in which an image becomes its object, as of Stan Laurel's transactions with his fist/pipe, what Wittgenstein said of the secret name in Rumpelstiltskin: 'Profound! Profound!' But of course we know that there are those who will not have had the instrumental rationale for mimetic magic rendered lucid by such considerations and will be bewildered as to why we think so; what came to us as a solution is for them another mystery to be penetrated.

Closely related to name magic is the wider notion of thought/speech magic. John Beattie observes that even among ourselves it is obscurely felt that 'to say or to think something solemnly and emphatically enough is somehow to make it more likely to happen' (Beattie 1964: 204). Isn't this the self-same principle which, stylized and elaborated, has been held to rationalize much primitive ritual? Many rituals can be seen as collective wishing dramatized with whatever materials are to hand, assisted perhaps by chanted imperatives or optatives. The question is whether conceiving of this dramatized, objectified wishing as likely to influence its fulfilment can be made any less perspicuous to us, i.e., is any less intimately related to 'inclinations in ourselves', than conceiving it as expressive/symbolic merely.

Francis Cornford's account attempts to do justice to both views:

'Sympathetic Magic consists in the representation of the object of passionate desire. Primarily, this representation is mimetic – in other words, the realisation of the desired end in dramatic action. The emotion is satisfied by actually doing the thing which is willed. . . . In the earliest stage . . . the dramatic action and the desired effect are not distinguished. The rainmaker feels simply that he is making rain, not that he is imitating the fall of rain, in order to cause real rain to fall subsequently. When the faith in magic begins to weaken, some distinction must begin to arise between the mimetic action and the real event; some notion of causality makes its first appearance.

(Cornford 1957: 139)

This account is incoherent. If the rainmaker does not distinguish between the dramatic action and the desired effect what can it mean to say that 'the faith in magic begins to weaken'? Faith in magic is only called for if magic is already conceived as a means of bringing about ends independent of, and ulterior to, the magic ritual itself. But Cornford's havering does inadvertently illustrate the ease with which the transition from an expressive to an instrumental conception of mimetic rituals is conceived, a point on which Beattie also insists (Beattie 1964: 205, 212, 215).

A similar ambiguity infects the following remarks:

To the magician knowledge is power . . . . To form a representation of the structure of nature is to have control over it. To classify things is to name them, and the name of a thing, or a group of things, is its soul; to know their names is to have power over their souls. Language, that stupendous product of the collective mind, is a duplicate, a shadow soul, of the whole structure of reality; it is the most effective and comprehensive tool of human power, for nothing, whether human or superhuman, is beyond its reach.

(Cornford 1957: 141)

When Cornford says that 'to form a representation of the structure of nature is to have control over it' he could mean either, that in consequence of his representation of some aspect of nature the magician thinks he can actually influence her or, that the representation of nature itself constitutes control independently of any ulterior effect it may have.

If we resolve this ambiguity in favour of an instrumental

construal then we can treat Cornford, too, as testifying to the affinity between the relation in which Frazer's primitives stand to magic and we, in our metaphysical deliria, to language. Hallpike argues in his Piaget-inspired account of primitive beliefs that the mode of thought described by Cornford, which he calls nominal realism, is a phase through which all humans pass on their way to 'operatory' thought (Hallpike 1979).

When Wittgenstein spoke of 'the mythology of language' and of 'magic as metaphysics' ('bringing something higher under the sway of our words') it is probably nominal realism he had in mind. Faust's 'In the beginning was the deed' (which Wittgenstein cited in this connection) has been taken as an emendation of the first verse of John's Gospel but it may have been only an elucidation of it: 'In the beginning was the Word/deed.' Why is this (largely superseded) propensity of ours not as capable of illuminating at least a certain range of occult practices, as are Wittgenstein's instances of our expressive/ symbolic inclinings?

But some of the practices described by Frazer are out of reach even of the sign/referent magic with which I have been urging our inwardness. The principle that is exemplified in many of Frazer's examples of instrumental magic is that of an occult connection between vaguely isomorphic events, one which is independent of human willing but which may be exploited by it and against which precautions must be taken, 'analogy magic' in Walter Burkert's phrase. A familiar example is the folk view that a man dying by a seashore will live until the tide goes out. Yet here too, we have something which is far from alien to us. The principle is illustrated by an incident in *Great Expectations*. The convict Magwitch, about to recount his history to Pip, takes out his pipe to fill it, and thinking that 'the tangle of tobacco in his hand . . . might perplex the thread of his narrative' puts it back again. Does this not confer a degree of intelligibility on the following custom recorded by Frazer? Among the Ainos of Sakhilin 'a pregnant woman may not spin or twist rope for two months before her delivery, because they think that if she did so the child's guts may be entangled like thread' (Frazer 1967: 17). This might seem too remote from Magwitch's behaviour to be elucidated by it but consider the following which immediately succeeds it in Frazer's text:

For a like reason in Bilaspore, a district of India, when the chief men of a village meet in council, no one present should twirl a spindle; for they think that if such a thing were to happen, the discussion, like the spindle, would move in a circle and never be wound up.

(Frazer 1967: 17)

Doesn't this act as what Wittgenstein calls an 'intermediate case' thus suggesting how the impulse operative in the case of Magwitch might also underlie the Aino proscription on a pregnant woman spinning?

It is said that when Napoleon began crossing the Niemen to invade Russia his horse stumbled and someone commented, 'a bad omen; a Roman would have turned back'. Similar stories are told in connection with other ventures. If the connection between a stumbling horse and the miscarriage of an enterprise seems natural even to those who don't credit it, how much in Frazer's accounts of homeopathic magic can we find unassimilable? A clue to the depth of the homeopathic principle is provided when we reflect how different our feelings as participants in a Mounce-like *gedanken* experiment would be if, having pierced the eyes of a picture, we were asked to imagine that the subject of it went not blind but deaf.

There was a famous Singapore towkay who was convinced that if he ever stopped building he would die. During the Japanese occupation, when he had to stop because building materials were not available, he did indeed die. This story is retold, with variations, throughout the world, probably because it occurs, with variations, throughout the world. Don't we feel a peculiar appositeness in the relation of the compulsion to the apprehension?

I don't think that these examples work simply cumulatively, as Wittgenstein suggests. In Moore's notes he speaks of reducing our perplexity at a rite by finding similar ones since this will 'make it seem more natural'. This isn't the way it is with homeopathic magic since instances which have no weight at all as evidence of the extensiveness of a practice may nevertheless mitigate its opacity. Wittgenstein's own example of the mouse in *Alice* drying out the sodden animals by reading them 'the driest thing he knows' does this for word magic.

Something which can do this for the notion of image/object magic and yet is extravagantly incapable of acting as evidence (unlike Hemingway's 'spoken jinx') is a comic routine of Stan Laurel's. Finding himself without his pipe he makes a fist and stuffs tobacco into it. When he sets it alight – puffing on his extended thumb – smoke issues from his mouth. Isn't this a fantasy fulfilment of Frances Cornford's incoherent notion of a 'dramatic' action which is simultaneously 'its desired effect', a reversion to Freud's auto-plastic phase 'when the omnipotence of thought was a reality'?

The notion that an image may take on the property of its object (whether it is autonomous or derivable from Beattie's principle or the source of it – thought as a kind of picture) extends from myth, fantasy and fiction to folk belief; from *Galatea*, the toy figures in Hans Christian Anderson, The Commendatore's statue in *Don Giovanni*, *Pinocchio*, *The Picture of Dorian Grey*, M. R. James's 'The Mezzotint' and Anatole France's 'Le Jongleur de Notre Dame' to a multitude of weeping statues of the Blessed Mother. There is a peculiar appropriateness in the notion of an occult connection between image and object. If with every successive debauch Dorian Grey's national insurance number became paler until it was finally illegible, the story would lack something.

What does Wittgenstein imagine our predicament to be with respect to effigy burning, and other apparently homeopathic operations, from which his picture-kissing analogy is to rescue us? He imagines us to suffer from a temporary, remediable incapacity to imagine that such activities could have other than practical objectives: and the remedy is to remind us of the strength and pervasiveness of our ceremonial, celebratory, memorializing impulses – 'Human life is like that.'

Wittgenstein's argument seems to require that whenever we have a ritual practice which Frazer construes as intended to achieve some ulterior end we can bethink ourselves of some non-instrumental practice or inclination of our own which could more economically account for it. But have not the examples just expounded illustrated the equal or greater eligibility of instrumental accounts? What grounds can be given for rejecting them?

Attempts to make clear can fail for either of two reasons: either because the practice or inclination which is appealed to is itself problematic and lacking in perspicuity, or where this is not the case, because it is found too remote from the opaque, exotic practice it was intended to clarify.

Let us examine the first requirement. In order to make anything clear we need to know something which is already clear. Now what do we know which is already clear? What is it that confers perspicuity on a practice? Why did Wittgenstein think that kissing the picture of a loved one was clear? Or beckoning to someone we wish to approach us? Or, pressing our lips together when we wish someone to be silent? Or, striking an inanimate object in anger? Familiarity?

No. Mere familiarity with similar practices is not enough. For in that case, not only could instrumental magic be rendered as perspicuous as expressive, but it would also be difficult to see how the need for elucidation of the ritual activities, recorded in *The Golden Bough*, could arise in the first place. How can 'people of the Book' have found the occult practices recorded by Frazer puzzling or his instrumental accounts of them questionable? Did not Elisha remonstrate with Joash for striking the ground with his spear thrice only, thus passing up the chance of obliterating the Syrians completely; and were not the Israelites able to defeat the hosts of Amalek only so long as Moses's arm was upraised? Even those of us without Bible culture can't have escaped similar stories from other sources.

We are perfectly familiar with the notion of effective wishing from fairy tales (e.g. *The Three Wishes*) and from folk custom (the wishing well, wishing on a star, the fowl's wish-bone, etc., etc.). Are these disqualified from making clear because we think them fiction whereas we know that kissing the picture of loved ones is fact? This is not the reason. Some of these stories are perfectly capable of making clear in spite of their fictional status and others are incapable of doing so even if their factual status was not in question, because they are not clear themselves. Familiarity does not guarantee perspicuity whereas it is perfectly possible for a mere fantasy to provoke an awareness of inclinations in ourselves capable of conferring perspicuity on practices hitherto opaque or only vaguely comprehensible. If being reminded of the story of Rumpelstiltskin fails to make clear the reluctance of a primitive to reveal his name, it is not because it is fiction but because it has failed to 'connect with our own feelings and thoughts'. And if kissing the picture of a loved one makes clear it is not because it is familiar but because it does.

We can't dissipate our perplexity with respect to a practice by invoking examples of superstitious practices, anecdotes, or ideas which are themselves problematic, however familiar they may be. They must first themselves be rendered clear by persuading us to see them in a certain light. This can't be done with all the omens, superstitions and stories of the supernatural we are familiar with but only with a subclass of them in which we can recognize inclinations of whose independent existence they remind us. It is not the unfamiliarity of the story of the aborigine's mislaying of the object containing his soul which makes it perplexing. Even if it had been taught in multi-cultural compulsory religious instruction classes and so was as familiar as the story of *The Three Wishes* or *Rumpelstiltskin* it could be no less in need of elucidation.

What makes an inclination to attach an occult power to names and uttered thoughts such as Hemingway displayed *our* inclination and not just *my* inclination or *his* inclination? Whether or not you agree that Harrison, Brandon, etc., have succeeded in dissipating the opacity of the notion of leaping dances, for example, you will find yourself contradicted and you won't know what to say. Should discussions of the opacity or perspicuity of exotic practices stop with success or failure at attaining the suffrage of those addressed, or are there further steps to be taken?

The following formula suggests itself – a practice has been made clear when the person to whom the parallels and reminders which are to make it clear are addressed says it has been made clear. But, can't he be wrong, not only about the pertinent others who constitute the 'we', but about himself? Not only do reminders of Stan Laurel's smoking transactions with his thumb sometimes fail in making primitive magical transactions with simulacra less opaque, but even when they do succeed, someone may, nevertheless, come to feel that he was being sequacious, and on attempting to reassure himself may find that he is unclear as to how, in a case like this, he is to distinguish non-sequaciousness from perverse contradictoriness. His grasp of what counts as 'understanding' or 'making sense' wavers.

What, finally, is the upshot of all these considerations and counter-considerations? What is the value of Wittgenstein's contrast between explaining and making clear? And why does it matter whether or not we find instrumental magic clear?

Perhaps Wittgenstein's remarks should not be read for the light they shed on ritual practices since perspicuity bears so tenuous a relation to historicity; people do act for reasons of which we can make no sense and the sense we do make of them is often not the sense they have. The extent of Wittgenstein's contribution to the explanatory enterprise is that of removing objections to non-instrumental or non-ratiocinative accounts on the score of their implausibility by relating them to inclinations of our own. But the predominant value of Wittgenstein's remarks is not their contribution to the explanatory tasks of anthropology or pre-history but for the light they shed on our relation to exotic practices – on where we might seek those 'familiar images' of which we see in these practices 'a distorted reflection', in Levi-Strauss's formulation.

Those who attempt to address each other on questions such as these must recognize that they are questions in which many of their fellows will take no interest. The only satisfaction these seek from explanation is the satisfaction of having the phenomenon explained in the way in which only further information can explain (Ernest Gellner, Marvin Harris). But the enterprise of making clear encounters a more demoralizing difficulty. It is that those who do respond with perplexity to accounts of certain practices and who are in search of the satisfaction of which Wittgenstein speaks and which can only come about by being related to an inclination of their own, will often respond diversely to the parallels and analogies which are intended to produce such satisfaction. And when they do disagree as to whether the invocation of an 'inclination of our own' has succeeded in conferring perspicuity on a hitherto opaque practice they will have no means of resolving their differences. It is on their willingness to tolerate this state of affairs that the value they place on enquiries, such as those Wittgenstein invites us to undertake with respect to magic, will depend.

BIBLIOGRAPHY

Ambrose, A. (1979) *Wittgenstein's Lectures 1930–1935*, Oxford: Clarendon Press.
Ayer, A. J. (1980) *Wittgenstein*, London: Weidenfeld & Nicolson.
Beattie, J. (1964) *Other Cultures*, London: Routledge & Kegan Paul.
Brandon, S. G. F. (1973–4) 'Ritual in religion', *Dictionary of the History of Ideas*, New York: Scribners.
Chesterton, G. K. (1905) *Heretics*, London and New York: John Lane.
Cook, John (1983) 'Magic, witchcraft and science', *Philosophical Investigations*, vol. 6, no. 1, January.
Cornford, Francis (1957) *From Religion to Philosophy*, New York: Harper.
Drury, M. O'C. (1974) *The Danger Of Words*, London: Routledge & Kegan Paul.
Frazer, Sir J. G. (1967) *The Golden Bough* (abridged edition) London: Macmillan.
Fustel de Coulange, Numa St Denis (1980) *The Ancient City*, Baltimore and London: Johns Hopkins.
Goethe, J. W. von (1949) *Truth and Fantasy from my Life*, edited by J. M. Cohen, London: Weidenfeld & Nicolson.
Guthrie, W. K. C. (1950) *The Greek Philosophers*, London: Methuen.
Hallpike, C. K. (1979) *The Foundations of Primitive Thought*, Oxford: Clarendon Press.
Harrison, Jane (1918) *Ancient Art and Ritual*, London: Home University Library.
Hudson W. D. (1987) 'The light Wittgenstein sheds on religion' in John Canfeild, *The Philosophy of Wittgenstein: Ethics, Aesthetics and Religion*, New York: Garland.
Levi-Strauss, Claude (1963) *Structural Anthropology*, New York: Basic Books.
Levi-Strauss, Claude (1966) *The Savage Mind*, London: Weidenfeld & Nicolson.
McGuinness, B. F. (1982)'Freud and Wittgenstein' in Brian McGuinness (ed.), *Wittgenstein and His Times*, Oxford: Blackwell.
MacIntyre, Alasdair (1970) 'Is understanding religion compatible with believing?' in Bryan Wilson (ed.), *Rationality*, Oxford: Blackwell.
Marett, R. R. (1927) *Man in the Making* (revised and enlarged edition), London: Thomas Nelson & Sons Ltd.
Moore, G. E. (1966) 'Wittgenstein's lectures in 1930–33' in *Philosophical Papers*, New York: Collier Books 1966.
Mounce, H. (1973) 'Understanding a primitive society', *Philosophy*, October; also in R. Beehler and A.R. Drengson (1978) *The Philosophy of Society*, London: Methuen.
Mitford, N. (1949) *Love in a Cold Climate*, London: Hamish Hamilton.
Pascal, Fania (1981) 'Wittgenstein: a personal memoir' in Rush Rhees (ed.), *Wittgenstein : Personal Reminiscences*, Oxford: Blackwell.
Rudich, N. and Stassen, M. (1971) 'Wittgenstein's implied anthropology', *History and Theory*.

Rhees, Rush (1982) 'Wittgenstein on language and ritual' in Brian McGuiness (ed.), *Wittgenstein and His Times*, Oxford: Blackwell.

Rhees, Rush (1971) 'Introduction to remarks on Frazer's Golden Bough', *The Human World*, no. 3, May.

Sabini, John and Silver, Maury (1982) *Moralities of Everyday Life*, Oxford: Oxford University Press.

Winch, Peter (1972) 'Understanding a primitive society' in Peter Winch, *Ethics and Action*, London: Routledge & Kegan Paul.

Wittgenstein, Ludwig (1967) 'Bemerkungen Über Frazer's The Golden Bough', *Synthese*, translation by John Berzelius; also in C. G. Luckhardt (1979) *Wittgenstein: Sources and Perspectives*, Brighton: Harvester Press.

Chapter Five

UNIVERSAL PRINCIPLES AND PARTICULAR DECISIONS AND FORMS OF LIFE

A PROBLEM OF ETHICS THAT IS BOTH POST-KANTIAN AND POST-WITTGENSTEINIAN

KARL-OTTO APEL

1. EXPOSITION OF THE PROBLEM AS IT IS RAISED BY PETER WINCH

1.1 In order to elucidate and display the problem exposed by the title of my paper, I will refer to a discussion between Peter Winch and myself which took place ten years ago at the University of East Anglia. Commenting on my conference paper 'Types of Social Science in the Light of Human Cognitive Interests',[1] Peter Winch gave an insightful survey of my claims in so far as they expressed a *hermeneutic* approach close to (and indeed inspired by) his own interpretation of the later Wittgenstein's work. However, he then expressed his misgivings and finally his critique of those presuppositions of my *transcendental-pragmatic* claims that are indebted to a Kantian or a Peirceian confidence in a priori insights into universal principles, e.g. regarding the necessity of 'regulative ideas' (and counterfactual anticipations) concerning an ultimate consensus about human validity-claims with regard to meaning, truth, and even rightness of norms.

Starting out from an analysis of particular cases rather than from universal postulates, Winch was prepared to admit that it is sometimes plausible to expect (and even to postulate as a presupposition of the discussion's making sense) that one would eventually reach a consensus. As an example he mentioned the case of two mechanics searching for, and discussing, their hypotheses about the possible cause of a motor defect in a car. But, on Winch's account, this presupposition would not be based on the *transcendental-pragmatic* insight that the idea of a serious argumentative discourse implies, somehow, the presupposition that it must be possible, in principle, to reach a consensus about a validity-claim – in the present example, a truth-claim. It would, rather, be based on a very special 'paradigm' of the 'inter-wovenness' of language use with activities and expectations of experience (in the sense of Wittgenstein and Thomas Kuhn). Hence Peter Winch would even 'hesitate to say, without considerable qualification, that the postulate of an eventual consensus holds generally within the context of natural scientific investigation'.[2]

As a crucial counter-argument against my transcendental-pragmatic postulate of a universal consensus as being an implication of the very notion of a serious, argumentative discourse, Peter Winch introduced an example from ethics. Referring to an essay by George Orwell, he confronts Gandhi's idea that 'for the seeker after goodness there must be no close friendships or exclusive loves whatever' with Orwell's rejection of this 'other-worldly' ethics by the following argument of a 'humanistic ethics'[3]: 'The essence of being human is that one should not seek perfection, that one is sometimes willing to commit sins for the sake of loyalty, that one does not push asceticism to the point where it makes friendly intercourse impossible, and that one is prepared in the end to be defeated and broken up by life, which is the inevitable price of fastening one's love upon other human individuals.'[4]

Winch's intention in confronting these two positions is not to argue in favour of one or other of them but rather to show that there are cases – presumably the paradigm cases of moral discourse? – where it makes no sense to expect, or to postulate, a possible consensus by arguments about the right position but where, nonetheless, every single person has to take a stand through judging his unique situation. In these cases one is called on 'to make a definite choice between . . . opposing ideals', and 'a man who chooses in one way need not think that anyone who, in such a situation made a different choice, would be mistaken'. Thereby Winch means to say that the person who makes a definite choice *does not logically commit himself to the judgment that anyone else in the same situation had to make the same choice.*[5]

By this argument, Winch obviously thinks to meet and to seriously question the universal validity (or at least the practical applicability in a moral discourse) of the abstract principle of 'the universalizability of moral judgements'. For he points for further discussion to a pertinent essay in his *Ethics and Action*[6] where he argues (again with the aid of a poet, namely, Melville) against Sidgwick's and Singer's version of the *universalizability principle*. In order to narrow the problem that I wish to share with Winch, let me try to distil his position from his essay in *Ethics and Action*.

1.2 There, in his argument with the proponents of the universalizability principle, he first makes it clear that he is not attacking the validity of the abstract principle in so far as it concerns 'the relation between judgments made by one and the same person' who is 'in the position of a spectator,' i. e., that he does not wish to question Sidgwick's thesis that 'one judgment, made by me as a spectator of another's situation, commits me to other judgments, also made by me as a spectator'.[7] Hence he explicitly accepts the universalizability thesis 'as applied to the relation between such judgments', emphasizing that considerations of 'consistency, intelligibility, and rationality do apply in moral matters'.[8] He is calling into question only the claim that the person judging his own action in a certain way 'must also be prepared to say: "And other people too, if they are to judge rightly, must make the same judgments as I have made concerning these situations." '[9] Or, more precisely, the claim 'that all statements of the verbal form "X ought to do so and so" (or "X has the right to do so and so") behave in the same way' no matter whether the place of X is filled by 'I, by 'He', or by 'She'.[10]

Now this thesis obviously suffices for Winch to call into question the following widely accepted versions of the universalizability thesis proposed by Sidgwick and Singer:

If, therefore, I judge any action to be right for myself, I implicitly judge it to be right for any other person whose nature and circumstances do not differ from my own in certain important respects.[11]

Hence to give a reason in support of the judgement that a given individual ought or has the right to do some act presupposes that anyone with the characteristics specified in the statement of the reason ought, or has the right, to do the same kind of act in a situation of the kind specified.[12]

Winch is contesting that these are *universally* valid, or more precisely, that they are applicable to 'a certain class of *first person*

74

moral judgments'.[13] In explaining this further, he is again careful to exclude current prejudices, as e. g. the suspicion that he might wish to defend 'special pleading or the making of an exception to a moral principle in one's own case'. In contradistinction to these suggestions, he says that he is interested 'in the position of a man who, *ex hypothesis,* is completely morally serious, who fully intends to do what he ought to do but is perplexed about *what* he ought to do.'[14]

Such a case presents itself, Winch suggests, if the agent, in his attempt at grounding his decision, is confronted with a conflict between two moral commands both of which can be based on universalizable principles.[15] In this case he is compelled to find out what is the right thing to do just for himself, that is, to judge his situation in such a way 'that deciding is an integral part of what we call "finding out what I ought to do" '.[16] It is such a 'first person moral judgment' that, according to Winch, cannot be universalized in such a way that the agent 'would be committed to implicitly judge it to be right for any other person whose nature and circumstances do not differ from his own in certain important respects'.

Winch finds an example for this case in Melville's novel *Billy Budd, Foretopman*[17] where the 'Captain, "Starry" Vere, R.N., captain of H.M.S. *Indomitable,* on active service against the French in the period immediately following the Nore mutiny, when further mutinous outbreaks aboard H.M. ships were feared at any time', was confronted with the following inescapable moral dilemma: he had to decide, by his judgment before a summary court martial, whether the foretopman, Billy Budd, had to be executed (or acquitted). Billy Budd had committed the capital offence of striking his superior officer, the master-at-arms of the *Indomitable,* Claggart, who, as a consequence, fell and died. However Budd's action was the expression of the circumstance that he was, on account of a speech impediment, prevented from answering Claggart's completely incorrect and unjust charge, made before the captain, that Billy Budd had incited the crew to mutiny.

The captain in Melville's novel considers and explicitly describes his situation as a conflict between his responsibility for the observation of the military law (the King's Regulation) and the strongly felt appeal of his 'private conscience', which he believes to be based on 'natural justice' and which tells him that

Billy is 'innocent before God'. In this situation, which Winch interprets as 'a conflict between two genuinely moral "oughts", a conflict, that is, *within* morality',[18] the captain decides in favour of execution since 'private conscience should . . . yield to that imperial one formulated in the code under which alone we officially proceed'.[19]

Winch takes that as an example of a first person moral judgment to which the universalizability-principle cannot be applied. He illustrates this assessment by the following confession: he himself, he intimates, could not have acted as did Vere, since he 'should have found it morally impossible to condemn a man "innocent before God" under such circumstances',[20] but he finds it impossible to criticize the captain's judgment. The point for him is that, in this case, neither he himself nor the captain need universalize their judgments.[21]

Winch emphasizes that this does not mean that he would deny the difference between what a man thinks he ought to do and what he in fact ought to do, as might be suggested by a version of the Protagorean claim that 'man is the measure of all things', according to which it would be senseless to ask who is right, since p might be true-for-A and not p be true-for-B. Winch asserts, contrary to this, that in the considered case of first person moral judgments, 'it can be that both are correct'.[22] The reason why this is possible is definitely suggested by Winch (as I understand him) by his comments on a passage he quotes from Hare's *Freedom and Reason*, which reads as follows: 'Since we cannot know everything about another actual person's concrete situation (including how it strikes him, which may make all the difference), it is nearly always presumptuous to suppose that another persons's situation is exactly like one we have ourselves been in, or even like it in the relevant particulars.'[23]

Winch claims that to admit this means to admit 'that, within the class of moral judgments to which this remark applies, ("preeminently, an agent's judgment about what he ought to do"[24]) the universalizability principle is *idle*'.[25] He seems to mean that it cannot be *applied*, since one never can know, with ultimate certainty, whether another person is in the same situation as oneself, this crucial condition of the principle's application being warranted, at best, only in so far as certain conventional roles may be attributed to unique persons. Winch especially stresses the parenthesized clause in Hare's text, 'including how it strikes him'. He comments: 'if we want to *express*, in a given situation, how it strikes the agent, we cannot dispense with his inclination to come to a particular moral decision.'[26]

This appears to me to be plausible since the 'inclination' – at least in the captain's case – may be understood as a necessitated disposition which, at least by implication, still belongs to the inescapable circumstances of the situation with which the agent is confronted. But then Winch illustrates the case by comparing the captain's situation with that of his senior officer who was for acquitting Billy, and he expresses the difference between both situations in the following words: 'faced with two conflicting sets of considerations, the one man was disposed to give precedence to the other, and convict.' And he concludes definitively: 'If such dispositions as this have to be taken into account in applying the notion of "exactly the same circumstances", surely the last vestige of logical force is removed from the universalizability thesis.'[27]

I should be inclined to comment on this by saying: 'Yes, indeed', since 'dispositions', as they are now characterized by Winch, obviously *anticipate the decision that is in question.* Thus they must, of course, a priori, abolish any chance of the universalizability principle intervening in the process of judgment formation at the point where the different persons could be confronted with the same situation, which, *ex hypothesi,* is the crucial condition for the application of the universalizability principle. (This also seems to me to be internally related to the reason why Winch tends to deny the difference between the cognitive problem of *finding out* what is the right thing to do and the volitional problem of *deciding to act* – possibly against one's insight into one's duty.)

But, even if I leave aside this last point (which perhaps only misled me), I cannot find it plausible that the impossibility of providing complete knowledge about another actual person's concrete situation should imply that the universalizability-principle must be idle, i. e. inapplicable to the situation of an agent who *tries to find out* what, for him, is the right thing to do.

Of course, if the agent who *has come to find out* what, for him, is the right thing to do, would feel entitled to connect his judgment 'This is what I ought to do' with the corollary 'And anyone else in a situation like this who comes to another result must be wrong', then he exposes himself to the reproach of being presumptuous or dogmatic. This is because he *absolutizes the correctness of his factual judgment* and thus ignores the *proviso of fallibility.* Does this mean, however, that the agent could not or should not, *in searching for the right solution of his decision-problem,* say to himself: 'I ought to find a solution of my problem which, if right, would also be binding "for any other person whose nature and circumstances do not differ from my own in certain important respects"' (Sidgwick), or: 'I ought or have a right to do some act that is in accordance with the presupposition "that anyone with the characteristics specified in the statement of the reason ought, or has the right, to do [so] . . . in a situation of the kind specified"' (Singer)?

I have the feeling that Winch, by falling a victim to (or exploiting) an ambiguity in Sidgwick's formulation, misses the point of the universalizability-principle. For Sidgwick's formulation could easily be modified to be read like this: 'If, therefore, I have to find out whether an action be right for myself, I have to (at least implicitly) judge whether it could be right for any other person whose nature and circumstances do not differ from my own in certain important respects.' One could even add: 'Any action I would be entitled to judge to be right for myself, I should implicitly judge to be right for any other person . . . etc.' Thus far it turns out (it seems to me) that Winch's special class of first person moral judgments does not represent an exception to, or even a counterargument against, the universalizability-principle as a normative principle of ethics but rather, it represents another problem: viz., whether it is permissible to universalize one's own fallible judgments by making them binding for everybody? It is, of course, not permissible.

It even appears to me that the captain in Melville's novel tries very hard to come up to the demand of finding a universalizable solution of his problem according to the mode of application that I suggested; although he could do so, I believe, only within the limits of his understanding of the principle. For he seems to have difficulties with connecting the universalizability-claim with the demands of what he calls 'private conscience', or at best 'natural justice', whereas his argument before the court martial, as Winch rightly observes, 'takes the form of putting the claims of the military code in a peculiarly impressive and compelling light'.[28] (I shall come back to this point later.) On the other hand, it seems to me doubtful whether one is entitled simply to state in a straightforward way, along with Winch, that the story seems to show 'that Vere did what was, for him, the right thing to do'.[29] For the captain's last murmured words 'Billy Budd, Billy Budd', even if they 'were not the accents of remorse', as Melville suggests, may nonetheless, perhaps, be interpreted as an expression of his lasting uncertainty about the rightness of his decision. This at least could be expected if one presupposes, as I do, that any such decision stands under the *proviso of fallibility*.

Any way, even on my interpretation one must admit that the application of the universalizability-principle becomes very difficult if (or when) the criteria for imaginatively identifying *those who are in the same situation as oneself* are no longer determined by certain conventional roles or institutions (e.g. that of an officer or a judge who are bound to certain codes of law) but are to be generalized in such a way that they may be applied to so called decisions of 'private conscience'. Many would even deny that there are, or can be, criteria for attributing equal rights or equal duties to unique persons beyond the domain of institutionalized or conventional norms. But, on the other hand, it seems clear too, that the *universalizability-principle* ('from Kant onwards', as Winch reminds us) is the outcome of the enlightenment's questioning precisely the *universal validity of all institutionalized or only conventional norms*. Hence, as a philosophical principle (like 'natural justice'), it is just not intended to be applied to limited classes of agents who are defined in terms of sociological concepts of membership, status or role, but rather to *human beings* as subjects of 'human rights' and corresponding duties – or to 'reasonable beings' (*'Vernunftwesen'*), to speak along with Kant and not, say, to 'Prussian officials' (*'Preußische Beamte'*), as was sometimes suggested in a popular German illustration of the 'categorical imperative.'

Now one could raise the question whether this 'transcendental' idea of a universalizability principle that would be applicable in a *post-conventional* and *unlimited* way, might be 'idle' in the sense in which Wittgenstein uses that expression in his critique of meaningless metaphysical language-games whose 'interwovenness' with possible activities and experiences, hence with real 'forms of life', can no longer be shown. Would it, perhaps, simply make no sense for a person who must come to a 'first person moral judgment' concerning the right thing to do, to ask whether a considered judgment could be universalized in such a way as to appear to be right for every other reasonable person who might be in a situation that does not differ from theirs in any relevant respect?

This seems to be the really serious problem that has been raised (though not solved) by Winch in his pertinent essay in *Ethics and Action*. Hence I will take up this problem and make it the subject of a renewed discussion in what follows.

1.3 However, before entering into this discussion, I have to remind the reader that for me the preceding interpretation of Winch's essay in *Ethics and Action* was only a roundabout way of achieving a better understanding of his comments on my 'transcendental-pragmatic' postulate. This postulate claims that it is an implication of the notion of a serious argumentative discourse to suppose that it is possible, in principle, to reach an ultimate consensus about validity-claims concerning meaning, truth, and even the rightness of norms. Now it seems clear after the preceding discussion that Winch would want to extrapolate his suggestions from *Ethics and Action* and apply them to the transcendental-pragmatic postulate in something like the following way.

Just as, on his account, it makes no sense to apply the universalizability principle to a certain class of first person moral judgments as exemplified by Melville's novel, so it should make no sense, either, to apply the postulate of an eventual consensus on a certain class of discussions as they are exemplified by Orwell's argument with Gandhi. Here, again, the example relates to the problem of moral norms that could be binding for a unique person. But the special feature of the problem is now constituted, not by the search after the right judgment as a basis for deciding how to act in a single case, but rather, by the search after the ideal of the good life (in the Aristotelian sense). The dilemma in this case (according to Winch) is that one has 'to make a definite choice between opposing ideals', e.g. Gandhi's 'other-worldly' ideal of asceticism and Orwell's 'humanistic ethics' of engagement in 'close friendships and exclusive loves'. [30]

Thus we are, here, arriving at a first comprehension of the meaning of the two interrelated problems that are exposed in the title of this paper by the phrase 'Universal Principles and Particular

(Incommensurable?) Decisions and Forms of Life'. In what follows I will try to deal with both problems from the point of view of a transcendental pragmatics (of language or communication). Therefore, I must first make clear how the transcendental-pragmatic account of argumentative discourse may be capable of grounding universal principles of philosophy, especially those of Ethics.

2. THE DIFFERENCE AND POSITIVE RELATIONSHIP BETWEEN THE LANGUAGE-GAMES OF EVERYDAY-LIFE AND THE ARGUMENTATIVE DISCOURSE OF PHILOSOPHY WITH REGARD TO THE PROBLEM OF GROUNDING VALIDITY-CLAIMS ACCORDING TO THE PRINCIPLE OF UNIVERSAL CONSENSUS

In the preceding section I have tried to comply to the best of my ability with the post-Wittgensteinian style of philosophizing as it is practised by Winch in his analysis of concrete examples. In what follows, I shall start in a rather post-Kantian style by introducing a universal principle of grounding validity-claims that, I suggest, can itself be grounded a priori and, though not functioning like an axiomatic basis for deductions, may at least serve as an ultimate point of view for the perspectives of a systematic 'architectonics' of philosophizing.

It seems plausible from the beginning that there must be an internal relation between the universalizability-principle of ethics and the transcendental-pragmatic thesis. This thesis states that the notion of a serious argumentative discourse implies the *regulative idea* of a universal consensus to be reached about all controversial validity-claims, as for example, those concerning meaning, truth and even the rightness of norms. The two principles obviously share the common presupposition that what can claim to be *valid – on the level of a philosophical argumentation about validity-claims –* must be capable of being reconfirmed as being *intersubjectively valid without limits; valid, that is to say, for everybody,* and that means: *acceptable by universal consensus.* This much granted, it seems clear, furthermore, that the transcendental-pragmatic principle *contains* the ethical universalizability principle; for ethical rightness-claims with regard to norms (i.e. normative judgments) are just one class of validity-claims.

On the other hand, there seems to be also a difference, at least in accent, between the two principles. For the ethical *universalizability-principle*, at least in the Kantian version, suggests that every reasonable being can discover a priori and by solitary thinking, which norm *is* universalizable, i.e. valid for everybody and hence acceptable by universal consensus. Contrary to this, the point of the *transcendental-pragmatic consensus-principle*, which is strongly inspired by Charles Peirce, is that we must enter upon a real communicative discourse about people's experiences and claims, in order to reach a universal consensus in the long run, knowing, at the same time, that each factual consensus (just as a solitary anticipation of the universal consensus) is subject to being *fallible*.

It seems clear that this perspective of a real consensus-formation by an unlimited and revisable procedure involves important consequences in respect to the application of the ethical universalizability principle. It means, on the one hand, that a transcendental-pragmatic *ethics of discourse* ('*Diskursethik* '[31]), which I, indeed, would defend, makes it a point to have the consensus-formation realized by bringing to bear the interests of all affected people, be it through their participation in the discourse, or be it through their advocates, or be it, as a last resort, through a single person's responsibly anticipating their possible arguments in a thought experiment. Now, since 'practical discourses', in contradistinction to the 'theoretical discourses' of the sciences, cannot wait for a consensus that is to be reached *only in the long run,* it becomes immediately clear, on the other hand, that a consensus reached in this way is always provisional in a special sense. On the one hand, even a genuine argumentative consensus of the affected persons about practical questions would still be fallible and revisable, in principle, as are the results of the theoretical discourses of the sciences. On the other hand, this provisional consensus would need to represent what may count as the right thing to do according to the universalizability principle – as must, on Kantian premises, a solitary decision based on a thought experiment (in the light, for example, of the 'categorical imperative').

Thus it shows itself that the postulate of a *universal consensus* as a principle of ethics is, on the one hand, an attempt at a *concretization* of the *universalizability-principle* : it shows how it has to be applied as a procedural principle of an argumentative discourse (real or fictional) which has to bring to bear the interests and experiences of all possible subjects of a possible redemption of the claims to universal validity. On the other hand, it sticks to the a priori intuition of the internal relation between the notion of *validity* as justified by arguments and the notion of a *universal consensus*, and thus shares a common transcendental presupposition with the universalizability principle.

In the first respect, the postulate of consensus-formation by argumentative discourse already suggests an answer to the following question: how could it be imagined that a *post-conventional version of the universalizability principle*, whose application is not restricted by social criteria of membership, status or role, could nevertheless be *applied* and hence not 'idle' in the sense suggested by Wittgenstein or, respectively, by Winch. It has to be admitted, though, that the conditions of its application suggested thus far are extremely difficult to fulfil, since any *real discourse* can of course only be an approximate realization of the *ideal discourse* that *would* guarantee a universal consensus, i.e. a genuine, sincere and self-transparent discursive consensus of all affected people (not of all who are present, possibly at the cost of the absent people). It is at this point where the real problems of a discourse-ethics (e. g. those which provide an ideal yardstick of an ethical valuation of the different possible types of consensus-formation, including those of a representative democracy) actually begin.[52] (I cannot adequately deal with these problems in the present context, but I shall come back to them later.)

With regard to the a priori intuition which, I suggested, constitutes the common transcendental presupposition of the universalizability (and the universal consensus) postulate, it may of course be asked, how it could be grounded as being a normatively binding principle, even if, as a 'regulative idea' in Kant's sense, it can only be approximately realized. Winch asks precisely this question with regard to my approach in his initially quoted comments. His question reads: 'What reason does Apel have for his claim that serious intellectual discussion implies such a commitment to an eventual universal consensus?'[53] As a possible answer from my perspective he suggests the following argument (which, however, he considers too abstract, in order to settle the question): 'I think he would want to say that, without this, the participants are not genuinely putting forward their views for criticism by others but are, as it were, disingenuously withholding something in their private domain as immune from criticism.'[34]

This argument could indeed be *part* of my possible answer, provided an appropriate context. Thus it would, for example, be a very good characterization of the attitude of those people who would behave in the following way suggested by Winch as an alternative to the disputants' subjection to the postulate of striving for an eventual consensus. Having first made the need for the subjection to this postulate dependent upon the special desires of the disputants (which I would of course not accept), he asks some rhetorical questions: 'What if Gandhi and Orwell recognize that any prospect of eventual agreement between them is no more than a pipe dream. And what if, as intelligent, realistic men, they therefore do not enter the discussion with the aim of reaching agreement. Does it mean that, to this extent, there can be no meaningful discussion between them from which they may both learn?'[35]

My answer would be: this may of course happen as a matter of fact; and there may be good reasons for it happening which I would even accept in my own case. And I would not be committed, either, to denying that in this event there remains a variety of meaningful types of communication from which the partners may learn, ranging from small talk or conversation to those serious forms which one might, in ordinary language, call 'discussion'. (There are also those forms which I would cluster around the type of negotiation or bargaining, through which even *agreements* can be reached, but, of course, not a *discursive consensus by arguments*.) In reality, there may be all kinds of transitions between these 'language-games', for the ideal types of a possible structural analysis can never be equated, in my opinion, with the empirical facts.

However, I would never admit that all this is compatible with entering what I call an 'argumentative discourse'. By that I understand that ideal type of communication that makes science and philosophy possible and which has, in fact, grounded their internal connection since the times of Socrates (experimental science having later integrated, as it were, the vote of nature into the human dialogue).

I could even characterize and delimit in a much sharper form what I mean by 'argumentative discourse' and by a language-game that commits the players to those rules (especially moral norms) that are internally connected with striving for consensus by arguments: I could simply point to that discourse which we are *necessarily* practising when we are trying to settle questions such as these about validity-claims – Winch and I ten years ago at the University of East Anglia, and I myself when I am trying to continue that discourse. We are necessarily exemplifying the structure of argumentative discourse because there is no other possibility than making the transition from whatever type of human interaction or communication to entering upon serious *argumentative discourse* and subjecting oneself to its moral norms, if one wishes to find out who is right, i.e. whose claims can be redeemed by arguments (and not, say, by open fight or by negotiations). And in a philosophical discussion we are entitled to suppose that all this has already been accepted, at least implicitly, whatever the psychological facts about the secret, private reservations of the participants may be.

Is this a far too 'abstract reflection on what we mean by expressions like "discussion", "inquiry", "intellectual seriousness",[36] so that it cannot cope with what we have to learn from concrete examples of human communication?

I think this suggestion rests on a misunderstanding of the *phenomenon* of the philosophical language-game (i. e. the philosophical sub-type of argumentative discourse) and its special relationship to *all* other types of language-games, especially those in which validity-claims are raised that can lead to conflicts. The misunderstanding goes back, as far as I can see, to the later Wittgenstein's style of analysis which has exercised so much influence and won so much authority in our time. For, in all his close studies of concrete examples, and his suggestions concerning the 'family-resemblances' between them and the contrast between functioning language games of everyday life and idling philosophical language-games, he never reflected on those structures of his own, those actually practised, philosophical language-games that make it possible – even for Wittgenstein – to speak about *language-games in general* and of their structure.[37]

(The same holds for the many followers of Wittgenstein's 'therapeutic' method who (vainly) try to avoid universal 'theoretical' statements. Richard Rorty, for example, tells us – by universal philosophical statements, of course – that we don't need context-transcendent universal principles or criteria and hence philosophical arguments that could be distinguished from literary discourse.)[38]

If I am saying that Wittgenstein 'never reflected on these structures', I mean to imply that *reflection* (in a non-psychological sense i.e. reflecting on one's role as one who argues and the validity-claims and presuppositions that are necessarily connected with that role) makes up the only cognitive way of becoming aware of the special structure of the philosophical language-game, especially of its unique relationship to all other language-games.

If one is willing to reflect on those structures then one can find out, with a priori evidence, that as one who seriously argues (or as one who asks a question in the sense of making it the subject of an argumentative discourse) one must have accepted a set of factual and normative presuppositions, which one can neither deny, nor even call into question, without entangling oneself into a *performative self-contradiction.* I want to enumerate here, without any claim to completeness, just the following presuppositions:

1   that the argumentative discourse of philosophy, along with the different types of scientific discourse, has the function of putting controversial validity-claims to the test by arguments which have the aim of coming to an eventual consensus about whether or not they are justified;

2   that it, in contradistinction to the language-games of everyday life and even to the different types of scientific discourse, has the function – not to be evaded by declarations of modesty or by attempts to retreat into rhetoric, literature, or *ad hoc* self-therapeutics – of finding out and stating *what the truth of things is in general* ('*wie es sich* überhaupt *mit den Dingen verhält*'). It has the function, that is, of making *universal* statements about, for example, universal validity-claims themselves and their possible redemption etc.;

3   that it, in particular, is the only *conceivable* instance (the meta-institution, so to speak, with regard to all institutions) by which conflicts concerning controversial validity-claims of moral and legal norms, hence, about the legitimacy of human institutions, may be *rationally* settled;

4   that it (through reflection on those moral norms it must itself
     necessarily presuppose, in order to function) can also provide
     an ultimate foundation of a *moral principle* (that of an *ethics of
     discursive consensus-formation*) which, by prescribing the
     procedural rules of practical discourses, can indirectly (via
     the results of the practical discourse) fulfil the function of
     rationally grounding concrete norms or institutions;

5   finally, that it – through self-reflection as in (4) – can also find
     out that it, together with the serious questions, always already
     implies the answer to questions like 'why be reasonable?',
     'why be responsible?', 'why be moral?': it implies a
     transcendental-pragmatic, reflexive answer to questions that,
     as is well known, cannot be answered without a *petitio principii*
     with the aid of formal logical operations.

Thus far *transcendental-pragmatic self-reflection*, i.e. reflection on the
function of the argumentative discourse, to be practised by everyone
who argues seriously, can, in my opinion, very well give an affirmative
answer to the sceptical question (for example, posed by Alasdair
MacIntyre and others): how could it be shown that there is a 'practical
reason', in Kant's sense, according to whose 'law' we *voluntarily* (by
'autonomy') subject ourselves to the 'categorical imperative', i.e., to
the universalizability-principle. Kant himself, having based his
transcendental reflection on the function of an (in principle) *solitary*
and *pre-lingual* 'I think' (or 'transcendental apperception'), could not
offer a *transcendental grounding* of the 'moral law'. He had to give up
this attempt in the *Critique of Practical Reason* in favour, on the one
hand, of a *metaphysical explanation* (based on the doctrine of 'Man as a
citizen of two worlds') and, on the other hand, of a somewhat
dogmatic affirmation that the 'moral law' is just a self-evident 'Fact of
Reason' that needs no further grounding.[39] Now, transcendental-
pragmatic self-reflection on the nature of *arguing*, by becoming aware
of those normative presuppositions that are implied in the notion of
an ideal argumentative discourse of an ideal communication
community, is indeed capable of deciphering, so to speak, Kant's talk
of 'The Fact of Reason' as referring to an *a priori perfect*, so to speak. It
can do so by showing that in serious argument (which, by the way,
cannot be *preceded* by any other mode of valid thinking), one who
argues has *necessarily* always already recognized (i.e. acknowledged)
the 'moral law'.

Of course, I am aware of the fact that the suggested method of *transcendental-pragmatic (i.e. non-psychological) reflection* is the last thing to appear plausible in our day. Logicians considered it the cause of semantic antinomies and proposed as a substitute the infinite series of meta-languages; and others, (e. g. Gilbert Ryle) asserted that reflection on the act of reflection must lead to an infinite regress.[40] I cannot adequately deal with this problem in this context, but, instead of taking a stand explicitly, I want to suggest one at least by asking the question: how is it possible that we *know with a priori certainty* that an attempt at psychological self-objectivation, as well as replacing pragmatic self-reflection of speech by a series of meta-languages, *must* lead to an infinite regress?

At any rate, if one seriously enters upon the suggested reflection on the presuppositions of argument one may find out that one cannot deny or doubt them without committing a *performative self-contradiction.* Furthermore, one may even find oneself in a position to 'observe' – of course not in the 'behaviouristic' way, but by hermeneutic role-taking – that every speaker in a philosophical discussion (especially those who practise the performative self-contradiction by asserting, for example, that arguing is 'practising violence') *shows* that he implicitly recognizes the transcendental presuppositions of argument. He even shows by the way he addresses his audience – especially if he tries to convince it of the contrary – that he cannot but *counterfactually anticipate* an *ideal speech-situation* and the possible *consensus about the claims concerning meaning, truth, and rightness* that are implied in his actual speech.

It is by pointing to these phenomena that I should answer the following question posed by Winch: 'To whom, or to what . . . is the aim of a universal consensus to be attributed . . . ?'[41] Winch sees a 'dilemma' in trying to answer this question: on the one hand, he recognizes that the answer must not depend on 'empirical facts about the participant's psychologies', but rather is to be derived, a priori, from the very conception of a serious discussion; on the other hand, he asks: 'What is it for a discussion to have aims and beliefs, especially if these are not thought of as in any way shared by the participants in it?'[42]

In answering this question, I would first deny that one could be entitled to suppose that the participants in a serious argumentative discourse (those who have not given up *that* language-game in favour of one of the variety of other possible language-games, be they serious or not, which cannot, in principle, solve the problem of redeeming validity-claims) *should not in any way* share those aims and beliefs that are internally connected with the institution of the argumentative discourse. Even if one admits that an individual participant in a philosophical discussion may secretly give up serious arguing, it would not make sense (precisely on Wittgenstein's premises, I think) to conclude from this possibility that participants in an argumentative discourse must not, as such participants, in any way share those aims and beliefs that they are supposed to share (and reflectively suppose themselves to share) if they are seriously participating. For this last situation is the paradigm-case.

Of course this does not mean that the participants in an argumentative discourse could not have very different private aims and beliefs *besides* those they must at least implicitly have if they are seriously participating in that language-game. They may in fact have all kinds of beliefs and aims, especially those controversial ones whose justification or critique makes up the subject of the discourse; for this is of course *ex institutione* compatible with their sharing common presuppositions concerning the rules and aims of the discourse. They may even have all kinds of dubious psychological ambitions, expectations, and reservations with regard to their chances in, or the relevance of, a particular discourse, so long as this does not seriously disturb their following the procedural rules of an argumentative discourse.

Hence I may answer Winch's question by stating that the beliefs and aims that are the transcendental presuppositions of the notion of serious argument, may very well be attributed to the human participants of the discourse. They need not, and perhaps never will in a pure form, be attributed to them as empirical subjects of their psychical states. Rather, they will be attributed to them in their role as members of the ideal community of argumentation, which is counterfactually anticipated by those who are seriously addressing the audience in an argumentative discourse. The best example I can provide for illustrating this answer was delivered by Winch himself by the following (for me, unforgettable) thesis which he brought forward in the discussion at the University of East Anglia and which I now quote from memory. He addressed his audience in a way that was obviously anticipating a possible consensus by saying something like this: '*We* can recognize that *we* cannot abstract in our discussions from the fact that *we* are particular, individual persons with different historical backgrounds, life histories and aims.'[43]

I think, this statement *shows* by way of a performative self-contradiction that *we* can and must be able to abstract from the latter facts, when we are reflecting on our role as subjects of the argumentative discourse of philosophy. For, on my interpretation, the first and the second 'we' in Winch's statement (although they, by their function in the address, also refer to the particular, individual persons present), in contradistinction to the third 'we', appeal to the participants of the discourse not as particular, individual persons, but as members, so to speak, of that indefinite, ideal community of argumentation of which we are in charge when we propose, defend or contest validity-claims. For Winch was not intending by his statement to say that, incidentally, the participants in that particular discourse could not abstract from their individuality. He wished to say that this is impossible, in principle, for human arguers as such.

However, isn't that indeed true just for *human* arguers as such, for the simple reason that they are human beings, with bodies that cannot be *separated* from the '*substantia cogitans*'? This question, I suggest, points to the reason why Winch had difficulties with the transcendental-pragmatic abstractions in general. For it is indeed not possible – on my account as well – to *separate* the transcendental functions of arguing from the particular, individual persons. And it was Descartes' mistake, in his dualistic metaphysics of the two substances, to confuse '*quod est clare et praecipue ad distinguendum*' with what can be *separated ontologically.* Still, Kant in his distinction between the 'empirical' and the 'transcendental I' (not to speak of the 'intelligible I') suggests a metaphysical separation according to which 'man is a citizen of two worlds'. But on the other hand, these metaphysical hypostatizations of abstract distinctions are not meaningless, I suggest, but point to a real problem and keep it present, so to speak, for a possible solution that might perhaps be post-metaphysical.

Thus far, I may have succeeded in making clear how *universal principles* (especially the postulate of striving for a universal consensus about validity-claims, which contains the universalizability principle of ethics) may be grounded according to the transcendental-pragmatic approach. But I have still to show how one could deal, from this perspective, with the problems of *particular existential decisions* and *particular forms of life* in so far as they, under finite conditions of human life, are not, and cannot be, *factually* solved on the basis of a universal consensus between those who must decide about actions or who must choose forms of life. I do not doubt that this is the dimension of the especially serious problems – partly beyond the limits of a *universalistic* ethics – that are exposed by Winch's examples. Therefore I will by no means trivialize these problems but only try to show their relationship to the universal principles in another light than Winch does.

3. THE COMPLEMENTARITY BETWEEN FORMAL REGULATIVE PRINCIPLES OF A UNIVERSALISTIC ETHICS AND DECISIONS FOR ACTING OR, RESPECTIVELY, CHOICES OF CONCRETE FORMS OF LIFE

In order to find out more closely how far the way of attaining a universal consensus may reach and where, or how, its limits are to be set, let us first come back once more to the dilemma of captain Vere in Melville's novel. I stated already that the supposed divergence between the captain's judgment and Peter Winch's own probable judgment in a case like that, and especially the point made by Winch that both agents in such a case would not be entitled to criticize each other for their divergent judgments, would not be arguments against the applicability of the universalizability-principle. They are, rather, implications of each man's being aware of his fallibility as a finite being who cannot take into account all possible arguments in applying the universalizability-principle on his situation.

Now proceeding from this interpretation, one might well imagine that, notwithstanding the facts of the story, on the level of a philosophical discourse (which means indeed: in a situation that is unburdened from the pressure of having to decide about one's action) the discussion about finding out how to act in accordance with the universalizability-principle in a situation like that of the captain, could be continued. And in the course of this discussion the participants might eventually come to a consensus (which I would suggest would be an achievement on the way toward the possible universal consensus) about the proposition that the

91

relation between the captain's and Winch's judgment is not, after all, just a symmetrical one. That is to say, Winch's alternative judgment could be considered to be based on arguments that, although they may appear a bit esoteric for a captain of HM's navy at Vere's time, and possibly even for a British captain during the Falkland's battle, nevertheless should have the future on their side.

For, from a philosophical point of view that combines a transcendental foundation of the universalizability-principle with a critical reconstruction of the development of moral consciousness,[44] one could argue somehow like this: Captain Vere, notwithstanding his being familiar with the idea of 'natural justice' and, of course, with the Christian belief that the personal conscience is 'immediate to God', seems to be strongly biassed towards the *absolute* liability of the 'Kings regulations', i. e. the *conventional* 'law and order' of his country. This attitude (which, on Kohlberg's account, would express stage four of the moral development which, on his estimate, is still representative of more than 80 per cent of the adult citizens even of modern countries, such as the USA[45]), it could be argued, has to be surpassed in favour of a 'post-conventional' one, which, being prepared to respect the legality of positive law, nevertheless maintains a principled reservation with regard to its *legitimacy,* that can be brought to bear in particular situations. (As a German philosopher who was an officer of the *Wehrmacht* in the Second World War, I feel strongly inclined to exemplify this last suggestion by what we had to learn in a dramatic way during our 'adolescence-crisis'. I do not say that we learned it at the right time, and still today it seems to be extremely difficult, even for the leading people in all countries, to accept the implications of what some philosophers and developmental psychologists have called the task of acquiring a 'post-conventional identity'. This would be based on a relativization – not a denial – of membership in a closed group which was naturally inherited or acquired by socialization, in favour of one's counter-factually anticipated membership of the ideal communication community, which is a community of human beings. One should not call this a 'utopia', I suggest, for a utopia is a blueprint of a new order of things that is conceived in a pseudo-concrete form, as if it could present a concrete alternative to the real world.[46] I am suggesting only a 'regulative idea' for a possible, but never finished, progress in cultural evolution.)

Having so far tried to outline the possible ways of a universalistic ethics, I do not wish to suggest that there are no factual limits to their successful applicability. For to assert this would, indeed, amount to suggesting a pseudo-concrete utopia of human life. The universalizability-principle of ethics, even in its concretized version as principle of consensus-formation through 'practical discourses', is, and must be, of course an abstract formal device. It cannot, and should not, prescribe a concrete form of life, which may be conceived, in its ethical aspect, as a unique sequence of more or less conscious decisions to be made in a finite span of life, within the context of an already existing socio-cultural form of life, and under the (never completely absent) pressure of time. The task of realizing such a concrete form of life, even if – or precisely if – it is conceived from the Aristotelian point of view as the objective of a *teleological ethics*, can never be fulfilled through *just applying the universalizability-principle*, although this does not mean, that this, strictly *deontological*, principle need not, or should not, be applied in any case of an ethically relevant decision.

I would, indeed, defend the thesis that Kant was right in putting the deontological problem of bringing to bear a universalizability-principle as of the first importance in ethics, instead of the Aristotelian (or rather Ancient and Christian) problem of realizing one's life as a good life in the sense of *eudaimonia*. This priority of the deontological point of view is justified, I suggest, precisely for the reason that ethics cannot, and must not, prescribe every single person's striving for a good life by a universally valid norm. Nevertheless it can and must demand that he or she tries to *realize his or her unique way of a good life under the restrictive conditions of the deontological universalizability-principle*.

However, I suggest that the Aristotelian problem of realizing the good life or *eudaimonia*, is a *complementary* problem of personal ethics for those who are consciously living after the break-through of the insight that is expressed by the *deontological universalizability-principle*. This means that persons on a post-conventional level of moral consciousness must comply with both demands. It also means, no doubt, that they must live under the tension between both demands. To speak more precisely: the tension to be lived through and coped with by the personal decisions under post-conventional conditions is a tension between *three complementary demands*: firstly that of the universalizability-principle, secondly those of the conventional morality and law of a socio-culutural form of life, and thirdly that of realizing one's own unique way of a good life. To cope with this tension by complying with all three complementary demands is what, in my opinion, defines the moral problem of realizing the 'post-conventional identity' as a person in our time.

By these suggestions of a systematical approach, I hope to have laid the ground for a satisfactory conclusion of my treatment of Winch's examples. And that means that I now may be in a position to compare the example of Captain Vere's decision with that of the different attitudes toward choosing a form of life that are attributed by Winch to Gandhi and Orwell. Vere's *decision* about what was the right thing to do, for him, in his 'limit situation' (*'Grenzsituation'* in Karl Jaspers' sense) may be considered to be only a single (though possibly crucial) element in the *process of choosing one's unique form of life* (the latter usually consisting of a sequence of more or less conscious decisions which are even fused into one another as constituting a single *style of life*). Hence the examples concerning Gandhi's and Orwell's divergent attitudes towards choosing a form of life as a whole, may be best suited for illustrating the *complementarity* of moral demands on the level of a post-conventional moral consciousness.

Before showing that, I want however to emphasize that, also in this case, we could conceive of a philosophical discourse in which the controversial claims would be discussed with the serious intention to reach an eventual consensus.

It could be argued, for example, that the life-situation of a youth like Romeo in Shakespeare's play, is very different from that of a public person who (like Gandhi) has to carry responsibility for representing justice in his relationship to everybody. The first may do the right thing (even as an example to others) by engaging himself to his love and by defending it, even as a human right, against impediments. There may, however, be limits to such an engagement which are set by other duties or at least by the obligatory precautions for avoiding wrong-doing. (Hence it is not self-evident that, as Orwell suggests, being involved in love or friendship must mean being committed to 'be willing to commit sins for the sake of loyalty,'[47] although this may often be unavoidable as a matter of fact.) A public person like Gandhi, on the other hand, may have good reasons (i.e. reasons that are acceptable

by universal consensus!) for abstaining from 'exclusive' friendships, especially those which may have risky political implications
– although it looks extravagant for us to be told (by Gandhi or
only by Orwell?) that he should 'seek perfection' through
pushing 'asceticism to the point where it makes friendly intercourse impossible'.[48]

But I don't wish to pursue this point any further since I can
agree with Winch in admitting that under the finite, factual
conditions of different socio-cultural forms of life, under which a
person has to choose his or her unique way of realizing a good life
in a sequence of personal decisions, factual forms of life (even
those which may count as examples for a good life) *cannot* be
based on the same choices. Thus far I can agree that the choices
of one's own form of life – just as the decisions about one's own
actions – are bound to be different from other people's choices.
But this, again, does not mean that the universalizability principle
could not, or should not, be applied at all but rather, that it has to
be applied by us human beings through fulfilling, at the same
time, the *complementary* demands that constitute the *conditio
humana*.

Now, in talking about the tension between three
complementary demands that belong to the *conditio humana* on
the post-conventional level of moral consciousness, I must be
careful to distinguish between the genuine reasons for the *moral*
tension and some apparent reasons that are based on fashionable
confusions. We have to distinguish here, it seems to me, at least
between three different accounts of the so-called 'incommensurability' of the different choices of forms of life:

(1) One account, which is quite irrelevant in respect of the
internal tension between *moral* demands, seems to be based, i. e.
insinuated, by the following fact: a good deal of the differences
and tensions between real forms of life – individual as well as
collective ones – is due to the fact that these forms of life have not
succeeded in realizing the good life. Cultural anthropologists and
philosophers with a relativistic bent of mind, however, will be
inclined to completely ignore this fact in favour of the suggestion
that forms of life (or, for that matter, 'patterns of culture') are, so
to speak, *of one piece* and therefore incommensurable, so that one
may not criticize them at all, if one is prepared, on principle, to
respect their diversity. On this account, it should have been a

priori illegitimate that, for example, the British rulers in India prohibited the Hindus from burning widows, or elsewhere, the natives from cannibalism and head-hunting. (Of course, one may also argue – according to the same logic – that the British may not be criticized for their prohibitions, since they just practised their own form of life.)

I think that this type of inflation of the right to diversity of unique forms of life, rests on the following fallacy: on the one hand, it has to be admitted and even stressed, that the coherence of moral and other features that constitute the totality of a form of life is, indeed, strong enough to exclude the possibility of *prescribing* a concrete form of life by a *universal* principle. This is the reason, I suggest, why the tradition of philosophical utopia, from Plato onward, which wants to construct a total order of life (of public and private virtue and happiness) is doomed to failure. And this holds even for those philosophies which cannot resign themselves to the fact that 'substantial' types of morality, in Hegel's sense (those that will cover more than the formal procedural principle of universalization) must always pay the price of being the result of contingent socio-cultural traditions. On the other hand, it is nonetheless fallacious to infer from this that it should also be impossible or illegitimate to morally criticize special features of concrete forms of life from the point of view of a universal principle. For the holistic coherence between moral and other features in a concrete form of human life is never strong enough to justify such a conclusion. (This holds especially for post-archaic, i.e. differentiated and reflected forms of life, it seems to me.)

(2) A second account that also inflates the morally relevant 'incommensurability' between individual and collective forms of life, is based on a similar fallacy. It seems to be motivated by a misinterpretation of the fact that the diversity of concrete forms of life, which has indeed to be morally respected, is not only constituted by the results of more or less conscious *moral* decisions but also by *other responses to the challenge of life-situations,* which may be completely beyond moral evaluation. This holds especially for those creative responses that are aesthetically relevant. They play however a delusive role in our context, because they usually make a crucial contribution to the visible, non-interchangeable physiognomy of a form of life (especially a 'pattern of culture') which, in

turn, suggests a complete unity of a unique 'style of life' that (it is concluded) can only be *destroyed* by the intervention of a universalistic ethics.

As far as I can see, this fallacy plays a decisive role in Michel Foucault's view of the history of ethics as he presents it in the last volumes of his *Histoire de la sexualité*.[49] As the paragon of true ethics there ranges the classical Greek ethics of '*souci de soi*', i.e. of self-realization through a beautiful style of life. The decay of this ethics is seen to have been initiated by the late Stoics (from Seneca to Marcus Aurelius) and completed by Christianity. They have put through (Foucault argues along with Nietzsche) a disastrous transformation of the classical ethics of '*souci de soi*' into morality '*d'une loi universelle s'imposant de la même façon à tout homme raisonnable*'.[50] Kant only opened a further way within this tradition by subjecting the 'individuality' of Man to his (transcendental) 'Subjectivity' and thus to the 'moral law'.[51] From the perspective of this reconstruction, Foucault came to formulate the fervent rejection of ethical universalism in his last public interview: '*La recherche d'une forme morale qui serait acceptable par tout le monde en ce sens que tous devraient s'y soumettre me paraît catastrophique*.'[52]

It is obvious that Foucault, like his master Nietzsche, is fascinated by the classical Greek ideal of the '*kalos kaghatos*' which made no distinction between the moral and the aesthetic part of a particular form or style of life. But, again like Nietzsche, he seems not even to recognize the problem of how to ensure that all human beings should be free to practise their equal rights of realizing their chosen form of life. Instead of reflecting upon this crucial motive and justification of the development of universalism in ethics and law, Foucault and his many 'post-modernist' followers are only prepared to equate universal normative principles with repressive coercion towards uniformity. Since I have dealt with this problem elsewhere,[53] I will at this place only suggest a retort like this: if in our day individuals or groups would try to realize their '*souci de soi*' without subjecting themselves to the restrictive conditions of universal normative principles, this would indeed be 'catastrophic'. It would be catastrophic not only from the moral point of view but also from the point of view of *protecting* the aesthetical manifoldness of the real forms of life. This shows, I suggest, that between this aspect of diversity and

97

ethical universalism – e. g. that of 'equal human rights' – there is no moral tension at all, but rather a complementarity without tension.

Now, having so far rejected, as based on confusions, two accounts of the reasons for the moral tension between the different demands that are to be coped with in choosing one's form of life, I will try to outline a third account which I indeed take seriously.

(3) I think, on the one hand, that *forms of life* – individual ones and collective ones – are indeed *incommensurable* in a sense. They are so in so far as they belong to *finite* living wholes which, nonetheless, cannot be reduced to combinations of common finite elements but rather, are different realizations of something *infinite*. On the other hand, *universal principles* of ethics as 'regulative ideas' are, it appears, something *infinite* that nevertheless has to be realized, as it were, by finite living beings in so far as they are reasonable beings. This, at least, is suggested by the fact that finite human beings as arguers can have *claims to universal validity*, as, for example, to intersubjectively valid meaning, truth, and rightness, and they must presuppose, in principle, that these claims are redeemable through universal consensus.

Now the *moral* tension between the three complementary demands, which, on my account, is characteristic of the *conditio humana*, seems to be caused by the fact that human beings, as reasonable beings, have to comply, always simultaneously, with both *infinite* and *finite* moral *claims* (for the requirements of finiteness, i. e. of realizing one's individual life and belonging to a concrete social group, also become *claims* on the level of one's morally relevant choices of a form of life).

This last account may appear to be still somehow metaphysically impregnated, recalling, for example, Kant's talk about Man as a 'citizen of two worlds'. This may indeed be the case – in the sense in which I suggested that the function of metaphysics in our day may be that of keeping certain problems open to more adequate treatments.

NOTES

1. See K.-O. Apel, 'Types of social science in the light of human cognitive interests' and Peter Winch, 'Apel's transcendental pragmatics' in S. C. Brown (ed.) *Philosophical Disputes in the Social Sciences*, (Brighton, Sussex: Harvester Press, 1979) pp. 3–86.

2. Peter Winch, loc. cit., p. 57.

3. ibid., p. 59f.

4. George Orwell, 'Reflections on Gandhi' in *Collected Essays and Journalism*, vol. 4 (Harmondsworth, Middlesex: Penguin Books) p. 527.

5. Peter Winch, loc. cit., pp. 59–60.

6. See Peter Winch, *Ethics and Action* (London: Routledge & Kegan Paul, 1972) pp. 151–70.

7. ibid., p. 152.

8. ibid., p. 154.

9. ibid.

10. ibid., p. 159.

11. ibid., p. 151, referring to Henry Sidgwick, *The Methods of Ethics* (London: Macmillan, 1907) pp. 384–5.

12. ibid., p. 159, referring to Marcus Singer, *Generalizations in Ethics* (London: Eyre and Spottiswoode, 1963) p. 367.

13. ibid., p. 159.

14. ibid., p. 161.

15. ibid., p. 162.

16. ibid., p. 165.

17. ibid., p. 170.

18. ibid., p. 158f.

19. ibid., p. 157.

20. ibid., p. 163.

21. ibid., cf. also p. 161.

22. ibid., p. 164.

23. ibid., p. 169.

24. ibid., p. 170, note 20.

25. ibid., p. 169.

26. ibid.

27. ibid.

28. ibid., p. 162.

29. ibid., p. 163.

30. Cf. S. C. Brown (ed.) *Philosophical Disputes . . .*, p. 60.

31. For recent explications of the program of 'Diskursethik' see e.g: J. Habermas: 'Diskursethik – Notizen zu einem Begründungsprogramm' in J. Habermas, *Moralbewußtsein und kommunikatives Handeln* (Frankfurt am Main: Suhrkamp, 1983) pp. 53–126; furthermore Wolfgang Kuhlmann (ed.) *Moralität und Sittlichkeit: Das Problem Hegels und die Diskursethik* (Frankfurt am Main: Suhrkamp, 1986); furthermore K.-O. Apel, 'Grenzen der Diskursethik?' in *Zeitschrift für Philosophische Forschung*, vol. 40 (1986) pp. 3–32, and *Diskurs und Verantwortung* (Frankfurt am Main: Suhrkamp, 1988).

32. Cf. my contribution to W. Kuhlmann (ed.) *Moralität und Sittlichkeit* . . ., pp. 217–64; furthermore K.-O. Apel, 'The problem of a macroethic of responsibility to the future in the crisis of technological civilization' in *Man and World*, 20 (1987) pp. 3–40.

33. Cf. S. C. Brown (ed.) *Philosophical Disputes* . . ., p. 66.

34. ibid.

35. ibid., p. 64.

36. ibid., p. 66.

37. I have brought forward this argument in all my comments on Wittgenstein's work. Cf. e.g. K.-O. Apel, 'Wittgenstein and the problem of hermeneutic understanding' in K.-O. Apel, *Towards a Transformation of Philosophy* (London: Routledge & Kegan Paul, 1980); furthermore 'Philosophical fundamental grounding in light of a transcendental pragmatic of language' in *Man and World*, 8 (1987) pp. 250–90, repr. in K. Baynes, J. Bohman, Th. McCarthy (eds) *After Philosophy: End or Transformation?* (Cambridge, Mass: The MIT Press, 1987) pp. 250–90, esp. pp. 264ff. and p. 271f.

38. Richard Rorty, *Consequences of Pragmatism* (Brighton, Sussex: Harvester Press, 1982).

39. See Immanuel Kant, *Kritik der praktischen Vernunft* (Akademie-Textausgabe, Berlin: de Gruyter, 1968) pp. 46f.

40. Cf. Gilbert Ryle, *The Concept of Mind* (London: Hutchinson, 1949) p. 195, and the critical comment on this argument in Hermann Schmitz, *System der Philosophie*, vol. 1 (Bonn: Bouvier, 1964) pp. 2f.

41. Cf. S. C. Brown (ed.) *Philosophical Disputes* . . ., p. 64.

42. ibid., pp. 64f.

43. Cf. my 'Reply to Peter Winch', ibid., p. 82.

44. Cf. K.-O. Apel, 'Die transzendentalpragmatische Begründung der Kommunikationsethik und das Problem der höchsten Stufe einer Entwicklungslogik des moralischen Bewußtseins' in *Archivio di filosofia*, LIV (1986) pp.107–59. See also note 45.

45. Cf. Lawrence Kohlberg, *The Philosophy of Moral Evolution* (San Francisco: Harper & Row, 1981).

46. Cf. K.-O. Apel, 'Kann der postkantische Standpunkt der Moralität noch einmal in substantielle Sittlichkeit "aufgehoben" werden?' in W. Kuhlmann (ed.) *Moralität und Sittlichkeit* . . ., pp. 217–64; furthermore K.-O. Apel, 'Ist die Ethik der idealen Kommunikationsgemeinschaft eine Utopie?' in Wilhelm Voßkamp (ed.) *Utopieforschung*, 3 vols (Stuttgart: Metzler, 1982) vol. 1, pp. 325–55.

47. Cf. S. C. Brown (ed.) *Philosophical Disputes* . . ., p. 60.

48. ibid.

49. Michel Foucault, *Histoire de la sexualité*, 3 vols (Paris: Gallimard – Bibliothèque des Histoires, 1976–1984), vol. 2: *L'Usage des plaisirs* (1984), vol. 3: *La Souci de soi* (1984). Cf. also Luc Ferry/Alain Renaut, *La Pensée 68: Essai sur l'anti-humanisme contemporain* (Paris: Gallimard, 1985) Ch. 3.

50. Michel Foucault in *Les Nouvelles littéraires*, 29 mai 1984.

51. Michel Foucault in 'Entretien avec Dreifus et Rabinow' in H. Dreifus/P. Rabinow, *Michel Foucault* (Paris: Gallimard, 1984) pp. 345–6.

52. Michel Foucault in *Les Nouvelles littéraires*, 28 juin 1984; cf. also ibid., *Entretien* du 29 mai 1984.

53. Cf. K.-O. Apel, 'Der postkantische Universalismus in der Ethik im Lichte seiner aktuellen Mißverstandnisse' in Klaus W. Hempfer/ Alexander Schwan (eds) *Grundlagen der politischen Kultur des Westens* (Berlin: de Gruyter, 1987) pp. 280–300.

Chapter Six

ON MORAL NECESSITY

LARS HERTZBERG

What categories one regards as central to moral thought is likely to determine the course of ethical inquiry in fundamental ways. All would agree that the concepts of goodness, of rights and duties, of virtue, belong to the province of moral philosophy. But how central are they? May there not be other categories equally important? Peter Winch, in several essays, has drawn attention to a range of concepts that moral philosophers have tended to neglect: those connected with the notion of moral necessity.

In 'Moral integrity' Winch discusses the following case: to save the life of a member of his community, a man kills the attacker who is about to shoot her. In doing so, he defies the principle of non-violence to which he and the community are deeply committed. Winch writes:

> How are we to describe the elder's position? . . . In the first place, it is quite clear that the elder thinks he has done something *wrong* in killing the gangster. It is not that he has abandoned or qualified his commitment to the principle of non-violence. The whole point of this principle . . . would be lost if it were thought of as subject to qualification in this way, and the life of the community still represents the elder's highest ideal . . . . But in the second place, it is equally clear that the elder would think that in some sense he 'had no choice' in the situation. That is how he *had to* act and if he had acted differently he would not have been able to forgive himself. My use of phrases like 'had to' and 'would not have been able to' in that last sentence may encourage some philosophers to think that what is in question here is a

conflict between a moral demand – in this case the principle of non-violence – and something 'purely psychological', a Kantian 'inclination'. Now . . . in so far as there is an implied *contrast* here between the psychological and the moral, I am quite sure that this account will not do. I said that, having killed the gangster, the elder knew he had done something wrong; but I also said that, if he had not killed the gangster, he would not have been able to forgive himself; i.e. that would have been wrong too, though perhaps in a different way. That the modalities involved on the side of killing the gangster are moral modalities is also clear from the fact that, in order to explicate them, notions like that of the innocence of the girl whose life was threatened and that of protecting the defenceless would have to be introduced. But it would be wrong to introduce them in the form of principles for the sake of which the elder was acting. They are involved in what I have called the 'perspective' of the action, but that perspective is not to be understood in the form of Kantian 'maxims' or Harean 'principles'.[1]

The reason moral philosophers have not thought it worthwhile to focus on the use of modal locutions in moral contexts, it might be suggested, is that they have been tempted to assimilate them to other uses of these locutions, uses which are assumed to be independently understood. As Winch implies in the passage just quoted, there are two opposite assumptions we may be inclined to make. On the one hand, we may think that these locutions are always just another way of invoking some moral principle or moral practice previously accepted. On the other hand, we may think that the necessity or impossibility involved in these cases are of no particular concern to moral philosophy, but can be understood in psychological terms.

I want to discuss each of these assumptions in turn. In Part I, I try to show that, while modal locutions do have a use in expressing one's commitment to a shared practice or principle, there is an interesting range of cases which cannot be understood in this way. Some of the examples discussed by Winch would seem to fit naturally into this range (although, as I shall try to argue, he himself is at times inclined to overlook this point).

In Part II, my aim is to show that an account of moral necessity cannot be helpfully given in terms of psychological incapacities, but rather the sense of incapacity that enters here is one that must itself be understood in moral terms.

I

1.1. In two recent papers, Peter Winch has brought his own thinking about moral modalities into connection with that of Elizabeth Anscombe. Professor Anscombe has drawn attention to the importance of what she calls 'stopping modals' in the teaching of various activities and in criticizing actions.[2] Among her examples are 'You can't move your king, he'd be in check'; 'You can't sit there, it's N's place'; 'You can't do that, it might hurt Mary'. She writes:

> In such a case you are told that you 'can't' do something you plainly *can*, as comes out in the fact that you sometimes *do*. At the beginning, the adults will physically stop the child from doing what they say he 'can't' do. But gradually the child learns. With one set of circumstances this business is part of the build up of the concept of a rule; with another, of a piece of etiquette; with another of a promise; in another, of an act of sacrilege or impiety; with another of a right. It is part of human intelligence to be able to learn the responses to stopping modals without which they wouldn't exist as linguistic instruments and without which these things: rules, etiquettes, rights, infringements, promises, pieties and impieties would not exist.
>
> (p. 101)

Questions about such modal statements, she points out, can in many cases be settled in ways comparable to those in which we settle disputes about chess rules (e.g. matters of law). Where a modal is supported by the appeal to a right, the appeal presupposes the existence of a practice in which the right is recognized:

> Truth about rights seems to fall into two kinds: what we may call theoretical, scientific truth on the one hand, which will be sociological or anthropological, and on the other

statements *within* the practice and the law of a certain society, statements in which we are going along with the language and continuing the practices which create the concept of a right and the particular rights together. A new statement of a right hitherto not acknowledged in the practice of the society can only be a proposal, and the idea of its really being a proposal which accords with an 'abstract truth' about rights must be the merest superstition.

(p. 141)

On the other hand, Miss Anscombe, as far as I can see, nowhere provides an account of how a stopping modal could ever be regarded as binding except in connection with a common practice (nor does she seem to recognize that there might be any call for such an account). It seems clear, then, that for Anscombe the sense of the claim that such and such a thing cannot be done depends in all cases on this being seen to be entailed by a current practice.

Peter Winch thinks that there is a close connection between moral modalities of the sort he has been concerned with and Miss Anscombe's idea of a stopping modal. This is brought out in his discussion of another example, derived from Joseph Conrad's short story, 'The Duel', and first brought to the attention of moral philosophers by R. F. Holland.[3] D'Hubert, having fought a duel with his fellow officer and antagonist Feraud, and having refrained from killing him, years later finds that this puts him under an obligation to keep Feraud from starving. Winch writes:

D'Hubert's reason for helping Feraud ('I had the right to blow his brains out; but as I didn't we can't let him starve.') . . . offers the 'special *logos*' of the modal 'we can't let him starve'. It indicates a peculiar claim that Feraud has on D'Hubert. Apart from saying what generates the claim (that D'Hubert had not exercised his right to blow Feraud's brains out), we cannot say much more about what the claim amounts to than to give some examples of the modals for which it would constitute the *logos*. (In fact it is Conrad's *narrative* that shows us what the claim amounts to.) This, I think, is quite in line with the account Miss Anscombe gives of such a *logos*.[4]

105

'*Logos*' is Miss Anscombe's term, referring to the theme of a stopping modal: it is used in support of the modal statement and indicates the nature of the impossibility in question ('because you promised', 'it's against the rules', etc.). The *logos*, however, does not refer to something that exists independently of the modalities themselves; its meaning is seen precisely in the modals it is used to support.

I believe that the phenomena to which Miss Anscombe is drawing attention are indeed important. We are inclined to overlook them, partly because we have a tendency to think that norms of conduct (at least if they are to be 'rational') must be capable of being supported by an appeal to some independently attractive end. Miss Anscombe reminds us that this need not be so. However, if without further ado we assimilate the appeals to moral modalities evoked in Winch's examples to Miss Anscombe's stopping modals, there is another important point we are in danger of forgetting, and it seems as if in this particular context Winch himself has forgotten it. We ought to be warned of a difference between the concerns of these two philosophers by the fact that the central examples of modal utterances imagined by Miss Anscombe are in the second person, whereas those of Winch are in the first person singular. The reason for this is evidently that the *didactic* use of these utterances is prominent in Miss Anscombe's concerns (as is natural in view of their close connection with current practices), whereas the utterances imagined by Winch are rather to be thought of as expressing the way in which the individual perceives a particular situation he has to face.

Thus, in Conrad's story, as I understand it, D'Hubert's remark is not to be taken as expressing a generally accepted norm concerning the relations between former duelists. We are rather to think of his reaction to Feraud's need as the mark of an exceptionally noble character, especially in view of the fact that Feraud had been viciously attacking him for years. In line with this, it would be misleading to say that Feraud had a claim on D'Hubert, as though this were something that anyone might have recognized. If that had been so, I do not think the story would have been, as Holland calls it, 'a remarkable portrayal of human fineness'. The claim, I would suggest, was only there for D'Hubert to assert: that was the way in which the situation struck *him*, and (I am inclined to say) no one else *could* have been struck by it in that way. This is not to deny that someone else in a situation like this might have said the words: 'He had to do it.' But I would be inclined to say that they would then have to be understood as expressing *D'Hubert's* perception of the situation, not the speaker's. (I shall, however, have to modify this claim later on.)

This granted, however, it is a matter of great importance that D'Hubert had need for the language of practices in order to express the way in which the situation struck him. The nobility of D'Hubert's character is brought out precisely by *his* seeing what to us is an extremely generous act as though it were simply what anyone would expect.

Assimilating moral modalities to Miss Anscombe's account thus obscures their importance for what makes an action or character admirable. There is, however, this similarity between the cases: Miss Anscombe's stopping modals (as we have seen), like the sorts of modal statements Winch had been discussing, do not require the support of an appeal to independently identifiable wants or needs.

The difference between them, on the other hand, can be seen the most clearly by contrasting what Winch, in discussing the case of the community elder, calls 'the perspective of the action', the *particularity* involved in this notion, with the way in which the concept of *logos* is introduced by Miss Anscombe. This difference, in turn, seems to be bound up with a difference in philosophical outlook, to which Winch himself draws attention in passing.[5] In her account of the learning of 'stopping modals', as well as of learning to speak, to count, etc., Miss Anscombe emphasizes what might be called the external aspect, the element of drill involved, at the expense of those aspects of the process that depend on the learner himself: on his spontaneous responses to the training. The learner, then, is seen more or less as a *tabula rasa*. The significance of the conventions is exhausted by what is conveyed in the training, and if it yields other results it must have been wrongly performed. On the other hand, the emphasis placed by Winch on the role of the learner's responses to the training leaves room for the thought that what the learner makes of the training (or fails to make of it) might be expressive of the particular person he is, of a particular way of taking the practice and its limitations. On this view (which is surely the right one to take) the way a practice is carried on depends on the ways in which individuals respond to such training, on the uniformity and the variety of their responses. This makes the practice what it is.

1.2. Winch's examples serve to draw attention to the inadequacies of a certain complex of thought conventionally surrounding the idea of a moral principle. Miss Anscombe's view of stopping modals is perhaps an instance of this. According to this way of thinking, modal statements can be taken to apply to individual agents and situations only as being instances of agents and situations of a certain type. Their application in particular cases thus always involves a generic commitment. Though a speaker may not be able to express that commitment in the form of a general principle (perhaps there will be no such way of expressing it), it will show itself in the fact that a determination to treat cases differently can only be meaningfully defended by an appeal to relevant differences between agents or situations, differences that are independent of the judgment made about the case at hand. (A similar point, I believe, can be made concerning the admissibility of transitions between 'I can't', 'You can't', 'One can't', 'No one can', etc.)

In the cases we have been discussing, however, the appeal to a moral necessity simply expresses a response to the particular situation at hand, rather like a perceptual judgment. It voices the claim that the way we would in most cases proceed, or reason, as a matter of routine, cannot be adopted, or be adopted without difficulty, in the present case: our ordinary ways of thinking get into conflict, or keep silent, or give the wrong verdict. This means that such an appeal cannot necessarily be shown up by a charge of inconsistency. Or better yet: there can be no 'ethically neutral' way of determining whether someone is being inconsistent: we might try to nudge someone into changing his judgment by pointing to other cases, but even if he does not agree with us, this does not have to mean that he is not making sense. Thus someone may regard a certain way of acting as excluded for himself, and yet think nothing of it when others act that way.[6]

These points are central to Winch's paper 'The universalizability of moral judgments',[7] in which, it appears, his thoughts about moral necessity are first beginning to take shape. (This may indeed be where the idea of moral necessity is first given prominence in British philosophy.) The case discussed there is the dilemma faced by Captain Vere in Herman Melville's *Billy Budd*: whether to sentence to death a man guilty in the eyes of the law but 'innocent before God'. Through reflecting on the conflicting claims of military law and natural justice, Vere is led to an understanding of what he must do . . . But somebody else in such a situation, considering those very same arguments, might conclude that the moral possibilities were different for him without necessarily making any further judgment about what the corresponding possibilities were for Vere or for anybody else and *without being committed to any such further judgment.* (my italics)

(Winch 1972: 168)

I agree entirely with this way of expressing the point. However, Winch also puts his position in a way that is, strictly speaking, misleading. He quotes R.M. Hare, an advocate of the universalizability thesis, who makes the concession:

Since we cannot know everything about another actual person's concrete situation (including how it strikes him, which may make all the difference), it is nearly always presumptuous to suppose that another person's situation is exactly like one we have ourselves been in, or even like it in the relevant respects.

(ibid.)

And then Winch comments: 'But if we want to *express,* in a given situation, how it strikes the agent, we cannot dispense with his inclination to come to a particular moral decision' (p. 169). This would mean that the inclination to judge this way or that is one of the circumstances that may have to be taken into account in assessing someone's decision. But when and by whom is it to be taken into account? By the agent in making the decision? But this would involve him in paradoxical self-reference. By a spectator (or the agent) after the fact? But this seems to blur a distinction one would wish to uphold: between respecting a decision and accepting it. (Winch himself obviously makes use of this distinction in his discussion about the community elder, as well as in saying, in the passage quoted above, that someone else reaching a different decision is not committed to making any judgment about what the possibilities were for Captain Vere.)

The reason why Winch is obscure here may be that his discussion still wavers between the language of moral principle (of 'right' and 'ought', of approval and disapproval), and that of moral necessity. The point to be made, I believe, is this: I might disagree with Vere's decision and yet find myself unable to argue with it; not, however, because I thought his inclination made it *right,* but because there was nothing there for my argument to get a grip on. We simply see the situation differently. (But the ways in which we see it are not part of the situation that we see.)

II

2.1. Following Peter Winch's suggestion in 'Moral integrity', I have tried to show that a plea of moral necessity or impossibility can be intelligibly made even without the support of an accepted principle or current practice. It is tempting to think that in such a case it must be possible instead to account for it in what might be called naturalistic terms, or else it seems this use of modal locutions will be left totally obscure. By this I mean the sort of modality involved, for instance, when a course of action is called impossible on the grounds that the intended result is not within our power, given the resources at our disposal; or again, because the attempt to achieve it would involve costs or consequences that we consider prohibitive.

An account of moral modalities along these lines, however, is likely to encounter an immediate objection of the following kind. In the normal sort of case, when some specific result is to be brought about, there is an effort to be undertaken which can be identified, independently of its success, as an attempt to achieve the result in question, and it is the failure of this effort that indicates (if not always conclusively) that the result cannot be attained by this person using this method. Such failures give a sense to the distinction between things under our control and things beyond it. (It is true that there are some actions we would describe as impossible in this sense although it is at least questionable whether there is anything we should count as trying to perform them – such as jumping over Mount Everest – but it is plausible to suppose that we consider them impossible because of the relation they have to things we actually try, and commonly fail, to do.)

Moral modalities, however, do not seem to involve the notion of trying in the same way. If someone claims he cannot perform an action but declares himself glad to try all the same, his claim can hardly be taken in earnest as an expression of *moral* impossibility. One may, it is true, try to do something, then find one cannot go through with it, but if this is to be regarded as the discovery of a moral impossibility, it must be understood as a discovery about oneself and one's relation to the action, not of something external. Moral modalities, accordingly, do not seem to involve the distinction between circumstances under the agent's control and circumstances beyond it, on which the naturalistic notion of necessities and impossibilities evidently depends.

A naturalistic account of moral modalities is discussed and rejected by Winch in 'Who is my neighbour?' (Winch 1987: 158f). He objects to it on the ground that it treats 'such modalities as imposing limits, not on what someone may *will*, but on what the will is capable of *carrying into effect*, given its presumed fundamental motivation'. Such an account, he thinks, is linked to the mistaken notion 'that morality is somehow based on and perhaps derivable from (an independently graspable) human nature'.

What is involved in the concept of what a person *may will* ? Winch does not have very much to say about this. Someone might, however, suggest that this concept is itself to be interpreted in naturalistic terms, and that it might accordingly provide an independent foundation for morality of the sort of which Winch is sceptical. An example of the sort of naturalistic account I have in mind is apparently to be found in Bernard Williams's paper 'Practical necessity'. He thinks of appeals to modalities in connection with action as expressing what he calls incapacities of character:

> What I recognize, when I conclude in deliberation that I cannot do a certain thing, is a certain incapacity of mine. I may be able to think of that course of action, but I cannot entertain it as a serious option. Or I can consider it as an option, but not in the end choose it or do it.[8]

What excludes an option, on Williams's account, is my recognition of constraints that I am incapable of overcoming or of objectives that I am incapable of surrendering. In the case we discussed earlier, an action was called impossible because it came into conflict with goals I happen to hold; in the case of character incapacities, the conflict is with goals that I cannot help holding.

The latter notion might be taken to explain why my regarding an action as impossible would not be compatible with my trying to perform it.

Among those constraints may be some that, as Williams puts it, 'obtain for distinctively moral reasons', e.g. because of what I see as other people's rights. This means that, for Williams, moral constraints are merely a *source* of incapacity: they do not, in themselves, constitute a particular sense in which actions may be said to be impossible. Moral constraints, then, make an action impossible only through their psychological effect on the agent.

Character incapacities are features of a person which can be identified independently of his own thought:

> These incapacities can be recognized also by the observer. The observer can, moreover, recognize a dimension of this sort of incapacity which the agent necessarily cannot register in his deliberation: that the agent could not think of this course of action at all, that it could not occur to him.
>
> (Williams 1981: 128f)

The strength of Williams's proposal, it might be thought, is that it offers an account of moral necessity in straightforward psychological terms. I want to show, however, that this is an illusion. The idea of being able to will something, I shall contend, can only be understood in an ethically relevant sense provided it is itself seen as an expression of ethical sensibility.

2.2. Let us consider what it means to be able or unable to *will* something. I suggested before that ordinarily the distinction between things under our control and things beyond it depends on the existence of something we can identify, independently of its success, as *trying* to do the thing in question. Obviously, this account does not apply in the present case.[9] A different grammar must come into play here.

Suppose someone is given a task and starts performing it, then stops, saying he cannot go on. And suppose it to be obvious that there is nothing about the external circumstances that would make it physically impossible for a man with his strength and skills to continue. In such a case what would be the significance of his claim to be *unable* (rather than simply unwilling) to go on?

Consider the role that the claim not to be able to do something will often have in human intercourse. Whatever the nature of the inability in question, making such a claim usually involves two things: on the one hand, a recognition of a demand that there is something one should do (or just a presumption in favour of one's doing it), and on the other hand an attempt to get the demand withdrawn or to get some of the consequences of one's failure to comply with it cancelled. Clearly, in such a context, a claim of inability will carry greater weight than a mere expression of reluctance.

A claim of inability may, of course, be countered with an exhortation to try harder. In some cases the claim may be defended by reference to the nature of the task, the agent's strength or skills in relation to those of others who have attempted it, etc. But where what is in question is an incapacity of the will, the possibility of testing it by reference to external evidence, as we have seen, is problematic. How then is it to be resolved? Maybe he did not set his mind to it sufficiently.

Perhaps it will be suggested that the claim to be unable to try to do something is based on a *feeling* of inability. But what would such a feeling consist in? Someone may feel strong aversion against carrying out a task he is given. But it should be clear first of all that he may go on in spite of this feeling. Besides, one may claim to be unable to go on even without a feeling of aversion, and the aversion, where it is present, need not be the reason for the claim.

I should like to suggest that the difference between someone who sincerely says that he cannot go on and someone who says he does not want to go on is in their *attitude* to the action demanded of them. While a person's self-knowledge, things he has observed about himself, may form the background of this attitude, it cannot be *reduced* to a matter of such observations, for anything known about a person's past behaviour is logically compatible with the assertion that he would be able to overcome his reluctance if only he tried hard enough.

These considerations might lead one to suppose that the inability to go on in a case like this is *constituted* by the sincere use of the words 'I can't go on', in much the same way as a person's intentions are constituted by his sincere expression of them. There is, indeed, some analogy between the cases, but there is also an important difference between them, which we might initially (if somewhat crudely) express by saying that, while a person is free to form his own intentions, he cannot freely decide what he is able or unable to do. Otherwise there would be no distinction between unwillingness and inability. Differently expressed: what a person says about his intentions is *decisive*, provided he is sincere and is not confused in what he says. But an audience need not accept a person's claim of inability as the last word. For although his words *express* his attitude they are not *about* his attitude. Their accepting or rejecting it is a matter of *their* attitude toward *him*. It is open to them to judge that he ought to try, or to try harder. So we might say: it all depends on what they make of him. Saying 'He should try harder' is like refusing to relinquish a demand, a refusal that one might try to justify by balancing the gravity of the demand against whatever circumstances, for this person, speak against trying to comply with it.[10]

Relinquishing the demand, on the other hand, might mean being prepared to be disappointed on the other: to accept that he is too weak. In other cases, however, no idea of *weakness* need be involved in accepting another's refusal.[11] On the contrary, acceptance may take the form of respect: the person who expressed the demand may come to see that by persisting he would put himself in the way of something he admires. Therefore he decides not to test the refusal (not because he despairs of succeeding, but because testing it would be despicable): so he accepts the action as an impossibility.

Thus, he may come to understand that the other sees the action, say, as dishonest, or cowardly, or mean. What moves him in this case need not be something we should call ethical; it might be the other's pride for instance. (The task of demarcating the ethical need not concern us here.) In either case, the impossibility reverts to whoever is making the demand. The important incapacity lies elsewhere, so to speak.

(We can now see why it is necessary to modify a claim that was made above, in discussing the case of D'Hubert. I made the point that, for another to say of D'Hubert 'He had to do it' would, in the particular circumstances of that case, be valid only if taken as expressing D'Hubert's perception of the situation. This must be modified as follows: for someone else to grant *that* form of expression to D'Hubert's view of things is to express his own respect for it. Otherwise, the natural form of expression would be: 'He *thought* he had to do it.')

We may respect someone's refusal to carry out a task because we understand how that course of action could be seen as coming into conflict, say, with the demands of honesty, or justice, or generosity. This does not have to mean that we see a conflict there for our part. Someone may respect, say, a conception of honesty that he does not impose on himself. This does not mean that he is dishonest. Maybe the word 'embodiment' could help us express this point: an understanding of what it means to be honest involves realizing that a concern for honesty may be differently embodied in different lives. This is connected with the fact that we primarily learn what a concern with honesty means in particular situations, as they enter our lives, not by the mediation of rules or by means of a drill. Hence the way we make this teaching our own is shaped by the particular persons we are and the particular lives we live. But at the same time we normally learn to see other ways of living as different embodiments of similar concerns. (Because there is this indeterminacy, there is scope for what we call matters of conscience.)

As I understand it, the attempt to account for moral modalities in terms of incapacities of character along the lines suggested by Williams assigns no essential role to respect or admiration. On that account, an appeal to such modalities will succeed *as* such an appeal only by convincing the other concerning the speaker's future behaviour. To believe him is to believe, for example, that it would be pointless to go on trying to persuade him. However, if the other does not believe him (if, for instance, he thinks he knows the speaker better than the speaker knows himself), there would be no reason for him to desist from trying, even if he thought the speaker sincere. This is the crucial point. For what has been suggested here is that appeals to moral impossibility or necessity may put an end to persuasion for reasons independent of what may be predicted about the other's behaviour. This, I would argue, gives such appeals their distinctive role.

Though the account given here has been critical of that offered by Williams, the two accounts are at one concerning this point: to accept an action as morally necessary or impossible for someone is to express an understanding of his life and character. The difference between these accounts lies in the fact that, unlike Williams, I have argued that the sort of understanding relevant here must itself be expressive of ethical concerns. Perhaps in this way it has helped bring out what is involved in a suggestion made by Peter Winch in discussing the case of Captain Vere.[12] According to Winch, in coming to see what he had to do, Captain Vere found out something about *himself.* And yet: 'The important point to make is that what a man finds out about himself is something that can be expressed only in terms of the moral ideas by consideration of which he arrives at his decision.'[13]

NOTES

1. Peter Winch, 'Moral integrity', reprinted in Peter Winch, *Ethics and Action* (London: Routledge & Kegan Paul, 1972) pp. 185f.

2. In 'Rules, rights and promises' as well as 'On the source of the authority of the state', both reprinted in G. E. M. Anscombe, *Collected Philosophical Papers,* vol. 3 (Oxford: Blackwell, 1981). They are discussed by Peter Winch in 'Who is my neighbour?', *Trying to Make Sense* (Oxford: Blackwell, 1987) and in the forthcoming 'Professor Anscombe's moral philosophy'.

3. See R. F. Holland, 'Good and evil in action', reprinted in his collection *Against Empiricism* (Oxford: Blackwell, 1980).

4. 'Professor Anscombe's moral philosophy'.

5. 'Who is my neighbour?' pp. 162f.

6. We find an instance of such an attitude in the life of Simone Weil. On several occasions, she insisted on imposing on herself the hardships of the unfortunate, thus virtually starving herself to death because she refused to have more to eat than the prisoners of war she heard about. This was evidently for her a moral necessity, but it was not bound up with any idea of a universal requirement: it simply expressed the way in which she saw her own life.

7. Reprinted in *Ethics and Action.*

8. Bernard Williams, *Moral Luck* (Cambridge: Cambridge University Press, 1981) p. 128. Concerning his view of the relation between trying and this form of necessity, see pp. 129f.

9. This is not to deny that we speak of trying even in cases where the source of difficulty is not a lack of physical strength or the complexity of the procedures involved. Thus, one may be told to try to enjoy oneself, to try to like someone, to try not to be afraid, etc. These are all, in a manner of speaking, cases of trying to want something. The point, however, is that 'trying' is not here the name of a specific procedure which can be identified independently of its result: nothing short of success will establish it beyond all possible controversy whether one has 'tried hard enough'.

10. Cf. the following remarks by Ludwig Wittgenstein:

> Man's greatest happiness is love. Suppose you say of the schizophrenic: he does not love, he cannot love, he refuses to love – what is the difference?!

116

'He refuses to...' means: it is in his power. And *who* wants to say that?! Well, what kind of thing do we say 'is in my power'? – We may say this when we want to draw a distinction. I can lift *this* weight, but I am not going to do it; I *cannot* lift that one.

(*Culture and Value* (Oxford: Blackwell, 1980) p. 77.)

The remark following these is apparently unrelated:

'God has commanded it, therefore it must be possible to do it.' That means nothing. There is no '*therefore* ' about it. At most the two expressions might mean the *same*.

A possible connection between these remarks, however, seems to be suggested in one of Wittgenstein's conversations with O. K. Bouwsma. (O.K. Bouwsma, *Wittgenstein. Conversations 1949–1951*, ed. by J. L. Craft and R. E. Hustwit (Indianapolis: Hackett Publishing Company, 1986) pp. 37f, cf. also p. 16). What Wittgenstein is saying, in brief, seems to be this: if someone sincerely holds the attitude expressed in saying 'God has commanded this' he cannot at the same time sincerely consider himself unable to do it, when what is in question is an ability to *want* to do something. The two attitudes simply will not fit into one space. The point is that this *is* a matter of attitudes: there is no truth in the matter of a person's ability to will something which one may grasp independently of the attitude one holds towards the action in question.

11. A similar point is expressed by R. F. Holland in the following terms: 'unlike external compulsions, this is a compulsion under which a man can act in character: indeed it can sensibly be claimed that in just such cases a man's action is most fully his' (op. cit., p. 122).

12. 'The universalizability of moral judgments' p. 168.

13. I wish to thank Robert Sharpe and the participants in the postgraduate seminar at Åbo Academy for their helpful comments on an earlier version of this paper. My special thanks are due to David Cockburn who patiently read and offered constructive criticisms of several versions of the paper. I alone am responsible for the errors that remain.

Chapter Seven

ETHICAL INDIVIDUALITY

RAIMOND GAITA

I

Many philosophers believe that Peter Winch has questioned the character of objectivity in ways which compromise the possibility of knowledge in social science and in ethics – in the social sciences because of the connections he draws between 'forms of life' and the conditions under which we find something intelligible, and in ethics because of his focus on the individual. Those who believe this often fail to notice that Winch undermines many of its assumptions. The belief that his emphasis on the individual compromises any substantial conception of ethical understanding rests on a failure to appreciate the extent to which he undermines a conception (common to both cognitivism and non-cognitivism) of what it is for something to be a moral problem (in what sense it is a *problem*) and therefore of what it is to try to find a *solution* to such a problem. David Wiggins has said that 'What we most badly need now in this field [ethics] is more options – more approaches not necessarily more "theories" or "isms"'.[1] We have had them but they have largely gone unnoticed.

A proper understanding of the character and importance of human individuality will alter our sense of both the moral subject and those to whom he is responsive. It is impossible to attend adequately to both of these in a single paper. In his essay 'The universalizability of moral judgments' (1972) Winch's attention is primarily on the moral subject: in later essays his attention is primarily on those with whom that subject interacts. This is merely a matter of emphasis: the two are interdependent and the concept which, for Winch, mediates between them is that of moral impossibility. The question what is it for a person to find

118

something morally impossible? may focus on them or it may focus on others – on what it is for another to be *that kind of limit* to one's will. In relation to the first of these emphases Winch's insight is that 'deciding is an integral part of what we call "finding out what I ought to do." '[2] In relation to the second it is the place he gives to Wittgenstein's remark that in relation to another human being 'my attitude towards him is an attitude towards a soul. I am not of the *opinion* that he has a soul.'[3] That Winch intends something different from the alternatives commonly believed to be possible is revealed by the fact that he can say both 'that there will not always be a position the acceptance of which will be definitive of a rational man of good will'[4] and that 'what is required is an account of other human beings which will make it possible to see how such knowledge can of itself impose bounds on our wills. An account that would achieve this is one which would make recognition of such moral bounds on the will a criterion for the knowledge in question.'[5] The first has earned him the reputation amongst some philosophers of being an 'irrationalist' while the second comes closer than most philosophers would think sensible to what is often called 'Socratic rationalism' – their thought being that Socrates was excessively rationalistic in his conception of the relation between moral understanding and action.

II

Winch's attention on the individuality of the ethical subject is most apparent in his essay 'The universalizability of moral judgments' and the critical passage is the following:

> One way of expressing what is puzzling about the class of propositions we are examining is to say that they seem to span the gulf between propositions and decisions. And we feel inclined to ask how *can* a gulf like that be spanned? A man in a situation like Vere's has to decide between two courses of action; but he is not merely concerned to *do* something, but also to *find out* what is the right thing for him to do. The difficulty is to give an account of what the expression 'find out' can mean here. What I have suggested is that deciding what to do is, in a situation like this, itself a

sort of finding out what to do; whereas I think that a writer like Sidgwick would have to say that the decision is one thing and the finding out quite another. It is because I think that deciding is an integral part of what we call 'finding out what I ought to do' that I have emphasized the position of the agent in all this.[6]

We may better see both the gap which the philosophical tradition has opened and why it needs to be spanned if we reflect on an assumption about the nature of moral thought which is common to both cognitivists and non-cognitivists. In contemporary philosophy it is most transparently at work in decision theory which depends upon the idea of a perfectly rational agent in whom practical reason works without error.[7]

Thinking (or reasoning) on this conception is impersonal in the sense that any rational agent can evaluate the situation of another agent and what his options are in that situation provided only that he has enough information. If I am a perfectly rational agent and you are too, then you can think as well as I can about my problem provided that you have all the information that I have. As far as *thinking* is concerned *no one's problems are necessarily theirs.* My problem might be necessarily *my* problem insofar as only *I* can make *my* decisions, but that comes *after* reasoning has delivered its verdict on what an agent such as I ought to do in a situation such as I am in; or, if mine is the kind of dilemma where there is no one thing which an agent such as I ought to do, then after reason has delivered its verdict on what my options are. Such a conception of the impersonal character of practical reasoning, insofar as it is reasoning, is by no means restricted to those who concern themselves with decision theory: indeed it is almost universal amongst philosophers and conditions a common conception of what will count as a good 'theory of what kinds of agents there should be'.[8]

Suppose I have an ethical problem. It is Friday and I must act by Monday. I have a very busy weekend ahead. You are as perfect a rational agent as there may be and you are a professor of practical ethics to boot. I give you all the information I can about my problem including, of course, all the information I can about myself – my desires, beliefs, and so on. I then ask that you hurry to prepare at least a range of options for me by no later than first thing on Monday morning. Meanwhile I continue preparing my lectures on moral dilemmas.

This is a parody of what it is to have a moral problem. It is not, in general, a parody of what it is to have a practical problem: one may do just that with many practical problems and although they remain personal problems in the sense that each person finally has to make a decision which only they can make, because it is they who must act, that fact is common to both the ethical and the non-ethical examples, and so cannot be what explains why it is a parody in the ethical case. Nor does it make a difference whether one is a cognitivist or a non-cognitivist in ethics: if one is a non-cognitivist one simply supplies the other rational agent with one's freely chosen moral principles.

I cannot argue here that the scenario I have just sketched ought to be treated as a *reductio* of a common conception of the kind of impersonality of anything that is properly called thinking or reasoning.[9] It is a common belief amongst people who are not philosophers that moral problems are, in a certain sense, irreducibly personal. This does not mean that there cannot be moral discussion, that one cannot learn from others, that one cannot seek advice, that there are not some who are morally wise and others who are morally foolish, and so on; but it does mean that all these will be misconstrued if one assumes that moral thinking is impersonal in the way that I have sketched. It also means that the necessarily personal character of a moral problem is a feature of moral *thought,* rather than a feature of something other than thought in a moral problem: I alluded to this when I said that the personal character of a moral problem is not to be accounted for by the truism that no one else can make a person's decision for them. All this means that the necessarily personal character of moral thought is internal to our sense of what it is to have a moral problem and of what thinking towards its solution may be. What kinds of practical thinking there are cannot be determined a priori: they must be discovered through an exploration of the grammar of various kinds of critical concepts in their diverse applications. In ethics it can be achieved only by close attention to the ways we express our sense of what it may be to seek a deepened understanding of good and evil and of the virtue and vices and of what the distinction between appearance and reality amounts to in relation to them. There is no other way to a philosophical understanding of the ways in which one may think well or badly other than by attention to the grammar of the extensive and, prima facie, *categorially diverse,* critical vocabularies with which we mark them.

Winch does not quite say what I have been saying. He seems to believe that the reason why moral problems are personal is because 'deciding is an integral part of what we call "finding out what I ought to do"'. I have suggested that is mistaken and I think that Winch may have been misled into thinking that the real problem was, at bottom, to achieve the right understanding of agency or of practical thinking in general: 'For Sidgwick ethics is a sort of calculus of action, in which actions are considered as events merely contingently attached to particular agents.'[10] And indeed, it might be said, in his defence and against me, that I have too easily secured the contrast between moral deliberation and some other forms of deliberation by distorting the nature of practical reasoning on non-moral matters to the point where it is *accidentally practical.*

There is some truth in this objection. The conception which I have sketched of the wrong kind of impersonality in practical thinking and which I contrasted with moral thinking *does* fail to reveal why practical reasoning is practical in a sense that implies more than that it is about practice and contingently applied in practice. It is of thinking about what to do and then applying the results of such thinking to practice, as though it were grammatically irrelevant to *the kind of thinking that it is,* that actually one must act. A sense of the inadequacy of such a conception may lie behind the sympathetic exploration of Aristotle's claim that the conclusion of a practical syllogism is not a proposition but an action, for if the conclusion were merely a proposition then it, and the thinking towards it, would be the same for us who must sometimes act and for beings who did not act but who merely contemplated their lives and amused themselves by thinking what one would do in certain circumstances if one happened to be an agent.

That cannot be the right understanding of practical thinking of any kind but it leaves my basic point untouched, for an account of that practical reasoning which I contrasted with moral thinking and which revealed that it was essentially practical, that is, thinking essentially *called forth in practice* rather than merely about practice and contingently applied to it, would still need to distinguish between when it was essentially personal in the ways that I have indicated and when it was not. We would still need to distinguish when a problem was essentially mine from when it was accidentally mine. But even though Winch failed to make that contrast clear, the fundamental thrust of his essay may be put like this: a certain sense of human individuality is internal to our understanding of what it is for someone to have a moral problem and to what thinking towards its solution may be.[11]

A further point needs to be made. In 'Particularity and morals' Winch discusses a play (*Rabbit Pie Day*) in which a commandant of a British transit camp immediately after the Second World War obeys orders to return Russian prisoners, to the Soviet Union, to almost certain death. Winch says that 'what warrants us in saying that what [the commandant] experiences is an instance of moral disgust is its connections with such notions as betrayal, breach of faith etc'.[12]

This last remark may seem obvious but there is an important point here and we see it if we ask what is the relation between such descriptions as 'betrayal', 'breach of faith', etc. and the modalities which express moral response and, in particular, what is their relation to modalities such as 'ought' and 'can't' or 'must'. One answer goes like this: for something to be a betrayal in a moral sense just *is* for it to be something that (morally) ought not to be done. Hare would say this and it may be widened to include modalities of necessity and impossibility. On such a (common) understanding of the matter such descriptions are moral descriptions only because of the prescriptive and deliberative modalities internal to them. Such a thin conception of which concepts philosophy will reveal to do the real moral work is tailor-made to the equally thin conception of the impersonal character of moral thought which I sketched earlier. Clearly it is not Winch's.

There is a mistake in the other direction: it is to think that such descriptions (Bernard Williams, coining an uncharacteristically ugly turn of phrase, calls them 'thick' ethical concepts)[13] do the real work and that the modalities expressive of moral response have no distinctively moral uses. I have given some reason for thinking this is not so and I do not think Winch thinks it is so. I suspect he believes, what, anyhow, I think is right to believe, that both moral descriptions and the modalities of moral response are *sui generis* and that they are interdependent. And this interdependence together with the emphasis on individuality will not comfort those who have hoped that attention to concepts such as cruelty, courage, betrayal, and so on, will support a relatively straightforward cognitivism.

If one believes that such descriptions cannot play the secondary role in our moral thinking and in our thinking about what it is to have a moral problem, which is assigned to them by philosophers like Hare, then we must attend more closely to kind of thinking involved in trying to achieve a deeper or more adequate understanding of what, for example, distinguishes genuine loyalty from its many false semblances. Socrates, Plato, and Aristotle were all troubled by this problem which R. F. Holland called the problem of false semblances. Of recent philosophers, to my knowledge only Iris Murdoch and Holland have thought it to be a fundamental problem.[14] Serious attention to it, at the very least, will lead to severe problems for the conception of practical reasoning according to which the impersonality of reasoning is such that each rational agent may, in principle, do another's ethical thinking for him.

III

In 'Particularity and morals' (1987) Winch objects to (Alan Donagan's) neo-Kantian construal of Judeo-Christian morality[15] by making the following comments on the parable of the Good Samaritan:

> The force of the parable comes from the sight I am asked to contemplate in imagination of this wounded man lying here in my path. That it is a man with whom I am confronted is of course essential. But though he is indeed – like any other man – an instance of humanity, he does not confront me under this aspect, but rather as a particular individual with his own nature and history. And it is important that the help I offer him should indeed take account of that individual nature and history, otherwise I can be charged with not really attending to him.

Of course the parable does also insist that help is due to any man who is afflicted solely by reason that that is what he is. That is the importance of the fact that the helper is a *Samaritan* and hence a traditional foe of the man he helps. But my point is that what is going to count as genuine 'help' will be discerned only by one who attends carefully to the nature and circumstances of the particular individual who is afflicted.[16]

Winch says that 'it is difficult to get the balance and emphasis right in stating this point'.[17] That may be misleading: what we need is not so much to get the balance and emphasis right as to introduce something new.

It is part of our common understanding (but strangely ignored by most moral philosophers) that human beings are individuals in the way nothing else in nature is. It is sometimes expressed simply by saying that human beings are irreplaceable in the way that nothing else is. It is sometimes expressed more desperately – conceptually more desperately. Gregory Vlastos said that Plato had no understanding of 'the love of persons, worthy of love for their own sake . . . in the uniqueness and integrity of his or her own individuality'.[18] Hannah Arendt has said that we cannot bring out *who* someone is in descriptions, for descriptions are always of *what* someone is.[19] Neither of these attempts to express that mode of individuality to which I, too, am alluding is satisfactory, but with Vlastos, it is the phrase 'the integrity of his or her own individuality' which is important, and with Arendt it is the thought that there is a mode of human presentness which is not wholly explicable in terms of the impact of a person's individuating features. My claim is that this sense of individuality is internal to our sense of what it is to wrong someone.

It is strange and at a certain level, mysterious, that other people can affect us as deeply as they do. Our sense of the reality of other people is connected with their power to affect us in ways we cannot fathom, as is shown by the fact that our lives seem empty when we lose those we love or, in a different way, in the destructive nature of certain dependencies. Although we often cannot fathom this power, we accept it as part of human life: if we are plunged into grief or despair because of it we may hope that time will heal our suffering and that life will reassert itself in us. It is not so with guilt: time, working alone, is denied the right to heal guilty suffering which means that it cannot heal such suffering when it is lucid. What can heal it is as strange as the suffering: repentance, atonement, forgiveness, punishment.[20] We are so familiar with this that we have lost a sense of its mystery. We are perfectly familiar with the fact that a person might kill himself because he became a murderer, even if he murdered a total stranger whose death would otherwise mean nothing to him and who was, if measured according to those qualities which are relevant to self-esteem, utterly worthless. We might condemn this kind of suicide as a confusion and as a corruption of a lucid remorse, but we find it perfectly intelligible and the fact that we do is part of our conception of the gravity of murder and of what another human being may mean to us. Any account of the seriousness of murder which does not give prominence to the way the murderer becomes haunted by his victim will be inadequate to the way in which remorse is an awakening to the terribleness of what was done. Many moral theories are inadequate in exactly that way: they are committed to saying that the murderer discovers in his remorse how terrible it is to become someone who broke a certain principle or rule, or that he was a traitor to Reason. The absurdity of this cannot be ameliorated unless the concrete individual who has been murdered assumes the kind of prominence I tried to convey by saying that the murderer is, in his remorse, haunted by his victim. But the accounts which I have criticized look upon that as extraneous to the murderer's understanding of the moral significance of what he has done. The contrary point that I wish to make is that a certain sense of his victim's individuality is internal to the murderer's understanding of the moral significance of what he had done and that this is part of what it is to be aware of the reality of another human being.

The power of human beings to affect one another in ways they cannot fathom is partly constitutive of that sense of individuality which we express when we say that human beings are unique and irreplaceable. Our need of certain other human beings is partly constitutive of a certain sense of their preciousness and of their reality but it is also, in some of its forms, destructive of it. That is why the need human beings have for one another has been a target for a familiar kind of moralism which fails to recognize that our sense of the independent reality of another human being, the acknowledgment of which is said to be threatened by need of that human being, is itself conditioned by the terrible effect that the loss of a human being may have on us. Something similar is true of remorse. One might say that remorse is the recognition of the reality of another through the shock of wronging them just as grief is the recognition of the reality of another through the shock of losing them. Both are liable to egocentric corruption: our dependencies, even at their best, tread a fine line between awakening a sense of the reality of another and submerging that sense in one of the many forms of egocentric absorption, and exactly the same is true of remorse. But the egocentricity is not merely *a* feature of the corruption, it is its central feature and is the opposite of what it corrupts. Love must sometimes find its expression in grief and our sense of the reality of other human beings must sometimes find its expression in remorse.

I said that it is strange that a person should kill himself because he murdered someone who, in every natural way, meant nothing to him and who, in every natural sense, was unworthy of anyone's esteem. I suspect that Kant and many other philosophers, in other respects quite different from Kant, find it strange too. They would prefer to say that it is not the particular person who is so important; it is the principle, or it is rational nature. They will say almost anything so long as he drops out and becomes merely an instance of something else that carries the moral weight. They will say that it cannot be him, John Smith, because would it not be exactly the same if it were someone else in the same circumstances? Isn't that already given in my example of a murderer who neither knew nor cared about his victim? His victim might have been anyone.

It is true that his victim might have been anyone, and that if it were someone else and the circumstances were the same then his moral response would have been the same. However, in remorse he is not haunted by everyman; he is not haunted by his principles; he is not haunted by the moral law; he is not haunted by the fact that he did what he ought not to have done (why should that drive anyone to despair?): he is haunted by the particular human being he murdered.

Should I not say that what is morally terrible is that he has killed *a human being* and that, of course, he will be haunted by the *particular* human being he has killed. If that is to counter what I have been saying, then it must imply that being haunted by this particular human being is extraneous to his and to our moral understanding of what he did, for otherwise, to say that what is morally terrible is that he killed a human being is only to say what is obviously true and has been acknowledged – it would have been the same if he had killed a different human being. But what is so terrible for him is not that he has killed a representative of humanity. The universality that I acknowledge when I say that it would have been the same if he had killed anyone else in relevantly similar circumstances will not yield an understanding of the moral significance of what he had done (not to him and not to a theorist) to which the individuality of his victim is extraneous and of only psychological interest. Nonetheless, it is true that he feels as he does because he has murdered a human being. But now there is no emphasis on the indefinite article. It means that he would not have felt this way if he had killed a cat.

Evidently what is needed is an understanding of the matter that reveals both why he would feel the same were it any other human being in relevantly similar circumstances, and why the particular human being he murdered is not devalued into a mere instance of something more general which is supposed to provide the ethical (non-psychological) dimension of remorse. An analogy would be someone grieving over a lost child. He grieves as he does because it is his child and would grieve so over any other of his children, but his grief focuses irreducibly and indivisibly upon *this particular child of his*. If it were not so, his grief would be as suspect as a remorse that had a representative of humanity or a moral principle as its focus. He loves his lost child because it is his child and he loves his other children because they are his children but in order to do that he must love them in their particularity.

The murderer's remorse is as it is because he has murdered a human being but in order for him to understand *that* his victim must remain with him in his distinctively human individuality for that is what it is to *be* a human being in any sense that makes the murder of a human being an immediately intelligible object of remorse. That individuality is obviously not detachable from the concrete historical human being. If he murders John Smith then John Smith does not become a mere instance of a unique mode of human individuality; the evil he did could not be captured by saying that he transgressed against a distinctive mode of individuality. It would therefore be ambiguous and misleading to say that it does not matter that it was John Smith he murdered, for, after all, he murdered John Smith, and the individual, historical, murdered, John Smith is the focus of his remorse. But it would have been the same if he murdered John Brown.

When Hare says that moral judgments are expressed in terms none of which are irreducibly singular,[21] he means that situations enter moral judgments irreducibly as *kinds* of situations, and that if John Smith is being judged then it is not only to John Smith that the judgment applies. There is some truth in this but we have already had occasion to see (Section II) that it is not so simple and we will again. For the present we should note that Hare ignores the significance to the grammar of the moral, that John Smith has a name and not a number.[22] Hare thinks of human individuality, as do many philosophers, as exhausted in numerical and qualitative distinctness.

My point should not be confused with the emphasis on partiality which has preoccupied Bernard Williams.[23] Or rather, its relation to partiality is complex. When I emphasized how strange it is that a murderer should be haunted by an anonymous tramp whom he murdered I did not mean to suggest that his remorse would have been more intelligible if he should feel it for murdering a friend. If it were it would not be that *kind* of remorse and this is captured in the claim that his remorse is for murdering a human being. To be sure, there will be dimensions to his guilty suffering if he murders his friend which will be absent if he murders an anonymous tramp. However, the deep terribleness lies in the fact that he has murdered a human being, but as I have already argued, that does not mean that his friend (from a moral perspective) is only a representative of humanity: it means that the nature of what he suffers in remorse because he has murdered his friend is conditioned by the fact that he should suffer it if he murdered an anonymous tramp. It is fundamental to an understanding of friendship *that it be bound by moral constraints which are what they are precisely because the evil of murdering a friend is the evil of murdering another a human being.* But the dialectic is such that in order to be seen as a fellow human being he must be seen as someone who could be someone's friend: that is a condition of his being within the conceptual reach of his murderer's remorse.

When I say that in order to be seen as a fellow human being the anonymous tramp must be seen as someone who could be someone's friend, I mean that he must be seen as someone who is subject to the demands which are internal to friendship, as someone of whom it is intelligible to require that he rise to those demands, no matter how often he actually fails to do so. That is compatible with him having been such a nasty fellow that nobody could befriend him, for it is to see his nastiness from the critical standpoint of what is required for friendship: he is not like a bad-tempered dog. The general point is this: for the tramp to be within the conceptual reach of his murderer's remorse he must be seen to be 'one of us', a fellow in a realm of meanings which conditions the way we may matter to one another. But friendship is in turn conditioned by what is disclosed in remorse: a friend is one who can be wronged and remorse teaches us what it is to wrong another. The point may be put more generally: the nature of remorse is underdetermined by what is internal to it – by what is necessary for someone to be within its conceptual reach. It discloses the fundamental determinant of our understanding of what it is to be a human being. It is fundamental because it radically transforms what conditions it: what it is to be a friend, what it is to be a husband, what it is be a lover – these are transformed under the shock of what a human being is revealed to be in the light of serious remorse.

The person who so evidently moves Kant, one who has been embittered and broken by misfortune but whose capacity to respond to the requirements of the moral law is not thereby diminished, is not a person who suffers remorse as I have described it. If he is a murderer then that his victim is dead does not matter except insofar as he must be dead if the other is to be a murderer. That is a manifestly inadequate conception of the seriousness of murder – that the fact that someone is dead matters only so that an action may be of a kind to fall under the moral law.

Is that a caricature of Kant's view? I think it is not. It is a consequence of Kant's position that a murderer may understand the seriousness of what he did though he cares not a fig for the fact that his victim is dead and if he lived in a community in which no one mourned the dead. Something like this must be true for Kant because although a person cannot be murdered unless he is dead, the Kantian division between inclination and duty excludes sorrow for his death as internal to the moral response: his death is internal only to the description of the deed as one which falls under the moral law. The murderer's moral response to his victim is determined solely by his sense that he violated the respect owed to him as a rational being: that he has suffered the natural harm of being killed is presumably relevant only to pre-moralized inclination – natural pity, perhaps. Kant insisted that the moral significance of murder is disclosed in a terminology that is proudly indifferent to anything that is conditioned by the fact that we are human beings in addition to being rational agents.[24] That is clearly revealed in the fact that for Kant, a person's capacity for moral response is in no way diminished by the fact that natural human feeling is completely extinguished in him. The distinction between inclination and duty undermines the right kind of internality between the evil of, say, murder as *sui generis* and the natural importance of death in human life. That is why the particular person's death appears unimportant against something more general – that one has violated rational nature in another.

One can see why Kant should think as he did. For one thing, our sense of the evil we do ought not to be dependent on the victim actually engaging our sympathies: he may be an utter stranger to whose fate we may be totally indifferent; or he may be so evil that one cannot feel anything for him, even though he was brutally murdered in an act of vengeance; or he may have welcomed death because he was so afflicted. But none of this alters the *evil* of his murder and that he suffered the evil of it as a distinct harm irreducible to whatever natural harms he suffered. One can see why those responses which are engaged by suffering and death as natural evils and which are dependent on the victim mattering to us in some natural way, should be judged to be irrelevant to the *evil* of murder. Much of this may be granted but it does not follow that the absence of such responses may not be seen as moral failings and, more importantly, it does not follow that they are not, in general, fundamental to our sense of what is an intelligible object of moral response.

The Kantian scheme undermines the internality of feeling and moral response even when the nature of that response and its object are *sui generis*. Kant often appealed to the idea that duty was owing and possible when feeling had died and that it was *required* whereas feeling could not be. His famous remark that Jesus' command that we should love our neighbour could not be taken literally because love cannot be commanded has often been quoted. It is certainly true that we must respect those we cannot love but it does not follow *that we could think of someone as an intelligible object of respect unless we also saw him as the intelligible object of someone's love.* It is compatible with the acknowledgement (which the Kantian point exploits) that we must respect those we cannot love, that we can see them as the intelligible object of respect only in the light of someone else's love.

IV

The direction in which I went in the previous section is not the direction Winch went although it should be congenial to him. He went the way indicated to him by Wittgenstein when he said: 'My attitude towards him is an attitude towards a soul. I am not of the *opinion* that he has a soul.' The prominence Winch gives to this is important because it restricts what he will count as the right account of the way 'knowledge can of itself impose bounds on our wills': it severely restricts the explanatory potential of the visual metaphors favoured by someone like McDowell who has said that a clear perception of the requirements will lead to virtuous action.[25]

In *'Eine Einstellung zur Seele'* Winch quotes this passage from Simone Weil:

> The human beings around us exert just by their presence a power which belongs uniquely to themselves to stop, to diminish or modify each movement which our bodies design. A person who crosses our path does not turn away our steps in the same manner as a street sign, no one stands up or moves about, or sits down again in quite the same fashion when he is alone in a room as when he has a visitor.[26]

Winch was discussing the passage from Wittgenstein which I have already quoted ('My attitude towards him is an attitude towards a soul [*eine Einstellung zur Seele*]. I am not of the *opinion* that he has a soul') and he argues that having 'an attitude towards a soul' is not consequent upon the ascription of particular states of thought to people, but is, rather, a condition of it.'[27]

Stanley Cavell makes a similar point:

> Ought not there . . . to be an objection to the argument from analogy concerning its narcissism. Call the argument autological: it yields at best a mind too like mine. It leaves out the otherness of the other.[28]

What Cavell tries to capture, or evoke, by the expression 'the otherness of the other' is a kind of dynamic interaction which is not a consequence, but the condition of what some philosophers call 'the ascription of mental predicate', or 'the attribution of mental properties or capacities'; which is not a consequence, but a condition, of intersubjectivity. The point might be put this way: we need a proper account of objectivity based upon a proper account of intersubjectivity, of the 'otherness of the other' or, as Wiggins puts it, of the 'alterity, of the otherness of the subjectivity of others'.[29]

The classical problem of other minds is to determine whether there are more things of a particular kind than one. At one level it is merely a kind of taxonomical problem: can I (the sceptical inquirer into what can be justifiably included in a book on what can be known to be) know that these things (bodies) are also another kind of thing (minds or minds *cum* bodies or persons). I could if I could know not only that this thing moved around in certain ways, had hairy legs, etc. but if I could also know that it could think and feel. The difficulty seems to be that whether or not they can think or feel is beyond my epistemic reach. But whether I think, as does the sceptic, that this is irredeemably beyond my epistemic reach, or whether I think that it is, albeit inferentially, within my epistemic reach, or whether I think that it is directly within my epistemic reach through intuition or some other mode of 'direct access', the sense of epistemic capacity, its proper objects and it's achievement is basically the same. Whether I get it inferentially or whether I get it directly, I get what philosophers tend to call 'propositional' knowledge – *that there are*, indeed, other things of a particular kind in the world. Contemporary philosophy, which is not much troubled by scepticism, thinks of other minds in the same way except that its problem is not whether there are other minds but *where else* they might be: do dolphins think?; do machines think?; does a brain in a vat think?

What Cavell means by 'the otherness of others' is expressed by Simone Weil when she says that 'the human beings around us exert just by their presence a power which belongs uniquely to them'. That is what is missed in speaking of human beings or persons as entities with certain properties and capacities which are assessed for their relevance to certain rules or principles of conduct, or which are thought to engage with our interests and desires in the same way as does recognition of the properties or capacities of anything else in nature.

The quotation from Weil is an excellent example of 'an attitude towards a soul' in the sense in which Wittgenstein speaks of it and it is also an excellent example of another human being as 'other' to oneself in the sense in which Cavell speaks of it. But it is also clear that someone may be, in this sense, 'other' to a slave owner. We have no reason to assume that the slave owner 'stands up or moves about, or sits down in quite the same fashion when he is alone in a room' as when his slave is in the room (although Weil was at least at times, inclined to say just that). She says immediately before the passage quoted by Winch, that 'it was not for want of sensibility that Achilles had, by a sudden gesture, pushed the old man glued against his knees to the ground. Priam's words, evoking his old father had moved him to tears. Quite simply he had found himself to be as free in his attitudes, in his movements, as if in place of a suppliant an inert object were there touching his knee.' And immediately afterwards she says 'But this indefinable influence of the human presence is not exercised by those men whom a movement of impatience could deprive of their lives even before a thought had the time to condemn them. Before these men others behave as though they were not there . . . .'[30] She speaks in the same tone of those who passed by the man tended by the Good Samaritan.

How far can this take us in understanding the slave owner's relation to his slaves or the Samaritan's response to the man in the ditch? Only some of the way. Take first, the Samaritan.[31] His behaviour is quite different from the behaviour described by Simone Weil when she says that 'no one stands up or moves about or sits down in quite the same fashion when he is alone in the room as when he has a visitor'. What she says is a good example of that kind of attitude to a soul which is relevant to the question: What gives me so much as the idea that another living thing thinks and feels? But the Samaritan's behaviour is not an instance of the kind of primitive reaction which is a condition for the ascription of mental predicates. It is offered as an example of what it is to love one's neighbour. When the lawyer asks 'Who is my neighbour?' it would not do to give an example of someone who turned away our steps: *he* is not the neighbour to the one who fell amongst thieves. Simone Weil tends to speak of those who walked past as though they walked past in the way they would if there were merely an inert *thing* in the ditch.[32] Perhaps they did, but if they did, it would seriously underdescribe the Samaritan's response to simply contrast it with such indifference, or to say he responded as to a soul, or as to a fellow human being, in the sense in which that is conveyed by the quotation from her essay on the *Iliad*.

In her notebooks Weil says that if a person with sufficient water in his canteen comes across another in the desert who is dying of thirst then he will give him water. She describes this as 'automatic'. That could be another example of a primitive reaction, or of the kind of attitude with which Wittgenstein is concerned in the *Investigations*. But such a person could be a slave owner, the one to whom he gives water could be his slave, and there be no inconsistency even if he were to appreciate the significance of what he had done. If he had an ear for even its faintest and most subtle intimations he would not need to free his slaves. It *is*, in one sense, a reaction to a fellow human being, as the kind of action which is constitutive of our sense of a fellow human being. But it is not the sense in which the Samaritan's actions were as to a fellow human being. The sense in which the Samaritan's actions revealed him as a 'neighbour' to the man in the ditch is connected with the concept of love and that emerges only in a culture which can distinguish genuine from corrupt forms of it. That does not mean that we cannot describe the Samaritan's actions as 'automatic': he acted without reflection. However, his actions were not merely in response to the suffering of another human being but to what it *means* for that human being to suffer as he does.

The quotation from Weil is also of limited help in

understanding the slave owner. When he rapes the slave girl he does not respond to her struggling as he does to the undergrowth against which he struggles when he tries to cut his way through the swamp. He does not respond to her struggle merely as an obstacle to be overcome if he is to realize his purpose (Weil tends to speak like this). He need not be blind to the suffering in her eyes and in her screams. He may try to shut his eyes, or suppress her screams. He may even be ashamed that he did not relent. (One cannot be in that way *unrelenting* in one's struggle against the undergrowth – as Diamond pointed out, to be unrelenting in the way that he is, is to be unrelenting in the face of a plea even though it may be only in her eyes.) He doesn't treat her as someone who would turn away his steps in a way indistinguishable from a lamppost, or as one whose presence would go unnoticed in a room, or as one who would not be welcomed as a fellow human being if he were marooned on a desert island. All this comes out in the fact that he may later recriminate himself for his lack of pity, but that does not mean that she is then for him, an intelligible object for his remorse. It does not mean that he could find it intelligible that he has violated something precious. He may have felt much the same when he beat his dog.

V

The power of human beings to affect us in ways I described earlier is not brute. We have first to take them seriously and to do that we must find it intelligible that we ascribe certain kinds of thoughts and feelings to them. I shall try to make the point clearer by commenting on Cavell's discussion of what he calls 'soul blindness'. He wants to understand what people might mean when they speak of 'seeing a human being as a human being' and he considers the claim that a slave owner does not see slaves as human beings. He replies:

> What he really believes is not that slaves are not human beings but that some human beings are slaves . . . . When he rapes a slave or takes her as his concubine he does not feel that he has, by that fact itself, embraced sodomy . . . he does not go to great lengths either to convert his horse to

Christianity or to prevent their getting wind of it. Everything in his relation to his slaves shows he treats them as more or less human – his humiliations of them, his disappointments, his jealousies, his fears, his punishments, his attachments . . .[33]

He then imagines a slave owner saying 'they are not human beings' and asks what he could mean. He concludes:

He means and can mean nothing definite. This is a definite frame of mind. He means, indefinitely, that they are not purely human. He means, indefinitely, that there are kinds of human. He means indefinitely that slaves are different . . . . It could be said that what he denies is that the slave is other, i. e. other to his one.[34]

Take that last sentence: 'he denies . . . that the slave is other, i. e. other to his one'. In this context his use of 'other' means something quite different from his use of it in the quotation in Section IV and the difference corresponds to the different ways we may speak of someone as a fellow human being. In this context Cavell means, I think, that the slave owner denies that the slave has his kind (the slave owner's kind) of individuality: the kind of individuality that shows itself in our revulsion in being numbered rather than called by name; the kind of individuality that gives human beings the power to haunt those who have wronged them, in remorse. If the slave owner could be haunted by the slave girl he raped then her days as a slave would be numbered. That does not mean that he would not rape her but now it would be as he would rape a white woman. The difference is that the evil he had done her would now be within the intelligible reach of his remorse. It was, I think, the mark of the racially based slavery of the southern states of America (when slave owners were unselfconscious and felt little need to invent rationalizations which focused on the empirical properties of their slaves) that whatever he did to his slaves was not within the conceptual reach of the slave-owner's remorse.

One way of characterizing remorse in its difference from some other moral reactions, would be to say that it is possible only over what has the power to haunt us. That power is a certain kind of individuality. It is, I think, what Cavell means by 'being other to his one'. The individuality, the power to be other to his one, which the slave owner fails to acknowledge in the slave girl he rapes, conditions and is conditioned by his finding it intelligible that certain moral descriptions apply to her – the kind which marks our sense of what it is to be a human being when we mean more than *homo sapiens*.

If we take up Cavell's invitation to see her as converted to Christianity then we may also imagine her married. In the eyes of the slave owner, her conversion and marriage must be in inverted commas, for in his eyes she ('they') must lack that form of inwardness necessary for a Christian understanding of them – the kind of capacity for a deepened understanding of which I alluded in Section II. His granting her that capacity is itself a form of her humanity being manifest to him, of him seeing her as another perspective on the world, (in the sense in which we use that expression to remind someone of the reality of another human being). It is internal to his sense that she may explore her sexuality with any depth which is itself internal to his sense of it *having* any depth and which alone gives sense to the idea that rape is a form of violation. For a Christian, Christianity offers a deepened understanding of sexuality in the light of which it is transformed, but that is dependent upon one having the depth to receive it, and that is not a brute fact about the species, and its acknowledgement in another human being is not an empirical perception. It has little to do with the kind of intelligence for which he bought her to do the accounts: as far as that kind of intelligence goes he may know that his slave girl is more intelligent than his wife and daughter. But if he acknowledged in her the capacity for a deepened understanding of sexuality which he would have to if he seriously believed that she had been married as a Christian, then she would be 'other to his one'.

He can rape someone who is married yet she will be beyond the reach of his remorse only if he sees her merely as 'married'. He rapes her as he does, that is, as a slave girl, because her sexuality is outside the (conceptual) space of the kind of pity whose character is determined by its taking a suffering human being as its object. In whatever way he pities her, it is not as one in whom he finds suffering which goes deep. If he pities her it cannot be as one who may be grievously wronged, as one whose sexuality has been violated, because his sense of what he can do in raping her is limited by his sense of what her sexuality can mean for her. (His slave-owning neighbour may think him cruel but then he may also think that he is cruel to his dogs.) It is true, as Cavell says, that when he rapes her he does not thereby think that he has committed sodomy. It is in some ways worse: she appears to him as sufficiently unlike an animal for him not to feel disgusted but sufficiently like one for her sexuality to have no meaning.

It's tempting to say that he treats her like an animal or as something half way between animal and human life – as though what suffering could mean to her was the same as to an animal but that she had, besides, certain properties and capacities which animals do not have. Or to put it another way: it is tempting to say he treats her as an animal of an extraordinary kind – one that can speak, do the accounts, and so on. That would be misleading and Cavell is right to point it out. This slave owner's responses to his slave are not as they would be to an animal, which is why Cavell says that the slave owner can mean only something indefinite when he says she is not human or not fully human. But Cavell seems to assume that 'human' as we mean it in this context is a relatively determinate sortal term. The slave owner may not know quite what to say if asked why his slaves are not human, but he most definitely means that 'they are not one of us'. When we use the expression 'human being' in this way we have, and could have, no determinate sense of its extension and, after a certain point, we can have no sense in advance (no sense informed by theory) of what we will count as a human being. It is, in that respect, quite different from the concept '*homo sapiens*'.

It is true, that the slave owner does not fail to see the kinds of things I have been referring to *because* he fails to see the slave girl as a human being. To fail to understand (know) such things *is* what it is for him to fail to see her as a human being in the only sense that is relevant, that is, as something more than *homo sapiens*. If he saw her as married (without the inverted commas) then (but not only then) he would have to take her sexuality humanly seriously and, therefore, be threatened by the realization of the evil he had done her. That realization is remorse. So I think Cavell is wrong to say that 'everything in his relations to his slaves shows that he treats them as more or less human', and that his sense of their difference is 'indefinite'. He treats them as many philosophers would have us treat human beings – as members of a species with certain empirically discoverable and morally relevant capacities.

There are definite moral descriptions, of what his slaves are, of what they do and suffer, which the slave owner must withhold. Why does he withhold them? To take the example of the raped slave girl again: perhaps he cannot see human sexuality as fully present in a black body, no more than he can see fully human sorrow in a black face, not just because it is black, but because these features cannot express it for him. Perhaps his sense of her sexuality is that 'they screw like monkeys'. He certainly thinks that 'it cannot be for them what it is for us' – nothing amongst 'them' really counts as betrayal for nothing really counts as being faithful. Perhaps he cannot hear dignity in their speech, or in their music. Cavell's slave owner and his friends thought of themselves as Christians: they thought of their slaves as 'Christians'. He and his friends could think of themselves as Christians only because they could think of themselves as serious respondents to the question: what is it to be a Christian? That is not a capacity of the same kind as the capacity to speak, to remember, to think, or to be self-conscious, and its acknowledgement in another is not of the same kind as the acknowledgement of such capacities.

Did his slaves not discuss what becoming Christians meant to them? Did he not overhear them? He probably did but what does one assume that he heard and what, in this kind of context, is to be able to hear? Does he hear the inwardness that informs authoritative and authentic speech? He knew they could be clever; he knew they could speak in imitation of their masters; he knew that they could speak the lines of the Bible. But if he could not hear the affliction in their music, how could he hear Christian inwardness in their prayers? Yet clearly he could not hear the affliction in their music, for if he did, then only radical self-deception could prevent him from seeing his actions under descriptions which would bring them into the conceptual space of a serious remorse. If he could hear the affliction in their music then he would rape the slave girl as he would rape a white woman.

I said that the slave owner *could not* have heard the affliction in their music. Should I not, at most, say that he did not. I would not say merely that he did not, for that does not capture the distance between him and his slaves, between his slaves and those he would not dream of making slaves even though he might treat them unjustly. If he rapes a white girl and is deaf to her agony, then I do not know how he has to change in order to hear the full depth of her suffering and to be seized by the horror at what he had done, but it is importantly different from how he must change if he is to see the evil he had done to the slave girl he raped. It is marked by the fact that in the case of the white girl, he keeps remorse at bay only through self-deception – through self-deceiving descriptions of her and so, of what he had done. If he has to deceive himself about the slave girl then she has reason to hope that her days as a slave will soon be at an end. Perhaps he will then invent empirically relevant differences between Negroes and whites: perhaps he will say that Negroes are less intelligent, or that they have a different evolutionary history: perhaps a pseudo-science will emerge. The time will then have come to ask him to demonstrate what the differences are and what relevance they have.

The racist taunt 'Would you want your daughter to marry one?' is instructive. If it revolts you that someone whom you think capable of love should be physically tender to people of a certain kind then talk of respecting them as a person begins to idle. It does not revolt the slave owner that someone whom he thinks capable of love should love and be physically tender to the white woman he rapes. What can be the proper object of tenderness can be violated – it is part of what gives sense to the idea that it can be violated. When I speak of someone whom he thinks capable of love I mean that he finds it intelligible to think of them as subject to love's claims even if they do not rise to them. We can only love those whom we acknowledge to be the intelligible object of the love of others. We cannot, unilaterally, make something intelligible.

The slave girl is not an intelligible object for her master's love. That means that in his eyes she is not an intelligible object for anyone's love. He does not think 'we cannot love them but they can love each other', for he speaks as he does of 'us' and 'them' because he denies that kind of meaning to their feelings, responses, actions, and lives. If he thought the slave girl could be loved by her husband, then he would know her as one who could return that love in wifely response. Then when he rapes her he would know that he rapes a wife; but that is what he does not know. If she were to become pregnant he could not see what she carries in pregnancy as something precious; nor can he think that she understands it as something precious, even if she says that it is and even if she kills herself in her grief after he forces her to abort it because he needs her to work.

Something is precious only in a world of meaning that the slaves are denied fellowship. That is why they are 'them'. That is why the slave girl's love for her husband and for her unborn child has no power of revelation for the slave owner. The slave owner knows that his slaves have interests, desires, feelings, hopes for the future, memories of the past; in short he ascribes to his slaves those capacities and properties philosophers list when they try to determine what the necessary and sufficient conditions are for being a 'person'. The reason they are slaves is not because he thinks that they lack them, or that they have them in only an attenuated way; nor is it because he is wilfully (self-deceivingly) blind to their moral relevance: it is because he denies them a certain content.

Rush Rhees said that there cannot be love without the language of love.[35] Without the language of love there could not be the claims of love and there is no love without love's claims. No doubt, there must be more than, and much that has to be before, the language of love: Rhees would be the first to point it out. There must be bodies with which we feel at home, through which love's tenderness can find expression. More primitively, there must be faces in which we can find depth and beauty. We could not love what did not have a face – which was of a *kind* which had no face or which (a machine for example) had a face only accidentally. (I do not mean that we cannot love a human being who has no face because of misfortune.) The slave girl had a face but it was not one her master could find in the poetry which informed the language of love which taught him what love was through its celebration. Peter Singer has said that you do not have to like Negroes in order to acknowledge their rights.[36] There is an obvious sense in which that is true, but he said it in a way, and it is often said in a way, that hides a terrible falsehood.

There is no point in telling the slave owner that his slaves are human beings (or fully paid up persons) and there is no point in challenging him to demonstrate that his slaves are different from him and other whites in some 'morally relevant' respect. Their differences, and their difference (in kind), seem apparent to him.[37] He cannot demonstrate them, but neither can it be demonstrated, to him or to anyone else, that they are not as he sees them. It could not be *demonstrated* that someone whose face appeared as caricatured in the *Black and White Minstrel Show* could not play Othello. It could not be demonstrated that someone with such a face could not mean the words he was given to speak because he could not suffer as Othello did and because of which Othello could speak with such power and authority. The reason why he cannot play Othello is not because he cannot utter those sentences and it is not because he cannot utter those sentences in such a way that, were they merely to be heard (over the radio, for example) they would move us deeply. It is because it is impossible for us to take them seriously when they come from a face like that: we cannot find it intelligible that suffering could go deep in someone like that. For the slave owner, the slaves' humanity is epistemically impotent. But they may have the kind of properties which philosophers generally believe to be morally relevant fully on display.

How does it become otherwise? Certainly not through philosophy, nor through science – no more than philosophy or science could teach us to see dignity in faces that all look alike to us. It would be like trying to *prove* that you could cast a black and white minstrel to play Othello. When we do come to see dignity in a face, or the full depth of human sexuality in a body, or hear the full depth of human sorrow in a song, or slip into conversation when previously there had been only instructing or commanding, then human individuality and a human moral subject become manifest together, one as the condition of the other. The slave owner was evilly mistaken about his slaves but not as he would be if he started inventing empirically relevant differences between them and those he would not dream of enslaving. That his slave girl was a Christian and not merely a 'Christian', or that she was a proper respondent to love's claims, or that her body could invite and worthily receive a tender caress, or that her affliction could lacerate her soul – these are not things he could learn from books whether they were scientific or philosophical, nor could he learn them by looking and listening more attentively in the sense in which that might yield more detailed empirical information. If he were to see his slaves like that then we would say that he saw them as human beings and we would rightly say that he had come to 'see things as they are', but the grammar of that should not be misunderstood.

VI

Winch argues (*ad hominem*) that it is a condition of the kind of unconditional respect to which Kant tried to give philosophical expression that one realizes that there often is no one position which must be arrived at by all who are rational and of good will.[38] The universalization of one's judgments concerning what one ought to do is often considered impertinent even when they are universalized only in thought. There will be fewer philosophical obstructions to seeing that a judgment that another person ought to do something is a concrete human act in relation to them and therefore itself liable to moral judgment, when one is rid of the mistaken conception of the impersonal character of moral thinking: it, together with the focus on a certain kind of 'ought', (as, so to speak, the bearer of 'the moral') made attractive the idea that it is *necessary* to universalize one's moral judgments.

Winch connects this criticism of Kant with a point he attributes to Cavell, namely that 'treating a person justly involves treating with seriousness his own conception of himself, his own commitments and cares, his own understanding of his situation and of what the situation demands of him'.[39] I raised the question of what makes someone an intelligible object of such serious attention. I concluded that it is, amongst other things, to be seen as one of whom it is intelligible to think (as the slave owner could not of his slaves) that he is capable of an increasingly deepened understanding of 'his own conception of himself, his own commitments and cares'. I argued that the acknowledgement that he has that capacity and a sense that there *is* something to be explored more deeply are interdependent. I have tried to show that the individuality which is a requirement of a serious conception of moral thinking, and the individuality which is a requirement of someone's being an intelligible object of remorse, are interdependent.

The connection with Wittgenstein, I believe, is less direct than Winch hoped it would be. The sense in which someone is a limit to my will, or 'other' to me, which is conveyed by the remark that 'my attitude towards him is an attitude towards a soul', I think is limited to the contexts in which it was discussed in the *Investigations* : limited, for example, to giving the right kind of answer to 'What gives us *so much as an idea* that living beings, things can feel?'[40] Wittgenstein's answer was that nothing gives us so much as the idea that they can for it is not a matter of our having an idea: 'I am not of the *opinion* that he has a soul.' If you take it as an idea then you will always give the wrong kind of answer to why we do not speculate about the mental life of stones and you will give the wrong account of the relation between our sense of another's subjectivity and our sense of them as a certain kind of limit to our will. That is why the point is important for ethics and not just for the philosophy of mind. And although the route between such concerns and the concerns of Section V is indirect, the kind of interdependence between certain ways of responding and the concepts which reveal these responses to be intelligible (let alone appropriate), I think, is of the same kind.

NOTES

1. D. Wiggins, *Values Needs and Truth* (Oxford and New York: Blackwell, 1987) p. viii.
2. P. Winch, 'The universalizability of moral judgments' *Ethics and Action* (London: Routledge & Kegan Paul, 1972) p. 165.
3. L. Wittgenstein, *Philosophical Investigations* (Oxford: Blackwell, 1953) vol. II, p. iv.
4. P. Winch, 'Particularity and morals' in *Trying to Make Sense* (Oxford and New York: Blackwell, 1987) p. 178.
5. ibid., p. 173.
6. Winch, op. cit., p. 165.
7. It is only because of such a conception of reason (elaborated further in the text) that there is any hope of introducing the kind of stability necessary for choice as Schelling puts it into 'a fluid and indeterminate situation that seemingly provides logical reason for anybody to expect anything except what he expects to be expected to expect'; this is because each rational agent is transparent to another *qua* rational agent. This provides the basis for 'collectivist' solutions to the various dilemmas.
8. I owe the phrase to Susan Hurley: it is from a paper she read at the Philosophy Colloquium, King's College, London, 1988.
9. I have argued this in detail in 'The personal in ethics' in P. Winch and D.Z. Phillips (eds) *Wittgenstein: Attending to Particulars* (London: Macmillan, 1989).
10. Winch, 'The universalizability of moral judgments', p. 153.
11. We may now see why a critic as sympathetic, astute, and as subtle as Wiggins missed the point when he came to discuss this essay and its bearing on truth as that might apply to moral judgments. Wiggins says in a footnote:

I note here that Winch spoke of self discovery in preference to self determination. But he deliberately blurs the effect of this by refusing to distinguish the process of discovery from that of decision – and in a manner presumably most unwelcome to unrestricted cognitivists. In dialogue with these or moral realists it is better, I believe, to say that the place where self-discovery comes in is that it supervenes on the deliberated decision and need not be part of that decision.

(D. Wiggins, op. cit., p. 182)

Wiggins misunderstands the point. He also fails to see how important it is to Winch's discussion and this is because of his susceptibility to the belief that the visual analogy for ethical understanding can be more fertile than Winch would allow. Iris Murdoch (*The Sovereignty of Good,* London: Routledge & Kegan Paul, 1970) said that two great metaphors dominate philosophy – the metaphor of vision and the metaphor of movement. Winch's lesson is that even if this is historically true it is a mistake to be decidedly partial to one rather than the other. Wiggins's partiality is revealed when he asks whether Winch's discussion might be of comfort to a strict realist because Winch's emphasis on the agent's perspective might be construed as likely to be the best perspective since he gets the best 'look' at his situation. To be sure Wiggins rejects that kind of realism and the idea that Winch might offer comfort to anyone inclined to it, but the fact that he could have mooted it together with his failure to see what is central in Winch's essay is why his diagnosis of why we need not universalize all our moral judgments goes less deep than does Winch's:

Human interests and concerns are as indefinitely various and heterogeneous as are human predicaments. Even moral interests and concerns are indefinitely various and heterogeneous. Therefore, in a world which was not made for us, and is in any case replete with economic and social conflict as well as conflicts of personality and preferences, there is simply no general reason to expect that a common moral consciousness will issue in some rational disposition to single out just one from among all the moral/practical alternatives apparently available in any situation.

(D. Wiggins, op. cit., p. 174)

12. Winch, 'Particularity and morals', p.168.
13. B. Williams, *Ethics and the Limits of Philosophy* (London: Fontana, 1985) p.140.
14. Iris Murdoch, op. cit. R. F. Holland, *Against Empiricism* (Oxford: Blackwell, 1980).
15. Alan Donagan, *The Theory of Morality* (London and Chicago: University of Chicago Press, 1977).
16. Winch, 'Particularity and morals' p. 174. It might at first be thought that Winch confuses the generality of a principle with its

universalizability, but this is not so as I hope my ensuing discussion reveals.

17. ibid., p.174.

18. G. Vlastos in 'The individual as object of love in Plato' in *Platonic Studies* (Princeton: Princeton University Press, 1973) p. 31.

19. H. Arendt, *The Human Condition* (London and Chicago: University of Chicago Press, 1958) p. 181.

20. See R. Gaita, *Good and Evil: An Absolute Conception* (London: Macmillan, 1989) Chapter Three.

21. R. Hare, 'Universalizability' in *Essays on the Moral Concepts* (London and Basingstoke: Macmillan, 1972).

22. The example and much else, I owe to Cora Diamond, 'Eating meat and eating people', *Philosophy* vol. 53 1978). She calls such things 'the source of morality' but that seems to me to underplay the interdependence between them and morality.

23. In many of his works, but see especially, 'Persons, character and morality' in *Moral Luck* (Cambridge and New York: Cambridge University Press, 1981).

24. I. Kant, *The Groundwork of the Metaphysics of Morals*, trans. Paton (London: Hutchinson University Library, 1969) p. 88ff.

25. J. McDowell, 'Is morality a system of hypothetical imperatives?', *The Proceedings of the Aristotelian Society*, supp. vol. (1978). We want an understanding of what it is for something to be a proper object of moral understanding and of the proper exercise of the capacity for it. Winch rightly judges that a proper erosion of the dominance of the visual analogy (not like Rorty's *Philosophy and The Mirror of Nature*, Oxford: Blackwell, 1980) is necessary for it and that it is located, not in Wittgenstein generally (not for example in seeing, in general, that the world cannot be prised apart from our concerns and interests) but in this remark and in a proper understanding of its importance to other parts of his philosophy. Or, one could put it this way: what one thinks Wittgenstein has to teach (or what may be derived from him) depends upon how one places that remark. If, for example, one thinks that his philosophy of mind depends upon it then one will read his remarks on language differently from those who think that the concern with rule-following mediates the concern with language and the concern with mind.

26. Winch, *Trying to Make Sense*, p. 146.

27. ibid., p. 146.

28. S. Cavell, *The Claim of Reason* (Oxford and New York: Oxford University Press, 1979) p. 395.

29. D. Wiggins, *Values Needs and Truth*, p. 70.

30. S. Weil, 'The Iliad, poem of might' in *Intimations of Christianity amongst the Ancient Greeks* (London and Henley: Routledge & Kegan Paul, 1976) p. 28.

31. See P. Winch, 'Who is my neighbour?' in *Trying to Make Sense*.

32. Weil has a point which can perhaps be put this way: no one will deny that there is a difference in the way we speak of human beings and

the way we speak of objects or things. However, if our sense that knowing that something is a human being is knowing that it is an entity with certain properties, then there is a question whether our sense of the difference in kind marks a sufficient sense of our difference between human beings and trees as objects of knowledge, and of the way in which they, as objects of knowledge, then engage with our interests and desires etc. This thing is a chair: it has certain properties and I have certain desires and certain principles and so I will act thus and so. This thing is a human being with certain capacities and properties: I have certain desires and certain principles and so I will act thus and so. This is one way of thinking of a human being as a thing.

33. S. Cavell, op. cit., p. 268.

34. ibid., p. 269.

35. R. Rhees, *Without Answers* (London: Routledge & Kegan Paul, 1970) p. 121.

36. P. Singer, *Animal Liberation* (New York: Cambridge University Press, 1975).

37. The distinction is made by Cora Diamond (op. cit.). She brings out that philosophers have assumed that the way we speak of the *difference* (in kind) between human beings and animals is based upon an (often exaggerated) sense of the *differences* between them.

38. Winch, 'Particularity and morals', pp. 174ff.

39. ibid., p. 177.

40. Wittgenstein, op. cit., p. 283.

Chapter Eight

HOW MANY LEGS?

CORA DIAMOND

But all this – the mysterious, far-reaching hair-line trail, the absence of sun from the sky, the tremendous cold, and the strangeness and weirdness of it all – made no impression on the man. It was not because he was long used to it. He was a newcomer in the land . . . and this was his first winter. The trouble with him was that he was without imagination. He was quick and alert in the things of life, but only in the things, and not in the significances. Fifty degrees below zero meant eighty-odd degrees of frost. Such facts impressed him as being cold and uncomfortable, and that was all. It did not lead him to meditate upon man's frailty in general, able only to live within certain narrow limits of heat and cold; and from there on it did not lead him to the conjectural field of immortality and man's place in the universe. Fifty degrees below zero stood for a bite of frost that hurt and that must he guarded against by the use of mittens, ear-flaps, warm moccasins, and thick socks. Fifty degrees below zero was to him just precisely fifty degrees below zero. That there should be anything more to it than that never entered his head.

'To Build a Fire', Jack London

I

In 'Understanding a primitive society', Peter Winch argued that conceptions of good and evil in human life are necessarily connected with our ways of thinking about the characteristic shape of human life: its relation to birth, sexuality and death.[1] My paper is intended to say, not quite the same thing, but something similar.

We start with a philosophical story of the usual sort. The ocean liner has sunk, and you can save only one of two people struggling in the water nearby. One has one leg; you have gathered from what you heard during the voyage that the loss of the leg occurred some time ago. The other person has two legs. You know virtually nothing else about them. They appear to be about the same age. They are both men or both women; it does not matter which.

Many contemporary versions of utilitarianism imply that it would normally be wrong for you to choose to save the one-legged person.[2] They have an even stronger consequence: that to choose to save the one-legged person is not just wrong, but is wrong for almost the same reasons for which it is wrong to cause a person to lose his leg in the first place. (I am excluding cases in which there was some good reason for causing someone to lose his leg, e. g., in order to save his life. I mean to include cases in which the loss of a leg is caused by negligence, or by more spectacular wrongdoing, like terrorist acts or deliberate attempts to maim.) If you choose to save the one-legged person rather than the two-legged, the number of legs in the world (or, better, legs attached to people) is down by one in comparison to what it would have been had you chosen differently. There being in the world fewer legs attached to people than there might be causes there to be greater frustration, less pleasure, more pain and so on than there would otherwise be. To cause someone to lose a leg is normally to cause something to happen which he very much wants not to happen; it will normally also cause a great deal of pain at the time. But many of the effects important for the utilitarian's evaluation of the act come after the initial loss. So let us now imagine a division, into two groups, of all the effects that the utilitarian takes into account. In the first group of effects are those of the first year, and in the second those after that year. From the utilitarian's point of view, a very great deal of what is wrong with what you do if you cause someone to lose his leg depends on effects after the first year. There is in the world more frustration, pain and so on, and less pleasure, or less adequate fulfilment of desire, than there would otherwise be.

But now consider a rescuer who chooses to save the life of someone who lost his leg a year before that choice, when the rescuer could instead save a two-legged person. We suppose, as before, that nothing more than that is known about the two possibly-to-be-saved people. In evaluating such a choice, the utilitarian puts into his calculations the probable consequences of saving the able-bodied person and not the disabled, and then the consequences of saving the disabled person and not the able-bodied. He looks at the probable satisfactions and frustrations and so on of the world with an average two-legged person in it, and compares those to the satisfactions and frustrations of the world with, instead, a person in it who lost his leg one year earlier. There are likely to be more frustrations and pains, and fewer satisfactions, satisfactions subject to greater limitations, if the world contains the person who lost his leg a year before the rescue. The frustrations and pains and lost satisfactions which make the difference here are comparable to those frustrations and pains and lost satisfactions that went into the second group of effects to which the utilitarian attended when he explained why it is usually wrong to cause someone to lose his leg in the first place. In the case of someone whom you cause to lose his leg, the pains after the first year, the pains in the second group, may well include resentment, of a sort which has no counterpart in the case of the one-legged person whose life you save. Or there may be the nuisances and inconveniences of a lawsuit, time diverted from more profitable activities to litigation. The second group of effects of causing a person to lose his leg may thus contain some kinds of effect to which there is no parallel in the case in which you, by rescuing a one-legged person instead of a two-legged person, cause there to be one fewer legs-attached-to-people in the world than there would otherwise be. Resentment in particular is certainly an important kind of effect, but I shall ignore it in the rest of this paper. Ignoring it (and ignoring the frustrations of prolonged litigation and the like), I shall first summarize what I have said and then generalize it.

From the utilitarian's point of view, it is wrong to choose to save a person who has lost his leg a year ago, when you could instead save a person with two legs, and the wrongness depends on effects of the same nature and extent as those which go into the second group of effects used by the utilitarian in explaining why it is wrong to cause someone to lose his leg in the first place. What I have said about a year holds equally of two years or ten, two months or a day or an hour. If you rescue someone with a disability, when you could instead have rescued someone about whom you know nothing to distinguish him from the first person except that he has not got that disability, what you do is, from the point of view of contemporary utilitarianism, not only wrong, but wrong for reasons which are like the reasons it is wrong to cause someone to be disabled in that way. More precisely: if the disability in question is the loss of x an hour ago, the reasons it is wrong to rescue such a person when one could rescue someone else instead can be found by considering the reasons it is wrong to cause a person to lose x, and then dividing those effects into effects of the first hour after the loss, and all others. The second group of effects accounts for most of the wrongness of causing such a disability, and equally explains what is wrong with rescuing a person who incurred the disability an hour previously instead of someone apparently similar but not suffering from that disability. The wrongness of doing certain things to a person, disabling him in significant ways, is for the utilitarian tied to the wrongness of choosing when you can to rescue someone suffering from such a disability when you could rescue someone else.

Utilitarianism nowadays is utilitarianism with frills on; and the frills disguise or soften the sharp lines of some of its distinctive features. So too with this feature of utilitarianism. There may be all sorts of utilitarian reasons for encouraging people to do things which appear to violate utilitarian principles. The utilitarian payoff from not encouraging rescuers to make a distinction between the disabled and those apparently not disabled may be considerable, or so it might be argued. (Not, actually, with very great plausibility. Someone inclined to rescue the wrong person might well, on the basis of similar inclinations, do a great deal of damage in a lifetime, and might set a bad example to others.) What concerns me is not whether utilitarianism can hold that we should not condemn the person who chooses to rescue a blind man, in anything like the terms in which we condemn someone who causes another to lose his sight. What concerns me is that utilitarianism should be in the position in which either it must accept that the condemnations in the two cases would appropriately be similar, or it must fudge something up to get out of what most people would regard as yet another ludicrous consequence of utilitarianism. It is no part of my argument to deny that utilitarian ingenuity could come up with something to patch this over. I am interested in what it shows about utilitarianism that there is something to be patched over here; and I am also interested in the ways in which other ethical views avoid such trouble.

II

I shall first say more about how utilitarianism yields the ludicrous consequence. It is frequently noted that utilitarianism ignores the difference between persons, and the fact that it does so is important in considering the relationship between utilitarianism and our ideas about justice. Justice does not come into cases of the sort with which I am concerned. (Justice, that is, does not require of us that we rescue either one of the two people rather than the other.) But the same ignoring of differences between people plays a role in these cases. Or, rather, something else does, which could be said to underlie the ignoring of differences between people. Utilitarianism does not care about whether someone's desires are frustrated; it cares about whether there are frustrated desires. More specifically, it cares about whether there are more frustrated desires than there might 'otherwise' be, whatever exactly the force of 'otherwise' is. The way in which the frustrations and pains of someone whom you have caused to lose a leg enter the utilitarian calculus reflects only the difference between the frustrations and pains there are because of your action or inaction, and the fewer or lesser frustrations and pains there would be if your behaviour had left the number of legs alone. In a situation in which, because of your choice, the number of legs in the world will go down either by one or by two, what enters the utilitarian calculus is what there will most probably be in the way of frustrations and pains, with each of the different actions open to you. What there will be is what settles it, not what you do to people or what happens to them through what you have failed to do.

It is possible for a thorough-going utilitarian to make a translation from the language of 'what there is' to that of 'what you are doing to people'. Let me explain what that would come to here, and why it is not a genuine taking into account of what happens to people through our actions and our failures to act.

Our ordinary way of looking at what happens to the two people affected by our choice of whom to rescue is this: the one who is saved has a great good, through our rescuing him; the one who is not saved suffers the loss that loss of life is. We do not normally think that a healthy person with one leg loses less in losing his life than does an otherwise similar healthy person with two legs; we do not normally think that a healthy person with two legs has gained more by being rescued than has an otherwise similar healthy person with one leg. Suppose that we were to accept some vague principle of the sort that when by our actions we must cause some loss to at least one person, we should (other things being equal) choose a course of action in which the loss we cause is a lesser loss. A non-utilitarian who accepted such a principle would be unlikely to understand it as requiring him to rescue (when he had to make a choice) people without disabilities. There can of course be a utilitarian reading of the principle. One can say: when a disabled person loses his life, there is usually a smaller loss of net satisfaction (considering his satisfactions alone) than when an otherwise similar person who has not got such a disability loses his life. Therefore, the disabled person loses less when he loses his life; therefore (even ignoring the effects of his disability on other people) the principle requiring us to cause as little loss and as little harm to people by our actions as we can requires us to save those without disabilities when no other consideration outweighs that one. Here it may look as if utilitarianism can talk about what we do to people through our actions, and about what happens to them through our actions. But suppose that we should want to say that the important thing that happens to one or other of these two people through our action is that he loses his life, and that (since we are talking about people whom we have no reason to take to be seriously ill or in any serious distress of any other sort, and about whom we know virtually nothing except for the presence or absence of some one disability) the loss of life is the same loss for one as it is for the other. Utilitarianism can try to make it appear as if that is not so, but only by taking a route that calculates what happens to a person by looking at what there is, and the things that 'there are' that it will take into account are those that enter the calculation of a total of good that there is, a total including all frustrations and satisfactions 'anywhere'.

Again, it is frequently said that utilitarianism regards moral agents as mere pushers of causal buttons. This is by itself an important point about utilitarianism. It leads to the utilitarian's characteristic disregard of all significant moral differences between actions and omissions, between doings and allowings-to-happen. What I have been drawing attention to is something else that is involved in the utilitarian view of the moral agent. Utilitarianism implies not only that your cutting someone else up is morally in the same class as your refusal to put adequate fences around your machines, if you know (or should know) that sooner or later someone will lose a limb because of your failure. It also and with far less justification implies that your rescuing the wrong person, the one who is already disabled, is an action of the same general moral category. Your choice has a causal relation to probable frustrations and pains of the same sort as does an action (or failure to act) leading to a comparable disability. Because of what you do, there are more frustrations and pains than there would probably have been otherwise. In the background is the utilitarian insistence that whatever reasons there are for avoiding disability in the first place are reasons for not choosing to rescue a disabled survivor of a disaster in preference to someone else. You are not causing any person to have a disability; but that is irrelevant to the utilitarian. What matters is that you are causing there to be a disabled person when there need not have been. You can do that in many ways. But just as the utilitarian insists that doing and letting happen are not in and of themselves significantly different ways of causing there to be a disabled person when there need not have been, so too a consistent utilitarian (and with the exception of John Stuart Mill they do go in for the most awful consistency) will insist that causing a person to have a disability and causing no one to have a disability but causing there to be one more disabled person than there need have been are not in and of themselves significantly different ways of causing there to be more disability around. The moral agent's relation to people is not merely that of abstract causer of things that happen to them. It is more distant even than that. He is primarily causer of there being more or less of satisfaction and frustration, pleasure and pain, or anything else that a utilitarian chooses to treat as the central stuff. That there is someone in particular whom he has affected by what he has done does indeed enter the calculations, but in ways which do not take into account the character of the difference between causing harm to someone and choosing to rescue someone less well off than others by utilitarian standards.

It should also be noted that the ludicrous consequence depends upon a utilitarian idea of what beliefs and actions are rational in the face of ignorance. The utilitarian is willing to argue that, since the one thing we know about the effects of rescuing the disabled person is that there is a disabled person where there might have been an able-bodied one, and since a disabled person is normally worse off than if he were not disabled, there is at least some reason for thinking, on the basis of the probabilities, that there will be less happiness altogether if such a person is rescued instead of an able-bodied person. But, given what we do not know about the case, and given what we do know about the variability and complexity of human life, a non-utilitarian might regard the willingness to draw any conclusions about effects on happiness overall as lunatic, not rational. Such willingness to draw conclusions is essential if we are to have a calculus of right and wrong, but it is just *that* that a non-utilitarian may reject, even if he cares as much about happiness as any utilitarian claims to.[3]

In what I have written, I have had in mind contemporary versions of utilitarianism, but it can be argued that what I have called the ludicrous consequence is a consequence also of older versions of utilitarianism, and in particular of Bentham's and Sidgwick's. Bentham's case is made slightly complex by the role in it of 'alarm', but the complexities do not make any really significant difference. In the case of Sidgwick, there is a direct connection between the ludicrous consequence and two of Sidgwick's fundamental 'rational intuitions': he says that it is a self-evident principle 'that the good of any one individual is of no more importance, from the point of view . . . of the Universe, than the good of any other', and adds that it is evident to him that as a rational being he is bound to aim at good generally and not merely at a particular part of it.[4] If you treat it as morally permissible to rescue a disabled person instead of an able-bodied one and you also treat it as wrong to cause disability when it is avoidable, you are violating those principles of Sidgwick's. You are saying that causing a disability in Alfred when you could avoid doing so is bringing about a bad state of affairs. So Alfred with a disability makes a total state of affairs that is worse than Alfred without it would make that total. But you say at the same time that there is no good moral reason for choosing to rescue the able-bodied person in preference to the disabled. But that is to say that Alfred alive with a disability and Basil dead is not worse than Basil alive with no disability and Alfred dead. If Basil dead and Alfred dead are equivalent in their probable effects on total welfare, then you are committed to saying that Alfred alive with a disability is not worse than Basil alive with no disability. But since Alfred with a disability is (you think) a worse state of things than Alfred without, and since Alfred alive with a disability is not worse (on your accounting) than Basil alive without a disability, you are treating Alfred without a disability as better than Basil without a disability, although by the terms of the example you know nothing that is a relevant difference between them. And that is a violation of Sidgwick's principles. In so far as, on Sidgwick's view, we are supposed to do what he calls aiming at good generally, we must therefore rescue Basil not Alfred if Alfred is disabled and Basil is not.

The same two principles of Sidgwick's underlie the idea, accepted in the familiar forms of utilitarianism, that, if we have a choice whether to rescue a larger rather than a smaller number of people, we must, other things being equal, rescue the larger number.[5] And that is why any version of utilitarianism which allowed the rescue of a disabled person instead of an able-bodied one, but did not allow the rescue of a smaller rather than a larger number of people, would have an ad-hoc-ness to it that would be repulsive to most utilitarians, whose reasons for accepting utilitarianism usually include a wish to reject any kind of apparent ad-hoc-ness in moral thought.

One could put the relation between the two types of case this way. Take the issue of saving the larger versus the smaller number of people, and ignore the separateness of people. That is, treat each of the two groups of people as a single notional person. Assume that the real people who are members of each of the notional persons are healthy and reasonably happy. Think now about the relation between the notional person composed of the larger number of real people and the notional person composed of the smaller number of real people. The relation between those two persons is analogous, from a utilitarian point of view, to the relation between an able-bodied real person and a disabled real person. Saving the notional person with more people-members is likely to result in there being more satisfaction or greater pleasure (or whatever the utilitarian goal is) than is saving the notional person with fewer people-members. From the utilitarian point of view, the notional person with more members is a relatively better-abled person. Utilitarianism will treat a larger number of saved legs-attached-to-people in exactly the same way it treats a larger number of saved people. The abstract relationship between the case of greater and lesser numbers of people and the case of able-bodied person and disabled person makes it extremely difficult to see how there could be a form of utilitarianism which would decide the two cases in different ways without losing the features which make utilitarianism attractive. It may be asked whether anyone who is attracted by those features would have any interest in finding a form of utilitarianism which treats it as morally permissible to rescue the disabled person rather than the able-bodied. The idea that it is wrong to do so, or that its wrongness is comparable to that of causing someone to become disabled (slightly less disabled), is hardly worse than much else that utilitarians cheerfully swallow.

III

I shall turn here to the views of Philippa Foot, but it will become clear only later why I say that she is at all attracted to utilitarianism. She has, after all, directed much energy to the exorcizing of utilitarian demons. Far from thinking of utilitarianism as attractive, she finds it radically wrong. Its radical wrongness is a matter of consequentialism; consequentialist thought makes use of a notion of good and bad states of affairs that she rejects. In arguing against the consequentialist view, she explains the place that a different notion of good and bad states of affairs can have within moral thought. What I want to show is that the demons have not been exorcized. The attraction of utilitarianism is still evident in the place that she assigns to the notion of good and bad states of affairs.

Here is her account. A person who has the virtue of benevolence must have as one of his aims the good of others; he

will regard it as a good thing when, for example, the results of
some distant disaster turn out to be less serious than had been
feared.[6] There is a kind of comparison of total outcomes that
benevolence may sometimes require. The comparison will not
always be the sort of comparison that a utilitarian would make. It
will, though, be similar in some cases – if, for example, there is
some question whether to rescue a larger rather than a smaller
number of people. I am not sure whether Mrs Foot implies here
that it would actually be wrong, other things being equal, to
rescue the smaller number. She says that 'benevolence would, we
may suppose, urge that the larger number be saved'.[7] And she says
that the benevolent person does have a general wish that loss and
harm be minimized.[8] She emphasizes very strongly, though, that
benevolence does not lead us to make a comparison of total
outcomes in cases in which one of the possible actions involves a
violation of the requirements of justice. We should not think of a
case in which an unjust killing would prevent several deaths as
one in which the 'best outcome' can be achieved only by unjust
killing. The judging of the goodness of an outcome cannot be
carried out in the manner that the utilitarian thinks necessary.
The person who has the virtues of benevolence and justice will
not see the outcome which involves unjust killing as a 'better
total', the way to which is unfortunately blocked by the
requirements of justice. What Mrs Foot says about the relation
between the benevolent person's assessment of outcomes and the
requirements of justice is not intended by her to apply only to
justice, although justice is the most important example of a virtue
whose requirements affect the benevolent person's assessment of
a situation. Benevolence is, as she says, only one of the virtues.
And her general claim seems to be that what is consistent with
one virtue cannot in general be determined in isolation from the
other virtues, although it may be possible in some cases to do just
that.

What is particularly interesting is Mrs Foot's criticism of
utilitarian theories of the 'ideal observer' type, which ask us to
imagine an ideally impartial observer whose benevolence extends
to everyone. She argues that these theories, which identify moral
right and wrong with the assessment such a being would make,
are question-begging in denying to the 'observer' any
characteristics other than the desire to increase happiness and

diminish suffering; all other virtues, and the desires corresponding to them, are missing. Such a being is not just not a perfect maker of moral assessments; he is not even a being whose *benevolence* is perfect. For benevolence does not always, in every case, aim at the highest possible overall welfare. What benevolence aims at in a particular case can be understood only through two things: its relation to other morally significant traits and the general end at which it aims.

What exactly then is the end that benevolence aims at when its direction is not in any way affected by other virtues? It aims at 'maximum welfare'. So Mrs Foot's view is that maximum welfare is not what morality as a whole has as its end, but that it 'appears *within* morality as the end of one of the virtues'.[9]

I need now to return to the question: can anyone be attracted to utilitarianism and yet want to avoid the ludicrous consequence? There is a sense in which Mrs Foot is attracted to utilitarianism: she gives the notion of maximum welfare a central place in explaining the end of benevolence. She does, though, want to reject the ludicrous consequence. The question is whether anyone who ties benevolence to a notion of maximum welfare, even in the way she does, has a problem rejecting the ludicrous consequence.

My aim here is to suggest that benevolence and its characteristic end or ends cannot be understood at all through the use of a notion of maximum welfare, or of notions explained through that one. For example, it is true, as Mrs Foot says, that a benevolent person is concerned with the avoidance of suffering.[10] But if 'avoidance of suffering' is explained in terms which tie it to maximum welfare, then benevolent people are concerned with something else. If 'avoidance of suffering' is explained in terms of a welfare sum, then suffering is avoided if one chooses to rescue an able-bodied person rather than an otherwise similar disabled person, if one has to make the choice. But the ordinary benevolent person, with *his* understanding of 'avoiding suffering', would not think that benevolence urged him to rescue the able-bodied person. Benevolence in such a case does not aim at maximum welfare; and its not doing so is not dependent on its relation to the other virtues of the benevolent person. It is not that friendship or justice or something else shapes what is consistent with benevolence in such circumstances. It is benevolence itself, considered here independently of its relation to other virtues and their associated desires, which is quite distinct from utilitarian benevolence: it is a different and more complex and more interesting set of dispositions and sensibilities.

I want to strengthen the claim that utilitarian benevolence and benevolence differ more thoroughly and more interestingly than Mrs Foot's account allows. That is to say, I want to show that the limited space that Mrs Foot allots to a notion closely allied to utilitarian notions is still too great. I want the lineaments of the unexorcized demons to be made sharper. To make them sharper, I shall consider two sorts of example.

Imagine that you are a concert pianist, and that your agent has, unfortunately and through no fault of your own, booked you to play a concert in each of two different cities the same evening. Both concerts are sold out; one is at a considerably larger hall than the other. Suppose that you decide to play at one of the halls, and that some people with tickets to the other concert come over in the hope of getting in, and suppose that a few seats are somehow found for them. Kindly people should, I should expect, be pleased by that; they might well say what a good thing it was. But if they are kindly people, and if one of their ends is the avoidance of suffering and disappointment, need they say that it would be best for you to disappoint the smaller audience? Many people would not take it that benevolence in such circumstances involved urging you to give the concert in the larger hall. But if benevolence does not urge you to choose the larger hall, it is not because some other virtue makes not doing so consistent with benevolence in this case.

That example suggests, I think, that benevolence, even when considered in isolation from other virtues, is not related in a simple way to sums of welfare. My second example is meant to support that suggestion more strongly. I need here to bring out a complexity hidden within a case that Mrs Foot uses. In order to illustrate how a benevolent person uses the phrase 'a good thing', she invites us to imagine such a person who has heard about a faraway disaster. It then turns out to be less serious than feared, and he speaks of its turning out so as a good thing. The case as she imagines it combines two significant features. There is a change in the seriousness of what has happened, but no change in what we may imagine to be the rather vaguely specified group of people among whom the victims are to be found. It will help to bring out what the issues are here, if we consider a pair of cases like hers in some ways but unlike it in others.

Suppose that we had all thought that a Boeing 747 had just crashed, and that everyone on it had been killed. We might indeed say 'What a good thing' if we found later that some people had indeed survived virtually unharmed (or if we had originally thought that the plane was full and later found that some passengers booked to go on the plane had been held up in traffic, and the plane had left without anyone else in their seats). We may contrast with that first case one in which the initial news is the same, but what we find out later is that the Boeing 747, which had indeed been in the area (and had been full), was not the plane that had crashed: it was in fact a smaller 727 that did so, and everyone on that plane has been killed: a smaller number. We do not so easily say, however benevolent we are, 'Oh, what a good thing that it was the 727'.

Look at the total welfare in these two cases. There is the total welfare as we estimate it on the basis of the original news, and the total welfare as we estimate it on the basis of the corrected reports. The original estimate of total welfare is the same in both cases; the corrected estimate we may suppose to be the same in both cases: we may suppose that the difference between the total number believed dead at first and the number found later to have died is the same in both cases. But the ordinary benevolent person may well treat the cases differently. And that is to say (again) that even when we are not concerned with the relation between benevolence and other virtues, the end which benevolence aims at is not to be explained in terms of total welfare. It is not because the total welfare is greater that we are pleased in the first case when we find that, amazingly, the crash did have survivors; or we should be pleased in the same way and to the same extent when we learn that it was the 727 and not the 747 that had crashed.

If he learns that a few have survived the crash of the 747 unharmed, or that a few by good luck were unable to get on the plane, the ordinary benevolent person is glad that some people have *escaped* death or terrible injury. (It is important that no one else has replaced those who have escaped death. The benevolent person in the case I am considering would not be pleased in the way he is if ten people had escaped death by being caught in a traffic jam, and ten people waiting at the airport had got on instead.) In the case in which the corrected news is that it was not a 747 but a 727 that had crashed, although one finds out that fewer people had died than one had thought, one does not find out that anyone has escaped death. (A person in the 747 cannot be said to have escaped death in this case, unless he had had some plan to go on the 727, or reason to go on that plane which he had not acted on, or something of the sort.)

For an ordinary benevolent person, as contrasted with a utilitarian, the fact that some have escaped death in one case and not in the other (escaped without being replaced), makes a difference to the way he sees the goodness of the state of affairs. For a utilitarian, the goodness of anyone's escaping death and not being replaced (in a case like this, in which we know nothing else about the people) is simply the goodness of there being one death less altogether. And so, although a benevolent person will sometimes be willing to compare states of affairs, and to say that one is better than another, the comparisons he is willing to make are not made in the style of the utilitarian. A benevolent person may use an expression like 'escaping death' in explaining why one outcome is better than another, why, for example, it is good that some people were unable to get on the 747 that then crashed. Here a utilitarian will ask: but what is there about an escape of death that makes that count in the comparison of states of affairs? What is there, he asks, that is good in that state of affairs that is not equally present in the case in which no one escaped death but fewer are killed? He lays down rules for what can properly count in the comparison of states of affairs or of outcomes. When we have no further information about the people involved, someone's escaping death counts only in so far as what it involved is one less death altogether. To allow it to count in any other way is to allow *who* does not die to enter the calculation of overall good; and that violates Sidgwick's great principle governing what counts in such calculations, the first of the two principles I quoted earlier. Although a benevolent person does sometimes make comparisons of states of affairs, he does not accept utilitarian rules about what counts in such comparisons. And to see that he does not, we do not need to turn to cases involving any virtue other than benevolence itself. Benevolence does not have as its aim maximum welfare or maximum anything; very little indeed is given of an understanding of benevolence by specifying something as its distinctive aim. I shall say more about benevolence in Part V.

(I should point out that my examples here are not meant to suggest that those comparisons of the goodness of states of affairs that a benevolent person is willing to make depend on Pareto efficiency rather than on total welfare, or that the number of people killed or injured or endangered by what we do and by what happens never affects a benevolent person's judgments or responses.)

IV

Much discussion of the apparently repulsive consequences of utilitarianism has focused on cases in which utilitarianism allows or requires us to do something which other moral theories hold that we are not allowed to do at all; or on cases in which utilitarianism treats certain failures to act or allowings to happen as having the same moral significance as those things we more directly do. Cases of this second sort are important, in ways very like the first sorts of case, to the conflict between utilitarianism and moral theories involving actions which are absolutely prohibited or viewed as far more stringently prohibited than they are by utilitarianism. The focus on cases of these two sorts encourages and is encouraged by our view of what the choices are for philosophical treatments of morality. We see utilitarianism on one side, and on the other views which conflict with it in their insistence on certain things we must not do. The interest of the rescue example is that it may help us to see somewhat differently what kinds of alternative to utilitarianism there are. In the rest of this paper I shall argue that if we do find ludicrous what utilitarianism is committed to on rescuing a disabled person, that reflects a difference between our moral thinking and utilitarianism, not primarily in what we take to be permissible or required but in ways of thinking about life, which bear on moral evaluation. There are ways of thinking about life which Sidgwick's principles direct us to treat as irrelevant to the question of what we should aim at. I shall try to show the character of the conflict.

I want to turn first to contractual accounts of morality. One thing is clear: such accounts will not in general have as a consequence that an able-bodied person ought to be saved rather than a disabled person, if a choice between them has to be made. Nor will they have the consequence that saving the 'wrong', the disabled, person is wrong for the same sorts of reason it is usually wrong to cause a disabling injury to someone. The question is whether their avoidance of such consequences is connected in an illuminating way with the reasons, whatever they are, for which most people who are not utilitarians would find those consequences ludicrous. That question is analogous to one with which John Rawls is concerned. He wants to show a connection between principles of justice which can be derived by a certain procedure and characteristics of that procedure which represent or model important features of our conception of ourselves and of our relation to society.

Rawls's own arguments are not designed to apply to such questions as whom we should save when we cannot save everyone; they are concerned with fundamental principles of justice for a society. But the contractual procedure he describes can be taken to have a wider application. As Rawls points out, on his account of justice, the search for 'moral truth' (on which our principles of justice should rest) is replaced by a 'search for reasonable grounds for reaching agreement rooted in our conception of ourselves and in our relation to society'.[11] A contractual procedure may then (or so it may be argued) play a role in such a 'replacement' of the search for moral truth, in any other part of morality in which we might instead reach agreement 'rooted in our conception of ourselves and in our relation to society'. It is possible, then, to imagine an argument like Rawls's but concerned, not with fundamental principles of justice, but with the question whom to save when all cannot be saved. An argument of the kind used by Rawls to justify the two principles of justice can be given, which will lead to a rejection of the utilitarian view that the able-bodied must be given preference. (I should specify that I am avoiding the case of war and any other similar special circumstances in which a serious justification can be given for treating some groups of people, in limited respects, as resources.)

For parties in the 'original position', as described by Rawls, it would be rational to accept that neither the able-bodied nor the disabled should (other things being equal) be given preference when not everyone can be saved. The parties in the original position 'aim to advance their own interest' and have no interest in maximizing the sum total of satisfaction.[12] And it is the utilitarian interest in that total which generates the ludicrous consequence. The fact that the Rawlsian parties aim to advance their own interests does not build into the contractual theory any kind of egoism. The situation is rather this. They can advance their own interests through securing for themselves primary goods; but primary goods are things which are generally necessary for securing what Rawls calls the 'highest-order' interests of the parties. These are the interests they have, considering themselves as moral persons: moral persons have characteristic powers and corresponding highest-order interests in realizing and exercising these powers.[13] So the fact that the parties in the original position have as their aim the advancement of their own interests, far from making the resulting theory a type of 'self-interest' theory, is the way in which the contractual arrangements represent the freedom and equality of moral persons. Free and equal moral persons, considered merely as such, can agree in rejecting principles which would give preferential treatment to the lives of the able-bodied. Anyone's life stands to the achievement of his highest-order interests in the same general way; the presence or absence of the kinds of disability I have been talking about makes no difference to that relation between life and highest-order interests.

I have sketched one sort of argument that can be made within the context of a contractual theory of ethics to show that such an approach would not lead to the ludicrous consequence. What I now want to show is that, while a contractual theory does not have the ludicrous consequence, it fails to illuminate what is really wrong with that consequence. I am not suggesting that that is an objection to contractual theories; such a theory need have no ambition to do everything that might usefully form a part of philosophical ethics. But my discussion does aim to make clear what falls outside the part of ethics that contractual theories can plausibly represent.

Let me put the contrast between the utilitarian view of whom to save and the contractual view this way. On the utilitarian view, what you have done for someone is reckoned, in connection with any question of right or wrong, relative to a conception of him as a locus of satisfaction. Other things being equal, the expected satisfactions of two people, about whom you know that they are roughly similar but differ in that one has some disability like lack of a limb and the other has not, differ in that the disabled person can expect more difficulties, frustrations, discourtesies and so on than can the other. Since the expectations of the disabled person are lower, you are doing less for him by saving him than you are doing for the able-bodied person by saving him: that is how the utilitarian reckons what he would be doing for each of the people by saving them. He must also take into account that he is doing less for others by saving the disabled person. On the contractual view, what you are doing for someone is told, in connection with those questions to which a contractual approach is appropriate (e.g. on Rawls's own view, in connection with questions of justice), relative to the idea of him as a moral person. Relative to the idea of people as beings with the characteristic powers of moral persons, what you are doing for any person in rescuing him is the same as what you are doing for anyone else in rescuing *that* person. If, for some reason, the person you rescued was incapable of exercising the capacities of moral persons, what you are doing for him in rescuing him could not be reckoned (in accordance with contractual theories like Rawls's) in the same way. But I have not been considering such cases.

What comes out in the contrast is that what you are doing for someone in saving his life is determined relative to some particular way of thinking of people. The difference between a utilitarian view and a contractual view of what you have done for someone in rescuing him depends on the difference between viewing a person for your purposes as a locus of satisfaction and viewing him as characterized by the powers of moral persons. And it should be apparent, then, that other general ways of viewing people will be tied to other ways of seeing what you are doing for someone in saving his life.

I need now to digress to take up a question which I have allowed to remain in the background. Whom *should* we save? There are two answers other than the utilitarian's. (1) We may say that we must try to save both people if we can, and otherwise either one, i.e., we may claim that there is no general principle giving preference to one rather than the other. Or (2) we may be inclined to say something different. We may think that the one thing that we know of that differentiates the two people is a reason for saving the disabled person. He has had things harder. So let him not be the one to be abandoned now. (Mrs Foot said something like that in discussion. I think it is a response that many people would find appropriate.) The thought here is not that the disabled person has a stronger right to be rescued than the able-bodied person; it is a different way of seeing fitnesses of things from any that can be well expressed in terms of rights. It does have something to do with justice, but not with justice thought of as it usually is in contemporary moral philosophy, in which it is tied very closely to the notion of a right. Although the second sort of answer is more interesting, I shall need to say more about the first.

That first answer, I have argued, can be given by contractual theories of ethics, in which it is tied to a view of people as moral persons with characteristic powers. Life is relevant to the exercise of those powers in the same way for any moral person. But if we see only the tie between the first answer and that contractualist mode of thinking about people, we shall not understand the force of that answer. (We shall misunderstand it in something like the way Kant misunderstands suicide in arguing for its wrongness on the basis of its relation to moral personality.) I want to make clear a connection between the first answer and a kind of abstraction different from that in a contractual view. That is, contractualism lets us abstract from all the particular features of the person who needs to be saved, apart from his moral powers. I shall illustrate this other kind of abstraction, this other notion of what the relevant features are of the person whose life is in danger, by a striking passage from Dickens's *Our Mutual Friend.* One of the thoroughly repulsive characters in Dickens's fiction, Rogue Riderhood, has been out in a rowing boat in the Thames in a fog. The boat has been cut in two by a steamer, and Riderhood has been under water for a long time. The body is grappled up and brought, quite rigid, to a Thames-side pub; but it may be that Riderhood is not quite dead. A doctor has been sent for, arrives,

> examines the dank carcass and pronounces, not hopefully, that it is worth while trying to reanimate the same. All the

best means are at once in action, and everybody present lends a hand, and a heart and soul. No one has the least regard for the man; with them all, he has been an object of avoidance, suspicion, and aversion; but the spark of life within him is curiously separable from himself now, and they have a deep interest in it, probably because it is life, and they are living and must die. . .

. . . If you are not gone for good, Mr. Riderhood, it would be something to know where you are hiding at present. This flabby lump of mortality that we work so hard at with such patient perseverance yields no sign of you. If you are gone for good, Rogue, it is very solemn, and if you are coming back, it is hardly less so. Nay, in the suspense and mystery of the latter question, involving that of where you may be now, there is a solemnity even added to that of death, making us who are in attendance alike afraid to look on you and to look off you, and making those below start at the least sound of a creaking plank in the floor.

Stay! Did that eyelid tremble? So the doctor, breathing low and closely watching, asks himself.

No.

Did that nostril twitch?

No.

This artificial respiration ceasing, do I feel any faint flutter under my hand upon the chest?

No.

Over and over again No. No. But try over and over again, nevertheless.

See! A token of life! An indubitable token of life! The spark may smoulder and go out, or it may glow and expand, but see! The four rough fellows seeing, shed tears. Neither Riderhood in this world, nor Riderhood in the other, could draw tears from them, but a striving human soul between the two can do it easily.[14]

What is it that is done for Riderhood, when Riderhood is brought back to life? Dickens presents a view quite different from both the utilitarian and the contractual view. The doctor and the rough fellows who struggle to save Riderhood are not utilitarians, and do not care a penny for any future satisfactions that Riderhood may have. They know him well enough to know that if he comes back to life, he will add to the total misery in the world and not the total happiness. Saving his life is tied for them to an impersonal view of what is at stake; but it is not the impersonality either of utilitarianism or of contractualism. They are not concerned with Riderhood's life in its relation to the exercise of the capacities of a moral person. It would be a mistake to go on to say that the rough fellows and the doctor and Dickens himself think that 'life is a good' or that it is 'intrinsically good'. It is a mistake not because it is straightforwardly false, but because it is not an explanation and directs attention away from what is important in the passage: a view of life and death, which cannot he captured in the language made available by moral philosophy of intrinsic and instrumental goods. Dickens is concerned with our sense of death as our fate, and with how that sense of death as common fate shapes our understanding of a situation, our conception of what counts in it. On the utilitarian view, the relevant characteristic of a human being which fixes what it is you are doing in saving his life (or, for that matter, in doing anything else) is his capacity for satisfaction; on contractual views it is the capacities of moral persons. More generally, the contractual view can explain what is done for someone in terms of the notion of a person as having, besides the characteristic powers of moral persons, needs, desires and a particular conception of the good. For Dickens, in contrast, the sense of death as common fate is tied to the idea of life and death as solemn and mysterious matters, and to that of death as our common enemy, an enemy of a special and terrible sort.

My overall argument in this part of the paper is going to be that ideas about life which are not ideas about rightness, goodness, or virtue enter our moral thought in many ways, and that moral theory, which characteristically ignores such features of moral thought, thus gives a distorted picture of that thought. You cannot see what is involved in our moral thought about such things as saving life if you do not see how we think about life; and you cannot see what we think about life if you take into account only certain limited types of thought: if you are willing to look at what we think to be good, but not at how we shape our notions of what we ourselves are. Those conceptions we have of what we are that we treat as available in moral theories (and that, in those theories, determine what counts in a description of a situation) exclude the sense of what death is that Dickens shows us at work. In philosophy we are familiar with the treatment of a person as a locus of satisfaction and as something the activities of which affect satisfaction at other such loci: such a conception of a person is tied to one type of impersonality. We are also familiar with the treatment of a person as moral agent or bearer of moral personality; and that conception of the person is linked to another kind of impersonality in moral thought, especially characteristic of Kant and followers of Kant. The doctor and the rough fellows and the others in the pub see in Riderhood a mortal man like themselves; nothing else about him comes into their understanding of the situation and its demands: this is another sort of impersonality in moral thought.

I need to say something more about what it is to think of him, and ourselves, so; in particular about why I used the words 'common fate' in speaking about what Dickens shows. I used the word 'fate' to suggest that death does not enter our thought merely as a type of event, biological death, which is to be expected by each of us with certainty. Death is something on which the human imagination has seized; we have made notions of what death is, what it means, notions of mortality which obviously are connected with biological death and its certainty; but what we have made is distinct. The imaginative grasp of death enters not only what the doctor and the rough fellows do, but also thought, theirs or ours, about what it is that they have done. It enters our vocabulary, even when we are merely describing what mortality has meant to others. Thus, for example, Alasdair MacIntyre writes about what death meant in heroic societies. He says that we might expect to find in such societies an emphasis on the contrast between the expectations of the man who has virtues and friends and kinsmen and those of the man who lacks such goods. But, he goes on, one central theme of these societies is that 'death waits for both alike'.[15] His intention is to describe their views, but he shifts in the course of giving those views into the language of those views: shifts out of academic prose into a personification of death in iambic meter. He can take for granted (without thinking about it) that readers will understand the fittingness of the shift in his prose, the fittingness to the subject matter of his shift to the language of death-as-fate, a language making use of the resources of poetry. This shift of language to what fits what death is for us is like the shift of Dickens's own narrative techniques in the passage I quoted: a shift from past to present tense and to a narrator who is one of 'us who are in attendance'. But it is also like the shift of *action* which Dickens describes, from the normal activities of a pub (one from which Riderhood is actually excluded) to activities focused entirely on saving a man's life, a shift to activities and responses made appropriate by our sense of what life and death are.

There is an important kind of parallel between contractual thought and what is presented in the passage from Dickens. To explain that parallel, I shall use the quotation from Jack London's 'To Build a Fire' with which I began this essay. There is implicit in it the contrast between being someone for whom fifty degrees below zero is precisely fifty degrees below zero, and being someone who does not stop there, but is led on by the fact of such cold. The contractual theorist is someone who 'does not stop there' with respect, not to fifty degrees below zero, but to certain features of human beings: the capacity to choose, to justify choices in talk with others, to regard things as good, features which could be looked at simply as parts of the natural world, characteristics of the species which have developed in the course of biological and social evolution. But contractual thought is led on by the facts here: seizes on these features, gives them imaginative weight. They are taken in imagination to play a central role in our understanding of what it is to be human.

Or take Kant. The starry skies above him were not just starry skies, but led him to thoughts about man's place in the universe; the moral law within was not just a matter of our use of 'the ordinary apparatus of value-language in order to commend or condemn' actions that, as a matter of psychological fact, we do care about. From a naturalistic or Humean view, reason may be seen just precisely as reason and nothing more, part of the way in which our actions are determined, part of the way in which we are able to satisfy our desires, whatever they may be. Reason does not (on such a view) show something special about the kind of creature we are or our place in the universe. Kant can, however, tell us stories (not, I mean, stories of what people do in real or imagined circumstances, although he does make some use of such stories; rather, stories about what reason *is*, like the imaginative tale of the relation between noumenal freedom and the empirical world), stories which help us make a connection between an imaginative grasp of what we are and the appropriateness of acting towards fellow possessors of reason in certain ways.

A contractual theorist like Rawls tells us stories of a somewhat different sort: about how people who know only certain facts about themselves, including in particular their having the capacities of moral persons, would choose rules to shape their social institutions. Such stories, like Kant's, can help us to make connections between an imaginative grasp of certain human capacities (which might instead be seen merely as those capacities and nothing more) and the appropriateness of certain kinds of social arrangements. Dickens, I am arguing, is in the same line of work. For him, the fact that we all die is not that fact and nothing more; it would be a failure of imagination to see it so, a failure with profound consequences for our capacity to live well. To understand its significance is to be able to make connections between a sense of who we are, what kind of being, and the way we live.

These are connections not only between the imaginative understanding of ourselves-as-sharers-of-mortality and a willingness to set to to save even a man like Riderhood; they are connections between our common fate and our capacity to enjoy life and to live compassionately. To make clear the appropriateness of certain modes of life to the kind of being we are (understood imaginatively), Dickens tells stories: that aim is especially clearly evident in *A Christmas Carol*, where the understanding of ourselves as 'fellow-passengers to the grave' is linked to living in what for Dickens is the spirit of Christmas. Instead of original contractors who make a choice based only on their knowledge of what their highest-order interests are as moral persons, we have Scrooge, who is able to live in a radically different spirit when brought to a live understanding of himself, not as 'moral person', but as a human being who was a child, who is capable of happiness and compassion, and who will die. He becomes capable of being touched by the characteristic temporal shape of human life; it enters his way of living, as (on the contractual story) our understanding of what rational contractors might do may enter the spirit in which we participate in political and social life.

There can be ethical theories which aim to see fifty degrees below zero just precisely as fifty degrees below zero. That aim is characteristic of many versions of utilitarianism. (Taken to be the aim of utilitarianism, it is the main target of Dickens's *Hard Times*.) The aim also characterizes some meta-ethical theories, and makes attractive the usual idea of the contrast between the descriptive and evaluative functions of language. One might divide ethical theories into those that do and those that do not tell stories (including metaphysical stories, or stories about beings suffering from queer kinds of ignorance of who they are), stories intended to bring us to an imaginative understanding of the kind of beings we are. My criticism of theories that do not tell us such stories at all, like utilitarianism, is that they are moral theories that have nothing to do with moral thought. It is a characterizing feature of moral thought that it is penetrated by our imaginative efforts to think about the kind of being we are and about the significance of such things as death, the passage of time, our moral capacities themselves, vulnerability to chance, the possibility or apparent possibility of happiness, and so on. The ludicrous consequence of utilitarianism, with which I began, is only one way in which the failure of utilitarianism to be in touch with those sources of moral thought that make it recognizable as such evidences itself.

The trouble with contractual theories and theories like Kant's is different. Moral thought is made what it is by thought about life: but thought which seizes on and makes something of and is infinitely touched by *various* things about life: not just by moral personality. The wonderful passage in Kant which I alluded to earlier, the conclusion of *The Critique of Practical Reason*, illustrates both the strength and the weakness of Kant. Moral personality and the most striking feature of the natural world are viewed by Kant with awe, and he sees this response not just as his own but as a profoundly appropriate response, tied for him to the contrast between our negligible place as mere animals in the natural world and our dignified status in a world with true infinity. The contrast goes with Kant's excluding from any role in moral thought any other understanding of our nature than that which takes moral personality as its distinguishing characteristic. Contractual theories share Kant's narrowness, although the imaginative vision of human life inspiring them is somewhat different. They allow two ways in which an imaginative understanding of what human life is can enter moral thought. Our idea of moral personality and its ties to the possibility of respect for others based on an understanding of our shared interests as moral persons has one central place in such theories; but our imaginative grasp of things other than moral personality, our thought about life, death, chance, happiness, time, love and the like, come into contractual theories in an altogether distinct kind of way: they are thought of only as elements affecting the conception individuals may form of how they want to arrange their own lives. They belong in the ragbag: people's thought about the good and the ends that they themselves pursue. I want to emphasize here that I am not suggesting the fault of contractual theories to be that of inadequate attention to how our notions of what is good and what our ends are shape our understanding of who we are. I am rejecting the idea that ethics takes as its starting point the right *or* the good *or* the character of a good person: that those are the essential elements in our ethical thought and that various types of ethical theory are determined by how they see the relation of those elements. Ethics comes from our thought about all the things that can strike us as revealing something significant about the kind of being we are. *That we die* and *that we are capable of moral choice* are side by side in this, and side by side with lots of other things.

The fault, then, of Kantian and contractual theories is not that they, like utilitarianism, reject the imaginative understanding of who we are as significant in ethics; it is that they treat the imaginative understanding of moral personality as utterly distinctive in ethical thought, which it is not. And that is why Kant on suicide, for example, barks up the wrong tree, and why, although contractual theories do not say that we must rescue the able-bodied person if we cannot rescue him and the disabled person, they are unable to present our understanding of such a case in an illuminating way. Elizabeth Anscombe once said that the utilitarian argument for respecting the prohibition on murder, that it 'makes life more commodious', is highly comic. Respect for that prohibition is what she calls a supra-utilitarian virtue, and she calls such virtues mystical.[16] Contractual theories, unlike utilitarian ones, are able to recognize with no difficulty that the wrong done in murder is not understandable in terms of its effects on the level of satisfaction. But, for such theories, premature death is most significantly the end of the opportunities

175

for the exercise of moral personality, and the interruption of the person's life plan. And that is still to miss the sense of respect for life, by cutting it off from the mysteriousness of life and death. If we are unwilling to make, in advance, any choice between an able-bodied and a disabled person, that reluctance has nothing to do with what is *fair*, or what treats moral personality with respect.

V

I want now to turn back to the other non-utilitarian answer to the question of whom we should rescue: the answer that it would be too bad to abandon the person whom we knew to have been struck earlier by misfortune. This response seems to me entirely natural for a benevolent person, but its consistency with benevolence suggests a different view of benevolence and other virtues from Mrs Foot's. What benevolence aims at in a particular case depends, in her account, in part on the bearing of the requirements in that particular case of other virtues. What is consistent with benevolence depends on them, as well as on the general aim of benevolence. My claim is that what a virtue aims at in a particular case is dependent not just on its relation to other virtues but also on its possessor's sense of the significance of multitudes of things. One of those things is vulnerability to misfortune, and the fragility of any good fortune in general, the fragility of our bodies in particular, our dependence on all these bodily parts continuing to hang together and to work; 'such forces within forces within forces, the marvel is that anyone is ever well'. The imaginative grasp of our shared vulnerability to misfortune, the sense of what that vulnerability means, may come out in the thought of its being appropriate to rescue the person who has lost a limb, if we cannot rescue both people. This is not a matter of some other virtues shaping what is consistent with benevolence, but of benevolence itself being a trait shaped by a sense of what it is to be human. Benevolence does not just wish for the good of others: it wishes for the good of others in the light of a more or less imaginative and full (but not usually discursive) understanding of human life. The emotions connected with benevolence are not just gladness at people's happiness and sorrow or sadness when they are made to suffer (and the range of reactive feelings towards those who cause others happiness or suffering). They include being touched by the facts here, the facts of our suffering and of our capacity for joy and delight, finding these things strange or troubling, being moved to wonder or deep confusion by them. That we have legs and need them and some must do without them at a cost that the person who has them can hardly imagine: these are facts like fifty degrees below zero. What we make of them we make of them; but benevolence bereft of any imaginative sense of such things, benevolence for which they remain mere facts, is poor benevolence indeed.

After quoting Jack London, I began this essay with Peter Winch's remarks, from the end of one of his articles, about the dependence of our conceptions of good and evil on how we think about the shaping elements of life itself, like mortality. I want to end with some remarks from the beginning of a different article of his, about Sidgwick's idea of ethics as a sort of calculus of action. In a footnote he connects that remark about Sidgwick's aims with the idea of a 'rational and normative system of ethics', and says that he is implicitly questioning the possibility of such a system.[17] Elsewhere he has emphasized that we should not think of reason in ethics as capable of determining that position, on any ethical issue, which a 'rational man of moral good will' would have to find acceptable. I have tried to show a particular line of connection between the two views. I have not, that is, tried to show that some answer to the question whom we should rescue is right. If we attend to what enters the answers we give to such a question, to what enters what may be our reluctance or refusal to answer, we may be able to see something of how imagination shapes our moral concepts, shapes what counts as the same and what counts as different, what is fitting and appropriate to what. That is not something to be done *for* us, or done once and for all, and embodied in a system that would ensure impartiality. If ways of understanding life and its queer or wonderful or terrible features are to be brought to moral thought, we cannot coherently suppose that limits may be set around how that is to be done. The utilitarians should be a warning of how the desire for systematized impartiality can denature moral thought. They may be quick and alert in the things of life (some of the things, anyway), but not in the significances. Peter Winch's work has always been directed to the significances.

NOTES

1. P. Winch, 'Understanding a primitive society' in *Ethics and Action* (London: Routledge & Kegan Paul, 1972) pp. 8–49, at pp. 46–7.

2. See for example, D. Parfit, *Reasons and Persons* (Oxford: Clarendon Press, 1985) pp. 358–61; J. Glover, *Causing Death And Saving Lives* (Harmondsworth: Penguin Books, 1977) pp. 67–8, 147–9.

3. I am grateful to Julie Ahmad for drawing my attention to the issues here.

4. H. Sidgwick, *The Methods of Ethics* (London: Macmillan, 1930) p.382.

5. See G. E. M. Anscombe, 'Who is wronged?', *The Oxford Review* (1967) pp.16–17.

6. P. Foot, 'Utilitarianism and the virtues', *Mind,* vol. 94 (1985) pp. 196–209, at p.204..

7. ibid., p. 206.

8. ibid., p. 207.

9. ibid., p. 206.

10. P. Foot, 'Morality, action and outcome' in T. Honderich (ed.) *Morality and Objectivity* (London: Routledge & Kegan Paul, 1985) pp. 23–38, at p.31.

11. J. Rawls, 'Kantian constructivism in moral theory', *Journal of Philosophy,* vol. 77 (1980) pp. 515–72, at p. 519.

12. J. Rawls, *A Theory of Justice* (Cambridge, Mass: Harvard University Press, 1971) p. 163.

13. J. Rawls, 'Kantian constructivism in moral theory', p. 525.

14. Charles Dickens, *Our Mutual Friend,* ch. 36.

15. Alasdair MacIntyre, *After Virtue* (Notre Dame, Ind.: University of Notre Dame Press, 1981) p. 117.

16. G. E. M. Anscombe 'Contraception and chastity', *The Human World* (1972), pp. 9–30, at p. 25.

17. P. Winch, op. cit. pp.153, 170.

Chapter Nine

'ETHICAL REWARD AND PUNISHMENT'

RUSH RHEES

Winch[1] discusses two statements which seem closely connected with one another in Wittgenstein's *Tractatus* 6.422:

1. 'that ethics has nothing to do with punishment and reward in the usual sense';

2. 'there must be some kind of ethical reward and ethical punishment, but they must reside in the action itself.'

(In what follows I shall look only at what is said about punishment.)

People might say that punishment was ethical if they meant that its aim is some betterment of those who are punished; or perhaps, if they held that the aim of punishment is some form of retribution. Winch does not ask about 'ethical' in these senses. He constructs an example of a prisoner who reflects on his imprisonment and what has led to it. He analyses the ways in which the crime and the stay in prison may become related in the man's thinking. He suggests that there might be in this an interpretation of the *Tractatus* phrase: 'a kind of ethical punishment'.

Both those *Tractatus* sentences are difficult; the whole passage is. They are interesting when we try to understand why he wrote them. And we are helped in this if we try to follow his own later criticisms. Winch does not do this. He seems to want to take those statements as they stand and ask what light they throw on his problem as he presents it: i.e., from the point of view of the one punished, rather than the view of a spectator. I think he misinterprets the remark about 'a kind of ethical punishment in which the punishment lies in the act itself'. And I think he has difficulties he might have avoided. (As always with questions of interpretation, it is at least as likely that he is on the right lines and I am wrong.)

What the *Tractatus* says about judgments of absolute value is difficult; at least I cannot understand it.

Some questions about punishment are connected with this. 'If a man has done wrong, he deserves to be punished.' Is there an internal relation expressed in that 'If . . ., then . . .'? – If we say: 'it is a rule of our practice' – we have still left 'deserves' unclear.

I want to look again at passages from Wittgenstein which have brought some of Winch's problems.

We speak of relative value and absolute value; and with examples it seems clear enough. 'Absolute' means 'not relative'; but – what else?

Does it suggest something like *'unconditioned'* or *'unconditioned necessity'*? These phrases would mean nothing in a description of facts; nor anywhere else, for that matter. And yet we want to say of absolute value that nothing can weaken it; (although this is misleading: as though it were like 'nothing can scratch a diamond' – as though 'absolute value' meant a limiting case of relative value: whereas the word 'value' has a different meaning here). And similarly with 'an absolute "ought"' (I think of Wittgenstein's example in the *Lecture on Ethics*), and 'absolute imperative'. We cannot *say* what this difference is, because (6.42, 6.421) 'There can be no ethical propositions. Propositions cannot express anything higher. It is clear that ethics cannot be expressed.'

Those sentences come after a longer paragraph, 6.41, and are conclusions from it: 6.42 begins: *'And so* there can be no ethical propositions.' 6.41, from which they follow, is difficult, but it may help to explain what he says about *'ethical punishment'* in 6.422, which follows it almost at once. There is the single sentence, 6.4: 'All propositions are of equal value.' And then:

6.41: The sense of the world must lie outside the world. In the world everything is as it is and happens as it does happen. *In it* there is no value – and if there were, it would be of no value.

If there is a value which is of value, it must lie outside all happening and being-so. For all happening and being-so is accidental.

What makes it non-accidental cannot lie in the world, for otherwise this again would be accidental.

It must lie outside the world.

If there *were* an ethical proposition, it would have to express or show a value which is of value; as it were, convey to you the value and that this has value. You would understand the value as you were given the terms and the form of the proposition: it would be commensurable with propositions in the world of facts: with possible transitions from one to another. But this is impossible; and *this* is what is meant by 'Propositions cannot express anything higher'. And here: 'what makes a value which has value non-accidental, must lie outside the world' is the same as: 'what makes it non-accidental must be something higher'. Obviously this 'non-accidental' does not mean 'logically necessary'. If someone wanted to say 'A value which is of value must be self-certifying', this could not mean *logically* self-certifying; the phrase itself shows this.

Tractatus 6.422:
When an ethical law of the form 'You ought . . .' is laid down one's first thought is: 'And what if I do not do it?' But it is clear that ethics has nothing to do with punishment and reward in the ordinary sense. So this question about the *consequences* of an action must be unimportant. – At least such consequences should not be events. For there must be something right about raising that question. There must indeed be a kind of ethical reward and ethical punishment, but these must lie in the action itself.

(And it is also clear that the reward must be something pleasant and the punishment something unpleasant.)

When there is a command by someone with authority to command, it must make sense to speak of *obedience* – of *obeying* and also of *not obeying* the command. Could we not speak of punishment, if we speak of disobedience? I think the point is that this ethical command cannot *include* the 'or else you will suffer so and so' which is not ethical. It cannot include a reason why you should obey it. This would annul the absolute imperative. The 'ethical law' would be something like a police regulation to keep order.

If we ask 'Why *isn't* it like a police regulation?' we may try to give a sociological account of the different situations in which people speak in the one way or in the other. But then we still have not said what 'ethical' is. And if propositions can state only facts, we shall feel that something is wrong.

Someone reading the *Tractatus* for the first time might think that all that those difficult passages were saying was, that ethical judgments are not reducible to statements of fact. To say that nothing ethical can ever be expressed in words at all – may leave the reader wondering what makes Wittgenstein say anything like that.

When I am told 'nothing ethical can be said', I may wonder what the *saying* is that is being ruled out. What is: *saying something?* This is the question of the *Tractatus*. At one level, we might ask: What is the difference between 'saying something' and just making a noise? The *Tractatus* answers by its exposition of the general form and structure of 'the proposition'. This gives also: the general form and structure of language. What it is that *makes* it language: how it has *sense*. In the *Tractatus* every proposition – whatever can be said – is a truth-function of elementary propositions which express *facts*. This cannot express what is ethical. It cannot express moral value.

What is formidable and also troublesome here, is the emphasis on 'the general form of a proposition', or 'the general form of language'. What makes language language must be the same, in every possible application and every possible subject matter. We might speak of the formal unity that language has, as we speak of the formal unity of a calculus.

By the time he wrote #65, for instance, of *Philosophical Investigations* (1937, probably) he said that part of his investigation which in earlier years had caused him the greatest perplexity, namely 'that concerning *the general* form of the proposition and of language' was not one of his problems now: 'Instead of suggesting something which is common to everything we call language, I say there is no one thing common to all these appearances, because of which we use the same word, – but rather, they are akin to one another in a variety of ways, and because of this kinship or these different forms of kinship, we call them all languages.' He goes on to illustrate and explain what he calls 'family similarities'. (These ideas come into the *Blue Book*, and especially into the *Brown Book* .)

In the *Investigations*, especially #100 to #109 and in rough notes pencilled in a manuscript notebook at the time of writing, he brings out what the confusions were which led him to think 'the general form of proposition' so important and to believe that 'whatever was language' depended on it. In the notebook he writes *about* his own earlier ideas. He had thought the business of logic was to bring to clarity that by which language is language. 'I grant that all this that we call language has imperfections, slag, in it, but I want to find and recognize *that* which *has* been defiled. That, through which it is possible for me to say something . . . . At that time I worked hard to remove any idea of an imperfect order in logic. "Every proposition has a definite sense" . . . . "A logically-unclear proposition would be one with no definite sense, i. e. with no sense." '

'Logically-unclear' meant, I think: 'with no clear logical structure'. (And what is the logical structure of an expression of absolute value?)

But he came to see later – *Investigations* #100 – that in taking the general form of a proposition to be that which makes language language – the form there must be in any complex of signs that can have sense – he was misunderstanding the role which the ideal or the model plays in the way we speak of or set forth what we are doing in our logical study of language. *'Wir missverstehen die Rolle, die das Ideal in unsrer Ausdrucksweise spielt.'* Suppose we have to do with a number of different 'systems of communication' of two or more people. We want to say that somehow they are all of them language. But what holds them together? We may describe their family resemblances by comparing each of them with a common 'model' or prototype: noticing the analogy between the language game and the prototype in one case, then the different analogy between the prototype and the next one, and so on. We may do this without taking any one of the language games to be the *fundamental* form of communication and language. The danger is that we may take the prototype or model to be *itself* the perfect form of language. This is what Wittgenstein had done with the general form of proposition. Whereas, in this examination, it is not one of the language games at all: it is related to each of the others as 'an object of comparison', *ein Vergleichsgegenstand*. This helps us, when we are comparing many different language games, to keep our comparisons on the road and treat them all from the same point of view. This may be important when we want to see how these languages are together; how they may be understood together. But we shall miss this if we think we are comparing them all with the *perfect* or fundamental form of language, and that the others fall short in various ways.

In fact, for an understanding of 'what makes them all language' the role of a prototype *of perfect logical construction* can be dropped altogether; although it helps avoid confusion sometimes, for certain questions. What holds the 'languages' together we see in the possible comparisons with one another within the family similarities. If someone asks 'What makes it language? What *is* language?', I should have to start by pointing to examples; and rely constantly on '. . . and so on'.

Why should there not be ethical expressions in a language, although they do not show the logical form of proposition? In the *Tractatus* 'what is higher' means 'what has absolute value'. And in the *Lecture on Ethics,* where these points are the same, he said (page 6): 'There are no propositions which, in any absolute sense, are sublime, important, or trivial.' But granting that there are no such propositions, can we express nothing that is sublime or important? Is there no language that is sublime or important?

Think of Wittgenstein's *Remarks on Frazer's 'Golden Bough',* which he wrote about two years later. Near the beginning he writes:

When Frazer begins by telling the story of The King of the Wood at Nemi, he does this in a tone which shows that something strange and terrible is happening here. And this is the answer to the question 'Why is this happening?': Because it is terrible. In other words what strikes us in this course of events as terrible, impressive, horrible, tragic, etc., anything but trivial and insignificant, that is what gave birth to them . . . .

Put that account of the King of the Wood at Nemi together with the phrase: 'the majesty of death', – and you see that they are one.

The life of the priest-king shows what is meant by that phrase.

If someone is gripped by the majesty of death, then through such a life he can give expression to this. – Of course this is not an explanation: it puts one symbol in place of another. One ceremony in place of another.[2]

The difficulty, in that passage from the *Lecture on Ethics,* is with the phrase 'no propositions which, *in any absolute sense* are sublime, important, or trivial'. If it meant simply that any printed sentence that says something important as we read it, might be reprinted in a setting and in circumstances which made it ludicrous and trivial – then of course I should agree. But that cannot be what he meant.

People might enact a parody of the life and death of the priest-king at Nemi which made it obscene and ridiculous. I have read that in the last century, in certain of the Irish funeral wakes, mourners would, on their return journey, enact an obscene and blasphemous portrayal of the requiem mass. Would this show that the prayers of the mass were not sublime or important in any absolute sense? Perhaps there is nothing sublime or important which cannot be presented somehow as contemptible. This does not detract from what is sublime and terrible in the first account.

The 'absolute' in that phrase of the *Lecture* is the same as in 'absolute value'. Wittgenstein soon gave up using it.

There are certain ethical judgments for which I have no answer to the question 'Why?' 'As far as I am concerned, it stops there.' (Wittgenstein's example: 'Well, you *ought* to want to behave better.')

I do not think these are judgments I could *discover* by any method, unless it might be self-examination. I may recognize them when I hear of them in someone else. (Soon after the last war a German Jewish lady, whose sister had been killed in a gas chamber at Auschwitz, published a book urging reconciliation between surviving Jews and other Germans. She gave lectures throughout the country making the same point. As she was coming out of the hall after a lecture, a man standing at the door held out his hand and said 'Thank you!' She was stretching out her hand in return, when she recognized him as the commandant who had been in charge of the camp when her sister was killed there; and she drew her hand back. Then after two or three seconds she stretched it out again and shook his hand. When I heard the story first, my feeling was that she ought not to have forgiven him. Hers was of a different order.)

I tell you that my friend in great distress has turned to me for help. You tell me: 'You must *help* him' . . . but then you give reasons: as if your first statement was advising me on the wisest course. I should think I had misunderstood you somehow.

The ethical law, which the *Tractatus* imagines in 6.422 has the form of an *imperative*. Whether he would have said that every expression of absolute value would have this form, I do not know. (For the *Tractatus*, I do not see how there could be an expression of absolute value anyway.)

The division between relative value and absolute value is prominent in what he says there. But in the *Lecture* he says that judgments of relative value can be reduced to statements of facts. And I do not see how an action could be justified by a judgment of *value* then: there could only be judgments of prudence, profitability. But neither could a judgment of absolute value be a reason for preferring one action to another.

I am saying only that I do not understand how that scheme and that terminology would be used in justifying or criticizing human actions. I understand a little of why he wrote about it in this way, and I hope I can refer to this in a minute.

Of course we do weigh preferences and we do regard certain 'values' – for example, loyalty to one's friend, as more important than, for example, personal advancement. And that statement of preference is not reducible to a statement of facts, in the sense of the *Lecture*.

That Wittgenstein was thinking about this, and that it led him to important changes, is clear from a short entry in a manuscript of 1931 (MS 110, p.119):

Every ethical justification of an action must appeal to the man to whom I want to justify it . . . to whom I want to make it comprehensible.

Here he is speaking of the *ethical* justification, i. e., by reference to value judgments – which will *appeal to* that particular individual.

Prima facie, at any rate, this would not have fitted with the *Tractatus* statement that 'what is ethical cannot be expressed'. And I do not think he would have spoken now of a fundamental division between what has relative value and what has absolute value. The phrase 'ethical punishment' might need explanation, but it would not appear baffling quite in the way it does in the *Tractatus*.

If I were asked whether 'punishment' is an ethical expression, I would say 'Yes'. But I should need to say more. (I take it we are keeping to the word as it is understood within a civil institution of punishment.) If I tell you that Jack has been put in prison, and if I then add 'That is his punishment', this is not a further description of what has happened to him – like adding that he is sharing a cell with another prisoner. You may say it is a reminder that he is in prison because he committed a crime. But I think it would be wrong to say that calling it 'his punishment' amounts to: treating the imprisonment *as* a form of condemnation of his actions, as an expression of a moral judgment. 'Why did they trouble to express it in this way? In writing, it would have been just as clear.' It would seem to push to one side the notion of 'What he deserved'. (He deserved condemnation as well, no doubt. But in his big-hearted way he might have been content with that.)

I have been troubled by some of Winch's phrases; for example: 'to think about the action's having been rewarded or punished is a way of thinking about the action itself. The relevance of the action's consequences e. g. imprisonment, according to this way of thinking, is as a "vehicle" which carries the thought about the action'(Winch 1972: 221). But I may have misread his emphasis. He is arguing against the view that in general punishment is inflicted simply as a deterrent.

When the *Tractatus* held that punishment in the usual sense has nothing ethical about it – or at least that if punishment is something that *happens* (like being put in prison), it is nothing ethical – this was because of the separation between 'the ethical', i.e., what has absolute value, and the world of events, in which everything that occurs is accidental: an ethical influence in the world of events is impossible, and it is impossible to will and produce anything of absolute value, i.e. anything good, in the world of events.

This made it impossible to give an account of the word or the concept of 'punishment'. When the *Tractatus* speaks of 'a *kind* of ethical punishment', this is something not of this world but supernatural. It cannot throw any light on punishment in the ordinary sense.

The remark which I have quoted about giving an ethical justification of an action, shows how far he had left his earlier position behind.

What had kept ethics, i.e. absolute value, and the world of facts apart had been his idea of the strict logical form of what can be said. When he saw the confusions in this, it was possible to look at

187

the ways in which people do speak of 'good' and 'bad' in the course of their lives; and also at the ways in which we may speak of 'moral issues' and 'moral problems' without those special words appearing.

Translated from L. Wittgenstein: *Eine Philosophische Betrachtung* (written 1936/37, published 1969):

Imagine a surface which has been painted in various colours . . . . The more familiar the shade of colour is, the stronger the impression it makes on me, by so much more am I inclined to call this the colour of the surface.

That is how it is if someone asks: 'What is the essence of punishment? – and someone replies, every punishment is *really* an act of revenge; someone else: the essence of punishment is deterrence, and so on. But are there not typical cases of society taking revenge, and again typical cases of measures taken for deterrence, and others of punishment for the improvement of the criminal; and are there not countless combinations and intermediate cases? So if we were asked what the essence of punishment is, or the essence of a revolution, or about the essence of knowledge, or of a cultural decline, or of an appreciation of music, – we would not try to give something common to all cases – what it is that all of them are really – in other words, an ideal *contained* in each of them; but instead of that, examples, as it were, centres of variation.

Someone might want to add: Yes, but the practice of the institution of punishment goes on through its different departments: police arrest, charging magistrate's court, criminal court and verdict, which if guilty leads to: sentencing to such and such a punishment, perhaps prison. The prisoner has been found guilty of a crime, and for this he is punished. The different ideas of what punishing *achieves* may not matter.

And there are certain features of what we are willing to call punishment. So for instance: a) The punishment is inflicted on the criminal 'from without': he cannot inflict it on himself. To the suggestion that this – inflicting it on himself – might be arranged, the reply would be: 'But then it would not be *punishment.*' b) The punishment must be unpleasant, painful to the criminal, it must make him suffer. To the query whether it might not be so devised that it did not cause pain, again the reply would be: 'But then it would not be punishment.' (I believe these conditions are very old.) And further: The criminal is divested of certain civil rights for the period of the punishment. So it must be inflicted by a body with authority to disfranchise.

One may remember these conditions when it is said that what is important in punishment is the expression of moral disapproval. I can imagine strong expression of disapproval without them.

We cannot speak of a punishment which is not punishment for anything. Although you might speak of a chain that was not holding anything. We cannot speak of a crime – we should not call it a *crime* – unless we could say: 'Whoever did that should be punished.' There are various ways of holding or detaining a man, various ways of seizing some or all of his possessions, various ways of depriving him of certain civil rights. If a man suffered any of these, we should not call it *punishment* unless it were done to him *for* something he has done. And he cannot (grammatical 'cannot') be punished for 'just anything' he has done; it is only when what he has done was a crime and (many would add) when it is evil.

'But this does not explain what punishing is.' Wittgenstein would object to the sentence I have placed in quotes. He would say: 'When do we ask – when would anyone ask – *what punishing is?*'

When we do, it is not because we do not understand the word, or do not understand what is being done in actual cases. You could explain by giving examples: 'That man has been sent to prison for two years, in punishment for his part in a bank robbery'; 'In punishment for obstruction the Court has ordered this man to report for sixteen hours of community service', and so on. These tell me nothing new. So what made me ask 'what punishing *is*', as though there were something queer about it?

I am confused about the relation or whatever is expressed by the 'for' in 'He is being punished for that crime'. Or: If someone says 'He has committed a crime, and therefore he must be punished', what is the necessity here? What is the *necessity* here?

The phrase 'the necessity of the punishment' would mean the same as 'the *reason* for the punishment'.

Kant argued[3] that nothing which we expect the punishing to achieve or bring about can be a reason for punishing. And this could make one ask: 'So there *is* no reason for punishing? Do we just punish without any reason?' Kant says, we inflict punishment on a criminal because and only because he committed a crime. Kant's point was that the utilitarian justification in terms of consequences that could be expected, always left the door open for exemption in particular cases. If the consequences of waiving the punishment of this particular criminal would be more beneficial to the society as a whole (perhaps because he had agreed to be the subject of certain dangerous medical experiments), he would be exempt from punishment, even though his guilt had been established. Kant thought that this way of thinking destroys the idea of punishment; destroys any connection between 'punishment' and 'law' and 'justice' – for which 'the equality of persons' subject to the law is important.

In the sentence 'He has committed a crime, so he must be punished', the *must* expresses an imperative. And this makes a difference.

If the judge had said, 'He has committed a crime', and added as an after-thought: 'so it might be as well if he were punished', the word would have become unclear.

'He has committed a crime, so he must not be punished' seems absurd.

How are the ideas of crime and of punishment together?

There cannot be a *reason* for punishing – a justification of punishing at all, of punishing as such. There may, of course, be a justification of means or methods of punishing.

We cannot ask what justification there is for punishing crimes. When Kant says that punishment must be inflicted on a criminal only because he has committed a crime, we cannot ask how *that* justifies it. We should have no idea what we were seeking.

On the other hand, any punishment is objectionable if it is arbitrary, if it springs from personal preference or antipathy. One reason why some people ask about 'The justification of punishment' may be the thought that: if I, as a private individual, were to lock my neighbour in a room in my house against his will and keep him captive, allowing him very restricted movements, for several weeks – or only for one – this would be an outrage and a crime on my part. I should be arrested and tried before the criminal court, convicted, and sent to prison. I should be kept in conditions at least as wretched as those in which I had kept my neighbour. When I did this, it was a crime. When the Court and the prison authorities do it, it is punishment. I am told that it was a vicious and inexcusable thing for me to do by the people who are doing it to me. The point could be made more carefully, but there is no need.

If I see a man knock a woman down and snatch her handbag, I impulsively start forward and shout: 'Stop that!' Suppose others reach the thief before me, but a man who was standing beside me when it happened is still there. I say 'Do you just let things like that happen? That was evil.' He says 'And if it's evil, it's evil. What of it?'

I want to say that the *reaction* – shouting 'Stop that!' and trying to do something about it – is what we mean by *seeing the action as evil*. The other – 'If it's evil, it's evil. What of it?' – is something like a contradiction. I could only answer: 'I just don't understand you.'

Perhaps some people would not find 'evil' a natural word. If they use some other in reacting with indignation or horror it is the same. We have the example of an utterance which 'fits' and of one which does not fit.

Where we speak of 'the fitting punishment' for this or that crime, there may be some analogy with such 'primitive' indignation at what is happening. And through this, perhaps, we have some understanding of the distinction between a punishment which is 'proper' and one which is 'arbitrary'. But of course there is much more involved here.

Punishing a crime is much more than condemnation of it. If he is found and convicted, the criminal is given a sentence that will make him suffer. At various times he may have experienced discomfort and pain worse than any of the physical discomforts of prison. But we have to understand the suffering that imprisonment does bring, if we are to understand what it means to speak of prison as punishment. The prison officers, on order of the Court, can treat him like this because he was stripped of certain of his rights as a citizen when he was found guilty of a crime; in particular he lost what we call the right of liberty (I will not try to define it here). He had had the right to come and go without let or hindrance on public ways and footpaths, to enter into contracts, of employment or other forms, to acquire possessions and dispose of them as he liked – and in general to go about his affairs free from damaging interference by others like himself, provided he respected the same rights in them. This latter – respect for their rights – is what he did not show when he attacked and robbed someone in the street. And this *breaking the security* of civil rights is an important part of his crime. The evil was not only in the bruising and other bodily harm and the loss of possessions suffered by the victim; it was also in that disrupting of civil rights and thereby weakening of the *trust* on which the normal living together of people in any community depends. With his own disfranchisement he is now excluded from leading a normal life with 'people outside', until his release.

At the same time, *nota bene*, he is kept, albeit in degraded status, within the society which recognizes its responsibilities towards him, and (in theory, anyway) offers 'readmission' when he has served his full punishment. (I think this holds in most western countries. It belongs to one conception of punishment among many.)

I want to imagine a society with a different relation to criminals. And I want to ask whether, with some very different way of 'dealing with' criminals, there would not be a different conception of the criminal's relation to his crime.

I will imagine that the incidence of those acts which we call 'crimes' is about the same in that society as in ours. And also that the number of those who have done those things and have been caught is about the same. Those who hold them captive would say it was obvious that they cannot let all these thieves, arsonists, kidnappers and the rest just run about scot free. But they have not a system of imprisonment, for a term specified in a sentence by the Court. Instead they have, extending over the whole country, an organization for *deporting* the convicts to another land or to islands. They are not allowed back, and questions of their rehabilitation when their time is up do not arise.

After 1770 there were, I believe, a few convicts sent to Australia from time to time. But I am assuming a practice applied to all convicts whose offence would have been judged deserving of (say) more than six months in prison.

If I am told that the expense and the difficulty of finding ships and crews, to say nothing of the docility of the convicts themselves, would rule this out, I agree. But I ask: Suppose some miracle made it possible and this were the practice, and that the use of prisons as we know them here, had died out: would this not have changed the conception of the relation of the criminal to his crime? Our own conception of this seems to go closely with our understanding (or want of understanding) of the nature of his punishment.

Where the prisoner is sentenced for a limited period (I will exclude capital punishment) the judge giving sentence will refer to the criminal's past acts, and anything said of the punishment's term is also a reference to his life when he is released. Meanwhile he will be 'here'. In this sense the punishment is centred on his crime and the event which that was and will be in the life he will have to live.

We have to live with very many criminals unknown among us; and among many crimes which are left unpunished because the criminal has not been caught. We understand the situation better because we know a little of the courts and prison system. The punishment of criminals can belong to the way life is lived round about us; it need not be something 'uncanny' as it might be if sentenced criminals were deported and, so to speak, swept away. That is one point in the comparison I was trying to make.

NOTES

1. P. Winch, 'Ethical reward and punishment' in *Ethics and Action* (London: Routledge & Kegan Paul, 1972).

2. L. Wittgenstein *Remarks on Frazer's 'Golden Bough'*, R. Rhees (ed.) (Retford: Brynmill, 1979).

3. I. Kant, *Metaphysik der Sitten* II, 2.

Chapter Ten

SELF-KNOWLEDGE AND THE REALITY OF GOOD AND EVIL

İLHAM DİLMAN

KNOWLEDGE OF GOOD AND EVIL

Some people speak of the knowledge of good and evil. They may say, for instance, that a particular age was marked by a decline in its knowledge of good and evil. Or they may say of an individual that he has lost contact with knowledge of good and evil. What is it that they have in mind and in what sense is what they refer to a form of knowledge?

Plato spoke in this way and he said some very striking and sometimes paradoxical things about such knowledge. For instance, he said that it is identical with virtue and at the same time expressed doubts as to whether it can ever be taught. He further claimed that a person who lacks such knowledge also thereby lacks self-knowledge. He spoke of one who lacks it as ignorant or deceived in himself.

This latter claim interests and puzzles me. But to understand it I need first to be clear about what those who speak in this way – and not everybody does – mean by knowledge of good and evil: what does the difference between having and lacking it amount to? Certainly what is in question is not something like knowing how to behave. Plato would have found no difficulty in the idea of teaching that. As he understood it moral knowledge had little to do with a knowledge of rules. Virtue, which he identified with moral knowledge, was not a social accomplishment for him, nor indeed any kind of accomplishment at all. He thought of it as a state of the soul.

Those who speak this way think of a person who has such knowledge as having access to and participating in a way of looking at things and seeing them which sets limits to forms of behaviour which would otherwise be open to him. These limits find expression in firmly held convictions that go through his life, and the sense of what he regards as important in life for him is bound up with these convictions. This way of looking at things also creates desires in a person which find expression in what he seeks and what he does. If we leave it at this, however, and say that a man who has knowledge of good and evil is a man who has deeply held convictions, we shall wonder what attributing 'knowledge' to him adds to this.

We may think: if it does not add anything then why not speak of him as a man of moral conviction and leave it at that? Why attribute knowledge to him? And if it does add something to what we say then it must be the claim that his convictions are true. But then who is to be the judge of that? In any case, is it not true that a man's moral beliefs and convictions determine what counts as good and evil for him, rather than the other way around? If so, how can his moral beliefs be characterized as true? For that to be possible, surely, what is good and evil must be *independent* of his moral beliefs. Unless this is so there can be no logical room for talking of knowledge here.

These objections may confuse 'believe in' with 'believe that', but they do not originate in such a confusion. Thus even when the confusion is cleared up the objections remain. What I mean is that a person may believe in something or someone, be prepared to stand by him and live his life by the light of his life, and he may still be said to be deceived or deluded for all that. A belief in something or someone is just as susceptible to deception as a belief that something is the case. So the problem of what 'truth' means here and what kind of 'reality' it presupposes remains.

Certainly these objections need to be answered even if that means or involves showing that they come from certain misunderstandings regarding the logic of 'true' and 'real' in the context of moral judgment. But the philosophical disquiet from which they come goes deep and so needs to be explored. The beliefs in question, I said, are part of the person's perspective on life. They are expressions of such a perspective, one in the light of which things have the sense and importance which they have for him so that, in particular circumstances, there are things which he must do and other things which are out of the question for him. That these beliefs go deep with him shows in his affective reactions to things – reactions of horror, pity, indignation, guilt, remorse, gratitude. The perspective itself finds expression in these reactions. For they carry in them a particular conception or view of things which evoke or inspire them. This conception is embedded in his moral vocabulary and the circumstances in which he uses it. The reactions are responses to the good and evil he sees in the things to which he so responds. They are expressions of his recognition of good and evil.

The disquiet to which I referred earlier makes itself felt here in further objections. Recognition implies truth, so that if a person is said to have recognized something what he claims must be true. But again who is to be the judge of that? The reaction itself cannot be the criterion of such truth. So must we not have something independent of the reaction against which to measure it? How else can we conceive of good and evil as independent realities?

If I were to say that to those who share these reactions what they react to is *real* this would hardly meet the objection: what guarantee is there that this reality is not wholly subjective? The reaction or affect no doubt 'confers reality' to its object in the sense of giving its subject a sense of conviction.[1] But what we need is for this reality to be *independent* of the reaction, to be accessible to the subject independently of the reaction, in short to be 'objective'.

There is some truth in this objection, but it is intermingled with what is confused. Obviously the reactions must be part of a coherent outlook, one that informs a man's life and convictions – even if this outlook has not been articulated by the man himself. Otherwise the conviction which any one of them carries for the person will not amount to anything more than a transitory feeling of conviction, it will not be something that goes deep with him. This is what the distinction between 'what is merely subjective' and what is not amounts to here. I did not say 'objective', for this is a dangerous word to use in this connection. It separates the object of the reaction from the sense it has for the subject in a way that is foreign to our conception of what it means to make a moral judgment. Certainly it is the moral values in which he believes which give the object of this reaction its sense, and these in turn exist independently of him. On the other hand, unless he makes them his own, so that they speak through him when he speaks for himself, this object will stand devoid of the sense he sees in it. Indeed, in such a case, the reaction is either not genuine or it is not what it purports to be. The term 'objective' thus leaves the subject out of the moral beliefs he holds and makes their object into something that stands outside his life.

The objection is right, then, in wanting to emphasize the independent reality of the aspect under which we see the object of our moral reactions, but suggests the wrong account of it in making 'objectivity' a requirement of this independence. The reality of this aspect, the good or evil to which the subject responds, is to be found in the significance it has in the life he shares with others, in the practices that have grown around it, in the language in which it is given expression, and in the art and literature in which it is brought into focus and reflected on. This is what gives the aspect a reality independent of those who affirm it in their individual lives.

It is in this way that while good and evil have a reality independent of the individual moral agent, this reality is internal to the moral values in which he believes. However, so long as he himself remains externally related to them, good and evil will have little or no reality for him. He will at best be able to say, 'This is considered just or dishonourable'; he will not himself find it so.

There is still a difference, I think, even here between genuine belief and knowledge, one that comes from the experience in which a person has contact with good and evil. This knowledge is a form of acquaintance and the contact in question is one that transforms his life. A person who has had such contact with good and evil has not only witnessed other people suffer evil, seen cruelty, callousness, betrayal and worse, he has been touched by what he has seen, he has responded to it. He may himself have been a victim of evil, even its agent, or nearly so insofar as he has been tempted. But he has recognized it as such and has recoiled from it in horror or suffered remorse. He has witnessed loved ones suffer it and he has felt pity for them. He thus knows by experience what it means to be vulnerable to evil, whether as victim or agent.

These affective responses of horror, pity, and remorse are expressions of a person's contact with evil. I say 'contact' for in them he recognizes evil for what it is, namely as something destructive of what he cherishes. It is the fact that there are things he cherishes, things in which his conception of goodness is rooted, that makes it possible for him to recognize evil. Its light is as necessary to the characteristic features of evil coming into focus as sunlight is necessary to the formation of shadows. Thus someone who cherishes nothing has no apprehension of the peculiar hatefulness and repugnance which forms part of the face of evil. A person's reactions of horror, guilt, and remorse are, therefore, inseparable from and at the same time expressions of his love for what he sees under the aspect of the good, a love which gives meaning and unity to his life. Indeed, in Plato's view, a person's knowledge of good and evil lies in just this love, it is his love of goodness itself.

To speak like this is not, of course, to speak of a love for a supersensible abstract object. If Plato spoke like this, if he located goodness in a world that goes beyond the reach of the senses, he was thinking of the way 'sensuality' in the broad sense forms an obstacle to coming in contact with goodness. So he suggests in the *Phaedo* that no man can *be* perfectly just (have virtue) or *know* perfect justice (have moral knowledge) in this world, while his soul is infected with 'the body', orientated by sensuality. Still a person's orientation towards goodness, a saint's knowledge of the good, he would have agreed, is something that finds expression in his responses and actions in *particular* situations. The reference to 'goodness' in the abstract, the way such a person's love and concern in these situations is described as 'directed towards goodness', is a way of indicating how his actions and responses are unified, what gives them unity. The goodness in question lies in their character and in the part of the soul from which they come. To speak of him as loving goodness is a way of referring to the affective orientation that finds expression in his actions and responses and to his relation to standards which belong to this orientation.

I said that it is the perspective of such a person's love that gives evil its characteristic face or aspect. But this dependence goes both ways. It is equally true that goodness has little reality for someone who has not woken up to the existence of evil. To have experienced it as agent, victim or witness to the suffering of a fellow creature, and to find it hateful and painful: this is what I mean by having woken up to the existence of evil. Without the pain, the pity, the remorse, the hatred, the recoil, whatever one has witnessed or experienced, one will not have seen the face of evil.

While knowledge of good and evil are thus interdependent, still the former has a certain logical priority over the latter. For in the contact which a person makes with goodness in love for it he takes part in that goodness. Goodness enters his soul, and so Plato has characterized such knowledge as virtue. In contrast, in the contact he makes with evil through the horror and repugnance it inspires in him, he turns away from it. We could say that to recognize evil is to turn away from it; it is in this recoil that a person knows evil. That is why Plato said that no one does evil voluntarily, that is with knowledge. The source of this recoil is the person' s love of the good; but not the other way round.

We could say that it is because he loves the good that he hates evil, but not because he hates evil that he loves the good. Someone may object that it is possible for a person to love what is destructive of what he hates. This may be true. But if his hatred is itself primary, if it is not inspired by any threat to something which he cherishes independently, then the love that comes from such hatred will be conditional. At any rate it will be an expression of 'self-assertion' in the sense in which Plato meant this in the *Phaedo*. This is not the kind of love he would have called a love of the good. But in any case, what makes the hatred directed to evil a hatred of *evil* is the way the person is related to certain moral values which determine his conception of goodness. It is this affective relation which embodies his love of the good.

That love takes its character from its object. Indeed, coming in contact with that object, goodness, transforms the love which the person gives to it. Thus goodness is not just something a person happens to love in the way that a man happens to fall in love with a particular woman. Given the right circumstances and the appropriate characteristics, he could have fallen in love with a different woman and given her that *same* love.[2] It is not so with 'love of the good', for that love is internally related to its object. I said that such a love is an expression of a certain kind of concern for people in particular circumstances and for one's own life in relation to such a concern. It cannot be a love of the good, however, unless it is related to certain standards which give it its moral identity.

A person develops the capacity for such love in his affective, moral development as an individual. This learning takes place in the context of his relationships, those in which he becomes who he is. He learns from what the others bring to these relationships – their concern and affection, their way of looking at and caring for things, their dependability and integrity. I have characterized what this learning makes possible as an acquaintance with good and evil through contact with these in one's affective reactions in particular situations. These are reactions in which one is oneself. Their moral identity, what makes them responses to good and evil, has its source in the framework which gives one a particular perspective on things as one comes to be related to it internally. The values in which one believes belong to this perspective.

We see now that while moral conviction is essential to knowledge of good and evil, it is not enough. It is essential, since without moral convictions, without values in which one believes, nothing can take on the aspect of good and evil. Things would only appear as pleasant or painful, likeable or detestable. But to have knowledge of good and evil one needs to have been touched by their operation in particular circumstances and to have responded to it. It is in these responses, I have argued, that one makes contact with good and evil. While this contact is thus made possible by one's moral convictions, it does in turn give them a depth they cannot have in the life of a person who has been sheltered from good and evil.

MORAL KNOWLEDGE AND THE RELATIVITY OF VALUE

The question we now have to face is one that troubles me, namely that there is no single conception of good and evil: where does this leave the idea of moral knowledge? When I characterize moral knowledge as contact with good and evil, what do I consider as counting as good and evil? What if you do not share my conception? But then what right do I or anybody else have to attribute moral knowledge to anyone or speak of him as lacking such knowledge?

To avoid confusion let me first distinguish between the *speaker* who attributes moral knowledge to others, and the *philosopher* who is concerned to understand what such an attribution amounts to. Interestingly Plato combined these two roles, he did two things at once: develop a particular conception of goodness *and* comment on what it means to know the good in *this* sense. What we now see is that the speaker must bring his own conception of good and evil into his attribution of moral knowledge and ignorance to others. This is not surprising since it belongs to the logic of the word 'know' that to claim that someone has some knowledge is to assent to the truth of what he claims.

In our case this means that to speak of people as having or lacking moral knowledge, good and evil must have reality for the speaker. This inevitably brings in the speaker's particular values. Such a claim, therefore, cannot be morally neutral, and in that sense 'objective', that is above the variety of the competing conceptions of good and evil to be found among men. There can be no neutral vantage point from which to adjudicate between rival conceptions of good and evil since such adjudication is necessarily moral in character. This being so, it presupposes a belief in or commitment to particular moral values which are inevitably at the level of the competing conceptions. This means that one cannot attribute knowledge or ignorance of good and evil to someone without *oneself* affirming their reality and, therefore, presupposing a particular conception of good and evil.

There is nothing logically vicious in this. The speaker, as *speaker,* sees only *one* conception of good and evil, there is for him only *one* such conception. This is as it should be and is true of any particular part of moral discourse; it applies to the use of the words 'true', 'truth', and 'deception' in such discourse. As *philosopher,* of course, he needs to take account of the fact that human life takes many different forms and throws up many different kinds of value and conceptions of good and evil. But this need not prevent him from making his own a particular conception, from having personal moral convictions. If as a philosopher he reflects at the level of differences, there is no inconsistency in his taking a stand on particular values as an agent and individual.

In his dialogues Plato throws this variety in human values and moral views into focus and pits them against one another, illuminating their different contents and the ways in which they differ from each other. At the same time he shows us what it means to step into the shoes of a thinker like Socrates and, through his eyes, to see individuals with very different convictions and conceptions of what is worthwhile in life as deluded. Callicles is a case in point. Socrates, and of course Plato, have reflected deeply on power, which Callicles worships, and on the way it transforms the lives of those who are attracted by it, come to love it, and give themselves to its pursuit. They know equally, and show, how the way of life which they themselves value ('the philosophic life') must seem to such a person. Callicles gives expression to it in the *Gorgias* and, in his turn, sees Socrates as deluded: 'when I see an older man still at philosophy . . . that man seems to me to need whipping . . . . However great his natural gifts, [he] will never be a real man'.[3]

In the *Phaedo* Socrates makes a contrast between 'viewing things philosophically' and 'viewing things self-assertively'.[4] It is for the way Socrates puts the self aside in the way he lives for the sake of truth and justice that Callicles thinks of him as a fool. As a philosopher Plato appreciates that there is a certain symmetry between Socrates' and Callicles' views of each other. Yet he is not afraid to let Socrates speak for himself persuasively and claim that power deceives, that one who lives for it is ignorant of good and evil.

One may still worry however: if the different conceptions of good and evil are, as I presented them, products of human life,[5] can there be much point in speaking of 'knowledge' in connection with good and evil? I agree that if the suggestion were that morality, whatever form it takes, is man-made and, therefore, that there is something artificial about men's conceptions of good and evil, there would be little point in doing so. But this is not part of what I have been saying.

Morality is not in any way something invented or constructed by men, any more than natural languages are so. Nor can it be. Its ideas and conceptions are thrown up by the forms of life which shape human beings. But there is nothing artificial about this process which is a socio-historical one, and while men are subject to it they also contribute to it in the way they are part of it. Nor, of course, is there anything artificial about the forms of life in which men's moral ideas take shape and have sense. In any case, these ideas give expression to and also extend certain primitive reactions of human beings and tendencies that are 'natural' to them.

Let us take, in very broad terms, two different conceptions of good and evil prominent among men: one sees goodness in care and consideration of others, in honesty, justice and respect for others, the other sees not so much 'goodness' as what counts as good in strength. It finds giving way to other people shameful and diminishing, and it gives precedence to such qualities as cleverness, toughness, independence, and the ability to look after one's self-interest over fairness and truthfulness. Now is it not clear that both these conceptions, however opposed they may be to each other, are rooted in tendencies in the human heart which cut across the varieties in human culture which I stressed earlier? Callicles was wrong to think that the tendencies he finds instantiated in history (Xerxes invading Greece and his father Scythia, to take two of the countless instances that present themselves[6]) 'justify' his moral values ('nature herself demonstrates'). But this does not mean that there is no connection between his views and these tendencies.

Simone Weil replaces Callicles' dichotomy between 'the natural' and 'the conventional' with one that contrasts 'the natural' with 'the supernatural'. However she agrees with Callicles that the claims of a 'morality of love' go against the grain of what is 'natural' to men. What impressed her, as well as Callicles and also Nietzsche, was how widespread these tendencies of 'self-assertion' are among men and how deep-seated in the human heart. But this does not mean that there is nothing else there which the orientation she characterizes as 'supernatural' extends. Simone Weil does not deny this. She speaks of these other tendencies as a seed implanted in the human soul by God. That is they have to be nurtured and will not develop 'naturally' or of their own accord. When she describes them as 'implanted by God' she means that we ought to regard them as a precious gift and not take them for granted. The orientation that is rooted in them is 'super-natural' in the sense that it runs counter to those orientations, of which Callicles represents an extreme form, which may be described as 'worldly' or 'of this world'.

My point is that what can grow into a capacity for generosity and devotion and the ability to feel gratitude is to be found in the human heart as much as the tendencies that make for self-assertion. I did not mean anything more than this when earlier I myself used the term 'natural' in connection with them. I wanted to emphasize that there is nothing artificial about any of them.

I said that they transcend the different forms of life that have developed among men in the sense that we find expressions of these same tendencies in different cultures. We find them there judging from the literature and other forms of art which have come to us from different periods in the history of diverse societies and from accounts of anthropologists – compassion on the one hand and self-assertion on the other, and the network of reactions that go with them. Each opens up onto a whole dimension of human life in which what human beings find important in the particular cultures to which they belong takes shape. For a person to have knowledge of good and evil is thus for him to have access to this dimension of life. It is this which gives point to the talk of 'knowledge' in connection with morality: to have knowledge of good and evil is to have access to a dimension of life which gives the whole of life a particular aspect. But, of course, unless one shared the particular conception of good and evil oneself one would not attribute moral knowledge to the person who has such access. The dimension of life in question would strike one as an illusion.

Talk of 'knowledge' in the sense under discussion, however, is not at home in connection with any conception of good and evil whatsoever. It has a natural home in moralities of love, such as the one expounded by Plato, where value is placed on knowledge and vision, but not in moralities of force. Callicles certainly thinks of Socrates as deluded in the sense of chasing after the wrong things, neglecting what would enhance him as a person standing for himself above everything else. These are judgments of value. But he does not think of Socrates – as Socrates thinks of Callicles – as lacking vision of a reality to which he has access. This is a moral difference, not merely a verbal one. It has to do with the pride of place given to truth as a value in the morality which Socrates expounds and defends. The values of fairness, justice, and honesty are bound up with this emphasis on truth as a supreme value – truth of the person as well as of claims and hypotheses.

SELF-KNOWLEDGE AND KNOWLEDGE OF OTHERS

The dimension of life to which a person's moral knowledge thus gives him access is one in which he finds himself and is measured. For him to lose touch with this dimension is to be alienated from himself. That is why, I think, Plato believes that a person who lacks moral knowledge cannot be said to know himself. But what is it for a person to find himself and in so doing to come to self-knowledge?

I argued that one cannot come to know goodness without coming to know evil, and vice versa. There is a certain parallel to this in the case of self-knowledge and knowledge of other people. For it is in his relationships with others, in activities in which he comes in contact with other people that a person finds himself. It is in our transactions with other people that we learn what makes us grow and be ourselves, that we develop our loyalties and 'find' or 'become' who we are.

Paradoxically here these two words mean the same thing. For in finding ourselves what we find is not something ready-made, waiting to be discovered. We find a mode of being in which we are ourselves, and this is something that we achieve. We emerge from naivety, innocence, falsity, a purely habitual existence, or one in which we are largely what others expect us to be, to 'become' authentic or true. This is what constitutes self-knowledge. For coming to it involves emerging from ignorance or returning from self-deception. The ignorance in question is a form of innocence, not having been exposed to life and learnt from such exposure. This is how one learns the 'separateness' of others and moves towards greater autonomy. As for the self-deception from which such a person emerges, it is a deception of the self. Such falsity is in the person, and not just in his beliefs about himself. Thus ignorance as naivety or innocence and self-deception are antitheses of self-knowledge.

Just as the truth of a moral belief is not its correspondence with an independent reality, similarly a person's truth, when we describe him as 'true to himself', is not his coincidence with a pre-existent self. If I may put it provocatively, there is no such pre-existent self, nor any pre-formed pattern particular to the person, pre-dating him as an individual. What he meets in life from the outset, what he makes of it, both open up his horizons and also set the direction in which he can move without falsity, determining what are real choices for him. There is no one, predetermined direction in which he must advance if he is to find greater authenticity. But as he makes his choices – friends, occupations, interests – commits himself in what he takes on, the direction in which he is to find such authenticity becomes more determinate. Unless he has been deceiving himself all along or chosen a life of pure conformity, it is within these limits that he will find himself.

If he has been false he will have to change direction. The further he has progressed along the path of falsity the greater the courage it will take to make a break, and the greater the inner resources he will need to throw away what has come to hold him together. Indeed, in shedding what now belongs to his identity, however false, he may have to face some difficult moral dilemmas. The process may be likened to ending an unhappy marriage of long standing.

Self-knowledge thus is not to be equated with 'knowing what one is like'. It goes beyond recognizing one's capacities, inclinations and vulnerabilities. It involves taking an attitude towards these and determining one's course in life. This may be described as knowing where one stands and what one wants, or more briefly knowing who one is. One may endorse or condemn different inclinations one has, one may decide to develop certain of one's capacities, to pursue certain of one's interests, and to give up others. In all this one may be authentic or false, one may act from conviction or out of fear. I am, of course, simplifying; the possibilities are more various than this. Self-knowledge is thus to be understood not simply in terms of what beliefs a person holds about himself, but also in terms of what attitudes he takes towards the object of these beliefs as well as towards other things. When he is true in these attitudes it is to *himself* that he is true.

We saw that Plato identified knowledge of the good with virtue which is a 'state of soul' and thus characterizes the person. A person who knows goodness is good in himself. Similarly, a person who knows himself is himself, he is true to himself. Knowledge of the good, we saw, involves contact with the good. Similarly, there is such a thing as 'being in touch with oneself' and it shows in what one wants, strives after, and in one's responses to things. A person who is not in touch with himself will, for instance, make exuberant promises, over-react to things, do things that he will regret, he will be thrown hither and thither by what the moment puts in his way. He does not have a realistic estimate of his capacities and limitations, sufficient regard for the claims of his past, for his present commitments and future possibilities.

Consequently his responses do not bear his true feelings, feelings that he has made his own. What moves him are not so much his convictions as the changing exigencies of the moment. Such a person has not come to self-knowledge.

This being in touch with oneself also involves 'self-acceptance'. This is not a form of resignation to what one is like. That would be a form of 'bad faith' – *pace* Sartre. It is a recognition and acceptance of what are possibilities for one, as these are delimited by one's sex, the accidents of one's birth, one's early experiences, one's physical make-up, health and innate talents, the choices one has already made and commitments one has undertaken. To recognize and, if need be, to reconcile oneself to these, to develop one's interests within the limits set by them, to make one's own the obligations they create for one within the parameter of one's convictions, is for a person to accept himself.

I said that it is in his relationships with others and in activities in which he makes contact with them that a person finds himself and so comes to self-knowledge. To make contact with them he needs to have an awareness of them as separate beings: that is in his affective responses to them he must not take them as extensions of himself, or as existing simply to please or frustrate him. A child moves towards such an awareness in the normal course of his emotional development, though he may never reach anything near a full awareness of it. To be far from it is also to be far from having found oneself and so from having come to self-knowledge.

To have moved towards a greater awareness of the separateness of others is to allow them to have an impact on one and to respond to them as persons in their own right. This may include caring for them, undertaking to do things for them, collaborating in joint activities, forming attachments to them, being pleased for, angry with and hurt by them, resenting their neglect, asking them for things, thanking them, seeking vengeance for their treachery, forgiving them, asking for their forgiveness, and so on. This is the stuff of the kind of transaction there is between human beings, transactions in which people recognize each other's humanity and take a moral attitude towards it, one that varies within certain limits. By the other's humanity I do not mean his being a human being – something a 'recognition' of which is inseparable from what Wittgenstein called 'an attitude towards a soul'. I mean his existence as a fellow human being. Recognizing his separateness is part of this. There is nothing paradoxical in this claim, since it is only for someone whose separateness I acknowledge that I can feel any fellowship. Otherwise fellowship degenerates into 'appropriation' or 'fusion of identity'. Now if a person is *himself* in his transactions with others and if he sees them *as they are* then he makes contact with them – provided that they too are themselves. Such contact is the form which one's acquaintance with another person takes. To be acquainted with him in the different modes of his being is to know another person.

As in the case of self-knowledge, this is not to be equated with finding out something about him: it goes beyond that. One can find out something about another person second-hand, by reading his biography, a reference or testimonial or by watching him. Although one may learn a great deal *about* him in these ways, one does not come to know *him*. If one met him face to face one could at best say, 'I know a lot about you'. To know him one would have to be the object of his response, a response directed to one as an individual, and one would have to respond to him him oneself.[7] There is obviously a difference between watching or observing a person and actually meeting him.

I said earlier that it is in making contact with other people, in the give and take which this involves, that a person learns about himself and grows. This is at one and the same time the contact in which he comes to know others. We have seen the sense in which this calls for courage and honesty, as well as regard for others. Even if, in this contact, a person does not learn something from the other, if he is honest and open he will still learn from the contact he makes: from meeting the demands which this makes on him. It is in this way that he will move towards greater self-knowledge.

A person is who he is in those relationships which mean most to him, relationships which engage his deepest loyalties, obligations, love, and gratitude. The first relationships of this kind are the network of family relationships into which he is born and in which he finds growth. Later come friendships, his work and colleagues, the demands these make on his moral resources, the interests and loyalties they engage, what he gives to them, his sexual loves, marriage, children, and other commitments. But what he learns in and from his earliest relationships, who he becomes in them and what he comes to be like, largely set the pattern for what he makes of these later relationships. Clearly I do not mean this in a restrictive sense, though that too may be the case, and often is. I believe this to be one of Freud's fundamental insights.

I made a distinction between *who* a person is, his identity, and *what* he is like, his character. The early relationships in which he first becomes who he is also provide the material, in relation to which he develops patterns of character on which he builds in the course of his experiences. These rarely alter radically. The process of growth towards self-knowledge involves taking cognizance of these patterns and an attitude towards them, endorsing or condemning them, accepting aspects of them, trying to change or resist them. Obviously a person's moral convictions, his regard for other people, his loves and interests, shape his attitude towards his own character, just as his character shapes his relation to the values that are the object of these convictions. The relationship is a two-way one.

Having seen how both self-knowledge and moral knowledge characterize the self, let us now turn to the relation between the two, try to bring together the two strands of discussion which I have pursued in parallel with each other.

MORAL KNOWLEDGE AND SELF-KNOWLEDGE

I said that one condition for our knowing others is that we should be capable of recognizing them as separate beings, able to choose and act for themselves, with concerns, convictions, longings, pains, and pleasures of their own – in other words, not there to please or annoy us, to facilitate or obstruct our schemes, to be manipulated or pushed around, having wishes and intentions the object of which we form no part. It is well known that it is this same orientation, one which excludes a recognition of others as separate beings, that also keeps a person's eyes closed to good and evil – or at any rate to good and evil as conceived in moralities of love. Thus Gabriel Marcel has pointed out that for someone who sees the world as revolving around him good and evil do not have much reality.[8] Pain and pleasure do of course, but this does not include the pains and pleasures of other people.

The possibility of good and evil presupposes a world of human beings with their separate lives and aspirations of their own, having to decide for themselves, responsible for their actions and prepared to acknowledge this in the case of others. There is no doubt that justice, compassion and respect for others require an awareness of the reality of other people, of their sufferings and hopes, their longings, struggles, success and failures. Unless a person can appreciate this reality and respond to others without referring their actions and intentions to himself or subordinating their claims to his own interests and desires he cannot feel any genuine concern or sympathy for them. Such concern and sympathy are among the responses in which a person's awareness or appreciation of the reality of other people finds expression.

This reality is a moral dimension of human life – I mean their separate existence as fellow human beings. It is a dimension in which various moral attitudes within a certain range are possible. We cannot speak of this reality from a morally neutral perspective. Such reactions as sympathy, gratitude, resentment, indignation, forgiveness, pity, and grief in which it finds recognition are constitutive of this form or dimension of life. Gratitude, for instance, involves a recognition of the goodness and kindness of other people, and so one who lacks it is blind to an important aspect of human behaviour. Such a person takes other people's goodness towards him as his due, or he sees it as an expression of their weakness or servility.

To know other people, then, one has to be able to relate to them as real people, capable of good and evil, with dreams of their own, ideals, ambitions, concerns, and passions. That is, one has to have access to this moral dimension of human life, share the affective responses which form part of it. One should want and be able to see others as they are, and not as people animated by fantasies that are projected onto them, whether by oneself or the ethos which surrounds them. This is part of caring for others. To care for them, to have regard for justice, to admire the courage a person has of his convictions, one needs to have an appreciation of other people as individuals in their own right.

It is in this way that in our development towards individual autonomy within a culture where justice, honesty and care for others are valued for themselves, our eyes open to the reality of good and evil and to that of other people *at the same time*. These two realities overlap, each is logically involved in the constitution of the other. Furthermore, this opening of our eyes is inevitably a change in us towards becoming ourselves and so coming to self-knowledge – becoming, that is, individuals with moral convictions and loyalties, and a life for which we assume responsibility.

It follows that if a person's eyes have not opened to these twin realities, if the things to which he gives himself keep his eyes shut to them, one who has access to them will be able to describe him as ignorant or deceived, as Plato did. Such ignorance or deception is in and of the self, it characterizes the self. But does this mean that self-knowledge is the prerogative of those we would call virtuous?

I hesitate to answer this question in the affirmative, though I think that Plato would have done so. Of course, for a person to be virtuous his virtuous actions must come from him. He must be authentic in these actions and so he must possess self-knowledge in *this* respect. But must the reverse hold as well: can we never attribute self-knowledge to him if he lacks virtue or moral knowledge? This is the question to which I said I would return.

Let us begin by considering the extreme case of a person who lives for himself alone and cares for little else: can we attribute self-knowledge to him? There are considerations which incline me to say that such a person is not his own master and can hardly be said to know what he wants. I would not speak of him as having found or come to know himself. Let us suppose that what he calls 'living for himself' is yielding to impulses of the moment – a case which Plato considers in the *Gorgias*. If he cares for little else and is unable to see beyond his present impulses, what would even 'self-interest' mean for him? What would self-satisfaction amount to in his case other than eating, drinking, and satisfying his sexual urges? Can such a person be even merry if, for instance, that involves drinking with companions? For can he have companions? Here I agree with Plato.

Let us next suppose that 'living for himself' means always putting himself first, subordinating everything to his self-interest. If what moves such a person is either greed or anxiety about being able to keep what he has, then I do not see how he could be said to possess self-mastery or to be in charge of his life. He may himself think of the way he calculates every move he makes as an expression of the mastery he has acquired over his destiny. But the way he clings to his self-interest in every situation and the consequent impoverishment of his life give the lie to this thought. A life which in this way revolves around a person's self-interest excludes a great deal of what is necessary to a full awareness of the reality of other people. Thus I do not see how, for instance, such a person can truly call anyone his friend.

These considerations lead me to think that his greed and/or anxieties must have prevented such a person from finding himself and arrested his development towards autonomy and self-knowledge. Here too I agree with Plato that what constitutes a lack of virtue is at the same time what leaves such a person devoid of self-knowledge. But let us be clear, the lack of virtue in question is indifference to *any* form of moral consideration.

When it comes to the case of someone whose behaviour we condemn, though we recognize that it comes from sincerely held beliefs which differ radically from those we hold ourselves, it is otherwise. We may, for instance, condemn a political assassin's actions. But would it not be rash and presumptuous to say, for this reason, that he does not know himself? Can we say this of him a priori, that is without further personal knowledge? If he is not doing what he is engaged in lightly, if he has thought about it deeply, if he is moved by considerations regarding the fate of those he loves, if there are circumstances in which he is prepared to give his life for them, if he takes full responsibility for his actions, would it not be ludicrous to say that he lacks self-knowledge or that he has not found himself?

I am not sure whether or not Plato would have agreed, but I will move on to a further case which decidedly raises difficulties for him: the man who likes to soil what is pure, corrupt what is innocent, spoil or destroy what is good. What attracts his hatred is clearly innocence, purity and goodness. So he recognizes these things, it would seem, as much as someone who loves them. It is goodness itself which attracts him, only perversely. Such a person is not insensitive or indifferent to goodness. He hates it and delights in evil. Should we, perhaps, say that he does not recognize the attractiveness of goodness, that in it which attracts others? Even that seems to me to be incorrect. For he does recognize goodness for what it is, appreciates that about it which renders it attractive. His hatred is an expression of envy. He sees the demands it makes on the self and so he cannot allow himself to receive it into his soul for fear of being destroyed by it. He thus hates it because he is both attracted and measured by it, being made to feel small and inadequate in its presence. Such a man, therefore, is not devoid of the knowledge of good and evil, as Plato conceived it, but his knowledge is twisted by envy.

The question of the relation between virtue and self-knowledge arose because, given what it means to have moral knowledge, to have it *is* to be virtuous, though this does not exclude the possibility of moral failure on particular occasions as Plato wrongly thought.[9] We saw that since self-knowledge is bound up with authenticity, and since moral action and judgments cannot be copied so that moral knowledge requires authenticity, there cannot be virtue or virtuous action without self-knowledge. But the converse does not hold: a person who has self-knowledge does not have to be virtuous. What is true, however, is that for a person to come to find and know himself there has to be things outside himself which he cares for, cherishes, and values. This in turn, we have seen, brings in his relationship with other people. In these relationships, whether friendly or hostile, co-operative or adversorial, he may be aware of their independent existence, their separate identities, or he may deny it, refuse to acknowledge the reality of others. Such refusal characterizes his mode of existence and affective orientation, it shows in the way he acts and lives.

It is this mode of existence which I have argued, excludes both self-knowledge and knowledge of good and evil. In other words, a person's capacity to act as a fully intentional agent and take charge of his life and his capacity to know good and evil are interrelated. He comes to acquire these capacities in relation to the moral norms which form part of the culture to which he belongs and in his relationship with other people. These relationships too are interrelated and, indeed, interdependent.

CONCLUSION

In this paper I have tried to bring out these interrelations, to give a broad sketch of them. But they need spelling out in detail and with care.

I have also tried to show that what we call 'knowledge' covers a wider spectrum of cases and exhibits a greater variety in its grammar than we are inclined to suppose in philosophy. The forms of knowing we have considered involve contact with something towards which the subject cannot be indifferent. One cannot detach the reality of its significance from his relation to the values in which he believes in the case of his knowledge of good and evil. Nor can one detach the reality which other people have for him, in the sense in which this enters his knowledge of them, from his relationships with other people. What those relationships amount to cannot itself be separated from what he is like in himself, from whether or not he is himself in those relationships. These are relationships which engage him as a person and not just his mind. They engage his emotions and bring into play his affective orientation. These emotions find expression in the responses which constitute the contact in which he comes to know what is in question. We have here forms of knowledge which stand in great contrast to the impersonal forms of knowledge in which the subject or person is detached from the object into which he inquires. Indeed enquiry is replaced by soul-searching here.

The questions I have discussed are questions in which I have come to be increasingly interested. Apart from Plato and, in passing, Sartre, I have not mentioned any philosophers – ancient, modern, or contemporary. This does not mean, of course, that I could have asked these questions without many of their contributions. However, among these, I would like to single out one whose contribution to moral philosophy I had in mind when I wrote this paper: and that is Peter Winch. I think enormously highly of his work and have learned more from it than I have been able to do justice to in this paper. I only wish I had been able to pull together the themes of this paper in a way that is more commensurate with the debt of philosophical gratitude I owe him.

NOTES

1. See Jean-Paul Sartre, *Esquisse d'une Théorie des Emotions* (Hermann: Paris, 1948).
2. See, İ. Dilman, 'Proust and solipsistic love' in *Love and Human Separateness* (Oxford: Blackwell, 1987) Chapter 7, Section 2.
3. Plato, *Gorgias* (Harmondsworth: Penguin Books, 1960) 485.
4. Plato, *Phaedo* (Harmondsworth: Penguin Books, 1960) 90 D.

5. Plato did not speak of the good, as he conceived it, as a product of human life. He said that it is to be found in a timeless world of forms distinct form the world, subject to change, in which human beings now live. I cannot here try to elucidate what he meant when he spoke like this. But despite appearances to the contrary, I do not think that his characterization and mine are in conflict.

6. Plato, *Gorgias*, 483.

7. See Dilman, op. cit., Chapter 9.

8. Gabriel Marcel, *Homo Viator* (London: Victor Gollancz 1951) Chapter 1.

9. See Î. Dilman, *Morality and the Inner Life: A Study in Plato's Gorgias* (London: Macmillan, 1979) Chapters 3, 9.

Chapter Eleven

THE PRESUMPTION OF THEORY

D.Z. PHILLIPS

I

Peter Winch's *The Idea of a Social Science*[1] and his paper 'Understanding a primitive society'[2] received widespread critical attention. But this has not been the case with his papers in moral philosophy reprinted in *Ethics and Action*. Why not? In all three contexts, Winch attacks the presumption of theory: theory which claims that it possesses the criteria of what is rational or worthwhile in human life. That presumption is so deeply engrained in contemporary moral philosophy that its practitioners have virtually ignored Winch's challenge to it. It is not surprising, therefore, on the rare occasions the challenge is recognized, to find it misunderstood, as we shall see in the second part of the paper.

In the philosophy of the social sciences and anthropology, the presumption of theory can lead to the following posture: '*We* know that Zande beliefs in the influence of witchcraft, the efficacy of magic medicines, the role of oracles in revealing what is going on and what is going to happen, are mistaken, illusory. Scientific methods of investigation have shown conclusively that there are no relations of cause and effect such as are implied by these beliefs and practices. All we can do is show them how such a system of mistaken beliefs and inefficacious practices can maintain itself in the face of objections that seem to us so obvious.'[3] By a consideration of examples, Winch is able to throw light on the possibilities of meaning which are shown in Zande magical beliefs, possibilities in terms of which people make sense of their lives. Winch believes that his treatment of these examples does help to bring out the significance which Zande practices *actually* have. Yet, it is important to note that the main thrust of

216

his argument would not be affected even if he were factually mistaken in this instance. The citing of such *possibilities* would still be of logical importance in weaning us away from the idea that what we find important, the ways in which we make sense of our lives, are underpinned by a necessity, such that this is all that *could* be important or make sense to anyone. In this respect, there would be a parallel with Wittgenstein's references to 'other possibilities' in *On Certainty*.

Winch's essays on ethics involve equally radical consequences for the presumption of theory. He insists that 'philosophy can no more show a man what he should attach importance to than geometry can show a man where he should stand'.[4] Unlike Winch's disputes with philosophers of social science and social scientists, however, his disputes with moral philosophers are not over common examples, such as Zande witchcraft. On the contrary, he has had an uphill battle to bring examples to their attention, examples which constitute telling counter-cases to the general claims of moral theories. Winch said, in 1964: 'In moral as in other branches of philosophy, good examples are indispensable: examples, that is, which bring out the real force of the ways in which we speak and in which language is not "on holiday" (to adapt a remark of Wittgenstein's). It is needful to say this in opposition to a fairly well-established, but no less debilitating, tradition in recent Anglo-Saxon moral philosophy, according to which it is not merely permissible, but desirable, to take trivial examples. The rationale of this view is that such examples do not generate the emotion which is liable to surround more serious cases and thus enable us to look more coolly at the logical issues involved. On such a view what is characteristic of the ways in which we express our moral concerns can be examined quite apart from any consideration of what it is about these concerns which makes them important to us. But "a moral issue that does not matter" is a mere chimera. The seriousness of such issues is not something that we can add, or not, after the explanations of what these issues are, as a sort of emotional extra: it is something that "shows itself" (again I deliberately echo Wittgenstein) in the explanation of the issues. And an issue the seriousness of which does not show itself will not be one that presents for our scrutiny those features of morality that we find philosophically puzzling.'[5]

In presenting his examples to us, we can ascribe to Winch the Wittgensteinian characterization he gives to Kierkegaard's work in *Purity of Heart*. Winch does not attempt to say what moral action is: he shows what it is by portraying various cases. Characteristically, philosophers try to tidy up this all too evident heterogeneity. Failure to do so, they seem to think, would commit one to saying that *anything* could be the object of moral approval or disapproval. Winch is committed to no such view. He criticizes 'moral philosophers who have made attitudes of approval and disapproval, or something similar, fundamental in ethics, and who have held that the *objects* of such attitudes were completely irrelevant to the conception of morality. On that view, there might be a society where the sorts of attitude taken up in *our* society to questions about relations between the sexes were reserved, say, for questions about the length people wear their hair, and vice versa. This seems to me incoherent. In the first place, there would be a confusion in calling a concern of that sort a 'moral' concern, however passionately felt. The story of Samson in the Old Testament confirms rather than refutes this point, for the interdict on the cutting of Samson's hair is, of course, connected there with much else:[6] and pre-eminently, it should be noted, with questions about sexual relations. But secondly, if that is thought to be mere verbal quibbling, I will say that it does not seem to me a mere conventional matter that T. S. Eliot's trinity of 'birth, copulation and death' happen to be such deep objects of human concern. I do not mean just that they are made such by fundamental psychological and sociological forces, though that is no doubt true. But I want to say further that the very notion of human life is limited by these conceptions.'[7] *How* these limiting conceptions are expressed, or how they are linked with other conceptions, including moral conceptions, varies enormously in different cultures, different societies, within the same society, and even between individuals. Yet, these conceptions give us a foothold in our efforts to understand the possibilities presented to us.

These possibilities, however, are not determined by moral theories. For example, Winch says: 'Hare's formalistic account of moral language seems to leave him with a problem about the source of the specific content of people's moral evaluations. He tries to overcome this (in *Freedom and Reason*) by taking an agent's own interests, desires and inclinations as a datum and then transmuting them into genuine moral judgements by means of the mechanism of universalization.' Leaving aside difficulties in this notion of transmutation and granting its possibility in the individual case, insuperable problems remain for any notion of a recognized shared moral authority. These problems are presented by Alasdair MacIntyre in *A Short History of Ethics*: 'MacIntyre asks why one agent's moral evaluation, the content of which springs from a consideration of his own interests and inclinations, should carry any authority at all for another agent who perhaps has quite different inclinations and interests. Will it not be simply a lucky chance if two agents manage to arrive at even roughly the same evaluations in this way? Moreover, even if they do manage to agree, will not each man's evaluation have authority for him only in so far as they are backed by his own interests and inclinations?'[8] Hare relies on his large assumption about the psychological unity of mankind, fanatics apart, to get out of these difficulties. The efficacy of Hare's assumption depends on ignoring the variety of examples Winch and others have brought to his attention. That Hare is ill-disposed to such examples, especially to examples from literature, is therefore not surprising.

Winch is far more sympathetic to MacIntyre's own suggestion that, in order to understand the authority moral considerations have for us, we must pay attention to the social parameters within which possibilities of good and evil are given; possibilities in terms of which people endeavour to make sense of their lives. The diversity which proved problematic for Hare's analysis at the level of individuals, thus takes a more promising form at the level of social practices. When MacIntyre speaks of different practices, Winch says, 'he means not merely different views about the specific needs human beings have, but also different views about the sense in which human beings can be said to have needs at all, and about the kind of importance in human life those needs have.'[9] Moral philosophy cannot provide a neutral standard by which an individual can choose between these diverse moral practices, since, as MacIntyre shows, the conception of such a standard is confused, a typical presumption of theory. 'MacIntyre maintains[10] that it is "arbitrary and illegitimate" in examining the logical structure of different moralities to specify as the logical form of moral argument that form which is characteristic of any one of them.'[11]

Winch's claim against MacIntyre is that he, too, falls prey to the presumption of theory, by claiming, inconsistently and surprisingly, that the Aristotelian conception of human nature is superior to conceptions of nature found in Christianity, the Sophists, and Hobbes, and that this can be demonstrated philosophically.[12] In opposing theories of human nature, Winch concludes that 'what we can ascribe to human nature does not determine what we can and what we cannot make sense of; rather, what we can and what we cannot make sense of determines what we can ascribe to human nature.'[13] This conclusion does not contradict what Winch said about limiting conceptions in human life. It would do so, only if those conceptions were thought of as given prior to the diverse ways in which we make sense of our lives, whereas their position as 'limits' is shown by the role they play in that diversity.

Moral theories distort the ways in which moral considerations are *constitutive* of certain ways of thinking. Moral theories can claim to be guides to conduct only because they conceive of morality itself as such a guide. The theories create a dualism between the agent and his world. The agent is depicted as acting on the world, effecting changes by so doing. Why should the agent bring about some changes rather than others? Morality, it is said, will guide us as to which changes should be made. Winch examines the various forms this assumption has taken in moral theories; an assumption which obscures the ways in which moral considerations may be constitutive of a person's thinking.

When a person proposes to act in certain ways, he may be faced with familiar obstacles: lack of money, lack of friends, lack of opportunity, etc. It can hardly be thought that morality is a guide around *these* difficulties. In fact, so far from ridding us of obstacles, morality seems to create obstacles to what we want to do. A man may contemplate acting in a certain way, but morality says, 'Not that way'. Winch comments: 'Morality, we are told, is a guide which helps him round his difficulty. But were it not for morality there would be no difficulty! This is a strange sort of guide, which first puts obstacles in our path and then shows us the way round them. Would it not be far simpler and more rational to be shot of the thing altogether? Then we could get on with the business in hand, whatever it is.'[14] As Winch says, this is the essence of Glaucon's case in Book II of the *Republic*. Each individual, he argues, would, if he could, pursue his own ends without regard for anyone else. Given that this is true of everyone, however, considerations of prudence restrict unrestrained self-interest. Rules become necessary to regulate the proceedings. By abiding by these rules, the odds are that an individual will obtain more than he would in a general free-for-all. But if a given individual could transcend these common conditions, for example, by possessing a ring that would make him invisible, he would no longer have any reason for abiding by the rules. Of course, the rest of society will condemn him, but, privately, every individual would take the possessor of the ring to be a fool if he did not take advantage of his situation. Glaucon's challenge has haunted moral philosophers and they have tried to answer it in their various theories.

Mill, by appealing to the notion of general interest, tried to show why an individual should abide by moral rules, even when it is not in his self-interest to do so. The notion of 'general interest' runs into the difficulties we have already mentioned which dog any attempt to found a *shared* moral authority on the basis of an individual's desires and inclinations. More consistently, but no less problematically, Philippa Foot tried to show, in her early papers, that moral considerations give every man a reason for satisfying them. This reason, she argued, had to do with the cost and penalties a person would have to pay if he ignored these considerations, cost and penalties which are unlikely to be avoided, but, as Winch says, 'Glaucon would have agreed . . . that most men are not in fact strong enough to free themselves from the shackles of convention and the question is: But suppose that somebody could, what then? And anyway situations in which men actually can and do act in ways which they know to be wrong and get away with it are not, after all, far to seek. What can be said to show them that they would not be fools not to do so?[15] Moral reasons can clearly not be used here as that would beg the question at issue.'[16] These tensions show why Glaucon's question cannot be answered on its own terms. The moral theories we are considering presumed that it can. But, Winch says, 'the question is: What advantage would morality bring? And the form of the question suggests that we must look outside morality for something on which morality can be based. But the moment we do this, then "what is commended is not morality itself", for surely if the commendation is in terms of some further advantage, the connection between that advantage and morality can only be a contingent one. And it does not matter how strong a contingent connection it is; it will still not be "morality itself" which is being commended.'[17]

How, then, are moral theories going to commend the good to us without falling foul of these criticisms? G. E. Moore and others who appealed to intuition, said that when we say something is good we are simply stating a fact about it. But, as Winch says, 'surely some further argument is needed in order to show why a man should aim at producing something of that kind'.[18] Moore simply says 'it is self-evident that men ought to do what will produce good things'. But, again, as Winch says, following John Anderson, Moore 'smuggles into what is supposed to be simply a property of something the idea of an essential relation which that thing is supposed to have to something else: namely, being desired by, or required of, human beings. So he gives the impression of having offered a reason why men should behave morally without in fact having done so.'[19]

If we want to appreciate the ways in which moral considerations can be constitutive of a person's perspective, it is important not to think of morality as the agent's guide in choosing between alternative courses of action. 'It may be at least as important to notice what he considers the alternatives to be, and, what is closely connected, the reasons he considers it relevant to deploy in deciding between them.'[20] The agent has a perspective on the situation. Indeed, it may be helpful to say that he *is* that perspective, one that may be informed by moral considerations. The moral possibilities expressed in his perspective are not self-generated, as Sartre thought, but are given in the language available to him in his culture. On the other hand, to understand what a person makes of these possibilities, how they enter his life, how they do or do not hang together there, we must understand, not the culture, but him.

Notice that Winch does not identify the agent's perspective with his will. He is anxious to avoid Kant's conception of the good will as the only thing which is good without qualification. The difficulty is, by now, a familiar one: once Kant gives his formal definition a positive content, namely, acting from a sense of duty, it is clearly not something which we can regard as good without qualification. To so regard it would be to force ourselves to call pure, actions we want to call corrupt, and to call corrupt, actions of moral purity or simplicity. Kant, quite rightly, wants to preserve the difference between acting from moral considerations (a sense of duty) and acting from inclinations external to morality. But, as Winch points out, there is just as much difference between doing something from a sense of duty, and, for example, simply paying a debt, making a gift, or being absorbed in play with one's children, as there is in the distinction Kant wants to preserve. Indeed, a person may criticize himself for simply being able to do from a sense of duty, what others can be absorbed in.

In criticizing moral theories, Winch is not wanting to replace them with one of his own. The presumption is in wanting there to be a theory here at all. In contrast, he asks us to wait on the possibilities he puts before us. He is not advocating them, or asking us to agree, morally, with them. How could he be, since he shows us differences? In seeing how the differences are just as important as similarities between moral points of view, we begin to appreciate what is involved in speaking of views, differences, disputes, problems, and disagreements in these contexts. We are rescued from the presumption of theory.

Yet, having said this, it brings us to the important question of how different moral possibilities are to be recognized. As one might expect, Winch gives no general answer to that question. He says: 'It is very common in philosophical discussion to find that a way of speaking and thinking which seems perfectly intelligible and acceptable to oneself is met with incomprehension by other people; and of course vice versa. In such circumstances one is bound to ask whether what one wants to say really does make sense or not . . . . Discussion will take the form of raising difficulties and trying to see one's way round them. Sometimes one will think one has dealt with the difficulties satisfactorily: sometimes that the view under criticism meets with difficulties so insurmountable as to be really incomprehensible. But if one recognized the possibility of being mistaken in one's initial belief that one had understood what was being said, or that one had shown it to be unintelligible, one can equally, after discussion recognize that one may have over- or underestimated the difficulties which have emerged in its course. But that does not mean that one's views are subject to the test of some ultimate criterion, the criterion of what does and does not belong to human nature.'[21]

The presumption of ethical theorists consists in laying claim to an ultimate criterion to determine the content of morality. They are like those philosophers of the social sciences and anthropologists we mentioned at the outset who knew what constitutes the essence of rational behaviour. The importance of Winch's work is in showing that a readiness to wait on examples in discussion carries with it no presumption about such an ultimate criterion. 'It means only that new difficulties and perhaps new ways of meeting the difficulties, are always lurking below the horizon and that discussion continues. Sometimes, if one is lucky, the discussion clarifies or extends one's conception of what is possible for human beings. But it is no use saying that this is contingent on what is or is not possible for human beings; for our only way of arriving at a view about that is by continuing to try to deal with the difficulties that arise in the course of the discussion.'[22]

I have quoted this passage at length because it describes so well Winch's own style of discussion in moral philosophy; a style of discussion with which I have been acquainted, not only in Winch's writings, but ever since I was one of his first honours students thirty-five years ago in Swansea. By presenting us with telling examples, he weans us away from the presumption that theories are necessary in ethics. He gets us to see that in their more ambitious claims, language is idling or on holiday in such theories. The state of contemporary moral philosophy would be very different if this lesson were taken to heart.

II

Given the lack of critical reaction to Winch's essays on ethics, it was something of a surprise to find Onora O'Neill calling attention, not only to them, but to what she identifies as a distinctive Wittgensteinian tradition in ethics.[23] She says: 'The wintry ethics of logical positivism and the cold spring of meta-ethical inquiry have supposedly been supplanted by a new flourishing of substantive ethical writing' (p. 5). This has taken two very different forms. On the one hand, there are the Wittgensteinian writings she has mentioned. On the other hand, especially in the United States, there are discussions of substantive legal, social and political problems. I shall simply note, that, with respect to the latter, O'Neill concludes that while actual problems are discussed, insufficient reflectiveness is involved in the over-simplistic solutions we are offered.

In contrast, she praises those influenced by Wittgenstein for the greater reflectiveness in their writings, a reflectiveness particularly evident in the use they make of examples. Yet, having said this, O'Neill has a major complaint against these writings: she accuses them of being 'more remote from moral life and in particular from the practical resolution of moral problems' (p. 6).

It is important to grasp, at the outset, that O'Neill has a conception of moral philosophy as a guide to human conduct. She never comes to grips with the fact that Winch is *challenging* that conception. For her, he is simply seen as someone whose examples lack the power to give us the moral guidance we need. O'Neill fails to appreciate that Winch is not offering examples which await our moral judgments. He is presenting *examples of people making moral judgments*. Winch wants us to note the complexity involved in these judgments, people not only show different priorities in judging between alternatives, but often differ in what they take the alternatives to be. What is an alternative to one person may not even be considered to be an alternative by another person. Winch is emphasizing that philosophy's task here, as elsewhere, is *descriptive*, one of noting that this is how it is where moral considerations are concerned. The presumption of theory is to think that this variety awaits an ordering to be determined by criteria it possesses. Opposing such a view, Winch says, 'All we can do, I am arguing, is to look at particular examples and see what we do want to say about them: there are no general rules which can determine in advance what we *must* say about them.'[24]

O'Neill observes, rightly, that Winch's examples are not theory-led, but she still calls them 'the pivot of moral thought' (p. 11). The examples, she is assuming, are meant to be a pivot for our reflections about what we ought to do: 'The Wittgensteinian approach to ethics by examples, depends on the possibility of arriving at "what we do want to say" in the course of reflecting on the example' (p. 12).

Having made this assumption, her complaint is that the examples Winch offers us take far too much for granted to give us the moral guidance we need. 'The method must presuppose sufficient community of moral views – an ethical tradition, perhaps, or a shared ideology – for there to be something which we (whoever "we" may be: and this is a large question) do want to say about a given example' (p. 12). But, O'Neill argues, in our fragmented world, it is just such a shared community of moral views that cannot be taken for granted. As a result, the examples Winch offers lack power, the power they need to guide us in solving our most pressing problems.

Given that O'Neill has misunderstood what Winch is trying to show, it might be said that there is little point in pursuing her criticisms any further. This reaction is a premature one, since O'Neill's failure to grasp the point of Winch's examples is illustrative of the very tendencies in moral philosophy which Winch is combatting. It is profitable, therefore, to examine O'Neill's complaints against Winch's examples in greater detail. We can find, in her paper, at least six complaints she brings to bear against a Wittgensteinian use of examples in moral philosophy, especially examples taken from literature.

The first complaint I shall note is the most interesting, namely, that *there are important differences between appreciating literary depictions of problems and facing problems oneself.* This is something Winch does not discuss, but it is something he would not deny. But O'Neill does not develop the differences either in any interesting way. The nearest she gets to doing so is when she says: 'Literary examples impose a spectator perspective; and in context the imposition is without costs . . . we do not have to do anything beyond "deciding what we do want to say" about the example and making sense of it. We do not have to decide whether to turn Raskolnikov in or whether to find Billy Budd guilty. The concern shown by Wittgensteinian writers on ethics for detailed examples understood in their context conveys an atmosphere of moral seriousness and closeness to moral life. But this is in some ways illusory' (p. 17).

What *are* some of the important differences between appreciating problems depicted in literature and facing problems in one's own life? We may reject the depiction of a character's development in literature as inconsistent or unrealistic. We may criticize a work saying, 'After a promising start, it falls apart'. But when loved ones, friends or acquaintances develop in ways we did not expect, we cannot put these developments aside as 'inconsistent'. They have happened, whether we like it or not. Things do fall apart after promising starts, but the 'falling apart' *is* our situation. People and events cannot be put aside like books. That is why learning to live with them is so very different. On the other hand, what our situations are, the possibilities open to us, would be very different but for the influence of literature, indirect though that influence may be. There are important, but difficult issues to be raised here, but they are not the ones O'Neill pursues. Her remaining five complaints are very different in kind.

Her second complaint against literary examples is *that the problems depicted in them are not our problems.* She says: 'Typically, the focus is on examples of completed action in a context which invites moral consideration or assessment, rather than on less complete examples of a situation which raises moral problems or dilemmas, as though the primary exercise of moral judgement were to *reflect* or *pass judgement* on what has been done rather than to decide among possible actions' (p. 11).

The first thing to be said in reply is that a problem does not have to be ours before we can learn from it. The whole point of Winch's depiction of *different* possibilities is to show us *how* different moral reactions and judgments can be. Consider, for example, Sophocles' depiction of Oedipus' absorption with what he has done. Winch says: 'Oedipus did not intend to kill his father and marry his mother; he would have acted differently if he had known the true nature of what he was doing but was in a position in which, in an important sense, it was not within his power to know this. On Kantian principles what we must say here is that Oedipus is in no way responsible for his actions (at least under these descriptions) and that no question of blame can possibly arise.'[25] Notice that Winch has no philosophical objection to anyone who holds this moral view: 'Now I realize that many people would in fact say this and I have nothing to say here against someone who, as a matter of fact, takes such a view. I do, however, have something to say against a philosopher who argues, on Kantian lines, that this is the only possible coherent view to take.'[26] Once again, the object of Winch's attack is the presumption of theory. The Kantian may hold on to his own moral view that Oedipus should not blame himself, but come to see as a moral possibility, the coherence of his doing so. He may come to see, as Winch says, that 'The pity we feel for Oedipus is inextricably connected with our realization of what he has *done* and with our understanding that these are actions for which he could not help blaming himself'.[27] The Kantian, while holding on to his moral view, is freed from the confusion of thinking that all moral possibilities *must* conform to it. So even where moral views do not change, appreciation of other possibilities is not the voyeurism O'Neill is tempted to make it. Even less can be said for her remark that Winch's conception of ethics flourishes 'mainly in the academies of a formerly imperial power', where, unsurprisingly, it focuses 'predominantly on judging what has been done' (p. 16). Embarrassingly for this piece of pseudo-sociology, the Wittgensteinian tradition in ethics has never been the dominant one in the context which, allegedly, should have made it so. On the contrary, it has combated the dominant tradition in which, sometimes, a kind of 'conceptual imperialism' seemed to flourish. After all, one of the main thrusts of 'Understanding a primitive society' was against the assumption that we possess, in our culture, all we need to understand cultures other than our own; an assumption which, on Winch's view, led to a condescending misunderstanding of Zande witchcraft. So far from being someone satisfied with current moral concepts, whatever they might be, as O'Neill suggests, Winch says: 'Our blindness to the point of primitive modes of life is a corollary of the pointlessness of much of our own life.'[28]

O'Neill's third complaint against literary examples is related to her second: *the invoking of literary examples takes an agreement in moral construals for granted, whereas, in our lives, the character of our construals is what we are uncertain about.* She points out that 'it is the authority of the text which imposes a largely shared interpretation of examples . . . . Nobody can reasonably speculate whether the interpretation of such examples hinges entirely on factors of which the author has neither told nor hinted. (It's hardly open to a Wittgensteinian to adopt principles of interpretation – whether radically subjectivist or deconstructive – which call in question the possibility of a shared, open reading of the text.) Consider how impertinent it would be to construe *Macbeth* as a murder mystery by adducing extratextual hunches, or to wonder whether Raskolnikov wasn't perhaps mistaken in thinking he had murdered Alyona Ivanovna, who survived his assault and was finished off by someone else, so that his entire experience of agitation, guilt and remorse is just misplaced. Even in a poor whodunnit extratextual importations are suspect; they are totally destructive of the literary examples on which Wittgensteinian ethical reflection builds' (p. 14).

O'Neill argues that the presentation of the literary examples determines the way they are construed by us. If her argument is to have any force, by 'construal' she must mean 'moral construal'. But does the authority of the text determine that *latter* construal? Sophocles' text certainly presents Oedipus as blaming himself for what he has done. His reaction is depicted as a moral reaction. That much the text asks us to recognize. The reader may be unable to accord it this descriptive status. But if he can see what Sophocles wants to show us, he need not agree morally with what he sees. O'Neill is therefore, wrong, when she says that the Wittgensteinian use of examples suggests 'that we can deliberate only in so far as we share the practices of those with or about whom we deliberate' (p. 14). If O'Neill were correct, Winch would have to contend 'that one is under an obligation to admire every single manifestation of integrity'. As Winch says, this would be 'a quite absurd moral doctrine'. He then gives an example of a terrible morality: 'The concentration camp commandant towards the end of Irwin Shaw's *The Young Lions* exhibited integrity of a peculiarly revolting sort from the point of view of Western liberal morality. He was morally revolting because of the unspeakable role he was playing; to say he was playing it with integrity is, for most of us, an additional count against him, not a point in his favour.'[29]

The fourth complaint O'Neill brings against the use of literary examples is that, *unlike the open-ended situations of life, these examples are complete and determinate.* She says: 'Unlike those who discuss pre-packaged examples drawn either from literary texts or from the outlook of some group of specialists, agents must first come to an appreciation or appraisal of actual situations and possibilities for action. To suppose that they can instantly recognize their situation as having a certain specification simplifies, indeed falsifies, the predicament agents face. An agent may initially not even realize that this is a situation which requires or permits action. Even one who sees this much may be at a loss as to how the situation should be described or construed' (p. 24).

It can be seen from this passage that O'Neill's objection seems to be to *any* determinate example, not simply to literary examples. It is extremely simplistic to suggest that all situations depicted in literature are 'complete', determinate, while all situations in life are open-ended. The determinate or the open-ended may be found in *either* context. Since O'Neill calls literary examples pre-packaged, I shall simply provide one counter-example from the countless cases which we can appeal to.

In Alice Monro's short story, *Something I've Been Meaning to Tell You*,[30] we meet two sisters, one of them, Et, envies the other's good looks. It is no surprise to her when her sister takes up with the local Romeo. Unexpectedly, however, he goes off with an older woman. Et helps her sister to get over a botched suicide attempt. Her sister marries her dull history teacher, a man much older than herself. Before long, the local Romeo is back in town and the original affair has resumed. Et is sad to see the husband deceived, but her attitude to what is going on is a complex mixture of admiration, condemnation, envy, and longing. The husband's health is not good, and Et keeps checking the level of the rat-poison kept in the house. The lover goes to the city for a short stay. Et has no reason to think that he will not return. Yet, when the husband, in the sisters' presence, says how much he misses him, Et finds herself blurting out that she had heard that he had taken up with another woman, reminding her sister that it had happened once before. The next morning, her sister is found dead in bed and the bottle of rat poison is missing. The local doctor puts death down to a heart-attack. Et's words were not premeditated. She wanted to bring things to a head somehow, but didn't quite know how. After the event, as the days and even years roll by, she wonders how to weigh her words. Sometimes she sees them one way, sometimes another. Whether she blames herself depends on the aspects under which she sees them, but they are never presented in a settled, determinate form. In old age, playing cards regularly with her sister's husband, there are times when she feels he should know what has happened. Often, it is on the tip of her tongue to say, 'There's something I've been meaning to tell you', but the years roll by and she never does. We, as readers, are invited to share the terrible ambiguities and ambivalences of the story. After all, what would be the 'something' which Et would tell? Further, what would the 'telling' amount to?[31]

It is not hard to find situations in our lives which share these ambiguities. Do we always know what we mean by our words? Did we mean to be honest or to hurt? When events occur subsequent to our words, do we always know the part to assign to our words in these events? The situation may remain permanently ambiguous, its shifting aspects not permitting any determinate description. In calling attention to such situations, O'Neill is not recognizing their possible permanence. On the contrary, for her, such situations are simply *preliminary data* awaiting further moral reflection. This is shown more clearly in her fifth and sixth complaints concerning what she takes to be Wittgensteinian attitudes towards moral dilemmas and moral disagreements.

O'Neill's fifth complaint is that: '*Many Wittgensteinian writers insist that deep moral conflicts cannot be resolved, so that there are ineliminable and tragic clashes of moral outlook*' (p. 16 fn.18 my italics). Let us apply this complaint to moral dilemmas. She is perfectly ready to admit that there are moral dilemmas. She cites Sartre's example of the young man who is torn between caring for his mother and joining the Free French.[32] She describes the dilemma as theory-led, but it is extremely odd to regard devotion to his mother or to the Free French as theory-determined. She says rightly, however, in the light of such examples, 'that moral principles and codes cannot make our decisions for us' (p. 10).

On the other hand, for O'Neill, these dilemmas are *preliminary* data, awaiting the kind of moral thinking which will make it difficult for them to be irresolvable. She accuses the first three essays of my *Through a Darkening Glass* of arguing that deep moral conflicts cannot be resolved. No such argument appears there. She responds: 'But one does not have to hold all moral disagreement is tragic and irresolvable because some is' (p. 16 fn.18). I would not dispute that. The a priorism concerning moral dilemmas has not been on the part of Wittgensteinian ethics, but on the part of those who insist that the irresolvability of a moral dilemma *must* be due to its being underdescribed. The dogmatism is theirs, not ours. For example, R. W. Beardsmore is quite ready to admit that many could not be faced with the dilemma of the wife who had to choose between her husband's life and becoming the mistress of a Nazi officer. For them, 'adultery' is ruled out on moral grounds. Beardsmore has no philosophical argument with this moral standpoint. He does object, however, to a philosophical claim that dilemmas of this form cannot arise for anyone. He considers such an argument by G. E. M. Anscombe.[33] 'No one', she tells us, 'can know in advance that there will be, in any given case, only two alternatives to choose from. There may always be a third way out of the difficulty.' Beardsmore replies: 'Her argument is objectionable for two reasons (a) because we may take our examples from novels or from our own experience, in which case we *already* know what the possibilities are, and (b) because if it is true that no one can know "*a priori*" that there will be only two possibilities, then it is also true that Miss Anscombe cannot know "*a priori*" that there will not be. And it is just this knowledge that she seems to be claiming.'[34]

O'Neill, surprisingly, pays no attention to Winch's discussion of the moral dilemma in which he shows why it is made artificial if it is thought of as the product of a clash of Kantian-like principles. For her, the force of the dilemmas 'derives from certain moral positions and principles which, tragically, lack the resources to resolve the problems they generate' (p. 10). The example Winch considers is from the film *Violent Saturday* ; 'a gang of bank raiders hide from the police on the farm of a strict, Dukhobor-like religious community, one of whose most fundamental guiding principles is non-violence. At the climax of the film one of the gangsters is about to shoot a young girl member of the community in the presence of the community's elder. With horror and doubt on his face, the elder seizes a pitchfork and hurls it into the gangster's back.'[35]

Winch says: 'According to a neo-Kantian position like Professor Hare's, the elder has had to make a "decision of principle", which consists in either qualifying, or perhaps even abandoning, the principle of non-violence according to which he has hitherto tried to live.'[36] But, as Winch points out, there are features of the situation which show such an analysis to be misplaced. It is clear that the elder thinks he has committed a wrong in killing the gangster. It is equally clear, however, that in acting, the elder did what he had to do.

Winch concludes: 'I said that, having killed the gangster, the elder knew he had done something wrong; but I also said that, if he had not killed the gangster, he would not have been able to forgive himself; i.e. that would have been wrong too, though perhaps in a different way. That the modalities involved on the side of killing the gangster are moral modalities is also clear from the fact that, in order to explicate them, notions like that of the innocence of the girl whose life was threatened and that of protecting the defenceless would have to be introduced. But it would be wrong to introduce them in the form of principles for the sake of which the elder was acting. They were involved in what I have called the "perspective" of the action, but that perspective is not to be understood in the form of Kantian "maxims" or Harean "principles". It will be objected that my account leaves no room for any discovery of, or decision concerning *the* right thing to do in such a situation and thus makes morality useless as a guide to conduct. But my whole point is that there is no room for the notion of "the right thing to do" in such a situation and that this shows yet again that morality is *wrongly* conceived as a guide to conduct.'[37]

O'Neill's sixth complaint against Wittgensteinian ethics is that by concentrating on examples of unbridgeable moral disagreements, *the examples will have 'little appeal for those whose lives confront them continually with heterogeneous practices'* (p. 16, my italics). O'Neill emphasizes, with Kant, 'that there can be no complete rules for judging particular cases' (p. 8). Kant writes: 'Judgement will be the faculty of subsuming under rules: that is of distinguishing whether something does or does not stand under a given rule . . . . General logic contains, and can contain no rules for judgement . . . . If it sought to give general instructions how we are to subsume under these rules, that is to distinguish whether something does or does not come under them, that could only be by means of another rule. This in turn, for the very reason that it is a rule, demands guidance from judgement . . . judgement is a peculiar talent which can be practised only and cannot be taught.' [38] O'Neill says that Kant goes on to liken judgment to 'mother wit' and to insist that 'its lack no school can make good'. She comments: 'However, he presumably means only that there can be no *algorithms* for judging and no formal instruction, for he allows that "sharpening of the judgement is indeed one of the benefits of examples"' (p. 8).[39]

It is in this complaint that O'Neill's misunderstanding of the role of examples in Winch is seen most explicitly. For her, the examples await our moral judgment. She does not appreciate that they are examples of *differences involved in what it means* to make moral judgments. For her, as for Kant, different moral construals of situations are construals of prima-facie moral significance (see p. 24) which are to be subsumed under a higher synthesis. It may involve 'coming to appreciate the actual case in a specific way, as falling under one rather than another set of descriptions and hence judgeable in the light of some rather than other practices or principles' (p. 24). O'Neill does not see that moral ideas may be *constitutive* of the descriptions people give of situations. Incredibly, she thinks that, in literature, 'the problem of rival appraisals of situations is greatly reduced' (p. 24), whereas, in fact, it is hard to imagine any literature of significance which does not give prominence to it. In any event, she misconstrues the *nature* of the problem.

One of O'Neill's concerns, one she shares with Kant, is for consistency in moral judgment. The principle of universalizability in ethics attempts to capture that concern. Winch acknowledges the importance of the principle with respect to the judgments an individual makes. Unless these judgments were consistent, it would be hard to attribute any moral seriousness to him. In particular, it would be a strong indictment against him if he did not judge himself as he judged others, and sought to make an exception on his own case. What Winch does *not* accept, however, is the further claim of the universalizability thesis, namely, that in order for an individual's judgment to count as a *moral* judgment, it entails his holding that anyone else, morally judging the same situation, *must* reach the same conclusion.

Winch argues against this further claim of the universalizability thesis by considering his reaction to Vere's decision in Herman Melville's *Billy Budd, Foretopman*, to condemn Billy Budd to death. Let us grant that Winch *has* shown that Vere is faced by a moral dilemma, that he is confronted by the 'ought' of private conscience and the 'ought' of military duty. Winch says that he could not have come to the same conclusion as Vere reached. He says: 'In reaching this decision I do not think that I should appeal to any considerations over and above those to which Vere himself appeals. It is just that I think that I should find the considerations connected with Billy Budd's peculiar innocence too powerful to be overridden by the appeal to military duty.'[40] According to supporters of the universalizability thesis, Winch *must*, if his moral view is to be called a *moral* view at all, come to the conclusion that Vere came to the wrong decision and acted wrongly. But he does not want to say this: 'The story seems to me to show that Vere did what was, for him, the right thing to do.'[41] Now, someone seeing what the story seeks to show, may disagree, morally, with Vere's decision. Winch has no philosophical objection to such a moral reaction. With respect to his own different moral reaction, 'The issue . . . is not, of course, whether (others) would happen to agree with this particular judgement of (his), but whether (he is) saying anything intelligible and coherent at all, whether (he is) in fact making any genuine moral judgement in speaking thus.'[42]

Only through the presumption of theory would we be led to deny the *possibility* of the moral differences between Winch and Vere. Such differences exist not only as between individuals, but also as between practices. O'Neill says 'Precisely because of the variety and transience of ethical practices to which Wittgensteinian writers draw our attention, we cannot easily lead our lives without raising questions which are not just internal to but about local practices. In doing so, however, we can still leave open the question of whether there is a rational or neutral standpoint from which all problems can be resolved' (p. 16). She accuses the Wittgensteinian failure to raise these questions of conservatism. True, the writers she refers to can make little of the notion of 'a rational or neutral standpoint' in this context, but they have not failed to raise the questions O'Neill refers to. What *is* true is that they deny that there is any *general* answer to them. People's reactions to the existence of moral perspectives different from their own will vary. Those reactions will themselves be informed, partly, by moral ideas. Moral ideas enter into the criticisms made in such contexts. One perspective may be hostile to another, even if the other seeks to co-operate. Compromise depends on how much value is placed on what it facilitates. Some will place high value on peace and commodious living, while others may be prepared, if necessary, to go down fighting. One practice may erode another or be swallowed up by a stronger or more prestigious one. When a person meets another who has values different from his own, either may change. All these possibilities have been emphasized by Wittgensteinian writers. Both at the level of individuals and practices, O'Neill complains, 'There is no neutral standpoint from which to discern who is the missionary and who is seducing missionaries into "going native"' (p. 15). But this complaint, like her others, only has force if one harbours a conception of moral philosophy as a guide to human conduct. But if one sees that relations between perspectives are themselves

235

moral relations for the most part, one ceases to be beguiled into a search for a 'neutrality' in which language is idling and even corrupting.

Winch does not deny that 'it is an important task for philosophy to make clear the distinction between corrupt and non-corrupt forms of the thought that something is worthy of admiration'. (On the other hand) 'neither it, nor any other form of enquiry, can show what is worthy of admiration. The idea that it can is itself a form of corruption and always involves an obscuring of possibilities . . . . Philosophy may indeed try to remove intellectual obstacles in the way of recognizing certain possibilities (though there is always the danger that it will throw up new obstacles). But what a man makes of the possibilities he can comprehend is a matter of what man he is. This is revealed in the way he lives; it is revealed to him in his understanding of what he can and what he cannot attach importance to.'[43]

III

Given that O'Neill has all these complaints against Wittgensteinian ethics, what alternative does she offer? She says, 'Kant presumably would have held that the shared capacities to reason and understand preclude radical incommensurability' (p. 23). For this reason, in his later writings, he 'turns to this issue, and discusses strategies by which we might arbitrate between competing construals of a situation, so emerging in reflective judging' (p. 23). When we see what these strategies amount to, we find that O'Neill's promises of a procedure which *contrasts* with Wittgensteinian ethics turn out to be rather empty.

The strategy we are offered is one whereby 'we may move towards overcoming discrepancies between disparate appraisals of one situation. They are strategies, one might suggest, not for finding that one shares a view with others but for seeking to share one. They can be thought of as strategies by which we seek to escape our 'private horizons' by following the maxim 'always to try to expand rather than to narrow one's horizon'.[44] When we adopt such strategies our 'reflective act takes account of the mode of representation of everyone else, in order, *as it were*, to weigh its judgement with the collective reason of mankind' (p. 26).[45] But what is this supposed to amount to and what is it supposed to achieve?

First, we are told that these strategies 'are indispensable when there is disagreement, and so the need to apprehend and appreciate others' appraisals and connect them to our own . . . . Even if we aim at manipulative or hostile rather than morally acceptable interaction with others we will be thwarted if we do not regulate our activity by such maxims. The wordly-wise need good judgement' (p. 26). So this is what we are offered: know there are moral points of view other than your own! But this is precisely part of what the Wittgensteinian discernment of differences emphasizes. This is the situation which, earlier, O'Neill found problematic.

But, second, the strategies are supposed to take us beyond this recognition. O'Neill says that 'we may need not only to see what other views of a situation are, and how they differ from our own, but may need to arbitrate discrepancies. One maxim which may guide us here is the so-called "maxim of enlarged thought" which enjoins us "always to think from the standpoint of everyone else".[46] Once we seek to share others' standpoints and so become aware of incompatibilities between standpoints, further reflection may lead us towards reappraisals in which coherence is restored' (p. 126). If sharing others' viewpoints simply means recognizing their existence, this leaves untouched the differences between them and the diversity of the relations between them. But, then, O'Neill speaks of *reappraising* standpoints and of *restoring* coherence without the slightest indication of what such 'reappraisal' amounts to, and as if the mere existence of moral differences constitutes a 'lack of coherence'. Compared with this, there is far more substance in the way Wittgensteinian writers have tried to show the variety of ways in which different moral perspectives may affect each other, and take account of each other.[47] It has far more substance than O'Neill's empty claim that 'our search for appraisals of actual situations is guided by considerations of coherence and interpretability to all parties' (p. 27).

Despite the emptiness of these promises, O'Neill presents alternatives in a disparaging light: 'To have reached the same "decision" by the toss of a coin or by mere whim would be something entirely different' (pp. 28–9). This would be her reaction, I suspect, to Winch's wanting to say of Vere: 'He did what was right for him.' Winch is aware of such reactions: 'To them it will seem that to speak as I have just spoken is to concede that anything goes in matters of morality, that morality is not a rational universe of discourse at all . . . . It will be said that if I do not admit that the right thing for him to do would be the right thing for anyone to do in the same circumstances, I am ruling out any possible distinction between what a man thinks he ought to do and what he in fact ought to do. And if that is so, how can it matter to a man what he thinks is right; since whatever he thinks is right will be right.'[48] Part of Winch's response is to say: 'It was clearly important to Vere that he did the right thing and he did not think that whatever he thought would be the right thing would in fact be so.'[49] Winch would say that this was *shown* in what Vere did. But if 'shown' is to mean anything, there must be *some* check such that some forms of behaviour would be reason for saying that a man did *not* do what was right for him, even though he may say he did. Without this check, to say that a man did what was right for him, would be no more, as far as O'Neill is concerned, than 'the toss of a coin'. It is all the more surprising, therefore, that O'Neill ignores the three examples Winch gives of such a check.

First, the circumstances surrounding the way in which Vere reached his decision may have been such as to show that moral considerations did not enter for him at all. For example, he may have applied the rules mechanically. We must always be alert to the possibility that we are missing features of a moral reaction different from our own, but there will be circumstances which cannot be called a genuinely moral context at all – 'our common understanding of moral ideas enabling us to judge what is and what is not a genuinely moral context'.[50] Winch's appeal to 'common understanding' has far more substance to it than O'Neill's appeal to the 'maxim of enlarged thought'.

The second set of limiting circumstances Winch presents are those cases 'where a man acts with every sign of moral concern, but where his ideas of right and wrong differ so profoundly from our own, that we are unwilling to accept his claim that he acted rightly'.[51] As Winch points out, the first set of circumstances constitute logical limits to what can be regarded as a genuinely moral context, whereas the second set of circumstances are an expression of our moral disagreements. The realism of these limits, which will be different for different people, contrasts favourably with O'Neill's appeal to 'the collective reasoning of mankind' and her claim that 'our search for appraisals is guided by considerations of coherence and interpretability to all parties' (p. 25).

The third set of circumstances Winch brings to our attention are those in which a person says he is concerned with moral considerations, but is, in fact, insincere or deceiving himself in saying so. He cites the behaviour of Raskolnikov after his murder of the moneylender as an obvious example.

We can see that O'Neill's fears that without a more 'systematic' approach in ethics moral perspectives become hopelessly relativistic, are unfounded. O'Neill hopes that 'the attempt to make sense of the nuances and complexities of situations, which is one of the most attractive features of Wittgensteinian ethical writing, might be incorporated in a more systemic form within an account of practical reasoning' (p. 27). What we have seen, however, is that the presumption of theory distorts and obscures the nuances and complexities involved in moral considerations. Had O'Neill seen this, she would not have wanted to go beyond Winch's examples. Instead, she would have been content to wait on them.

NOTES

1. P. Winch, *The Idea of a Social Science* (London: Routledge & Kegan Paul, 1958).

2. Reprinted in P. Winch, *Ethics and Action* (London: Routledge & Kegan Paul, 1972). All references to Winch's papers are from this volume.

3. Winch, 'Understanding a primitive society', p. 9.

4. Winch, 'Moral integrity', p.191.

5. Winch, 'The universalizability of moral judgments', p.154.

6. The necessity of such connections if the word 'moral' is to mean anything is excellently brought out by Philippa Foot in 'When is a principle a moral principle?', *Proceedings of the Aristotelian Society*, supp. vol. (1954), a paper unfortunately not included in her collection, *Virtues and Vices*.

7. Winch, 'Understanding a primitive society', pp. 43–4.

8. Winch, 'Human nature', p. 77.

9. ibid., p. 82.

10. Alasdair MacIntyre, *A Short History of Ethics* (New York: Macmillan, 1966) p. 148.

11. Winch, 'Human nature', p. 80.

12. For related criticisms of MacIntyre's later work, *After Virtue* (London: Duckworth, 1981) see my Critical Notice, *Mind* vol. XCIII (1984).

13. Winch, 'Human nature', p. 84.

14. Winch, 'Moral integrity', pp. 172–3.

15. For similar criticisms see D. Z. Phillips, 'Does it pay to be good?', *Proceedings of the Aristotelian Society*, vol. LXV (1964–5).

16. Winch, 'Moral integrity', p. 175.

17. ibid., pp. 175–6.

18. ibid., p. 177.

19. ibid.

20. ibid., p. 178.

21. Winch, 'Human nature', p. 88.

22. ibid.

23. Onora O'Neill, 'The power of example', *Philosophy*, vol. 61 (Jan. 1986). All references will be to this paper. Her footnote referring to the tradition she detects reads as follows: 'A basic source for this writing is Wittgenstein's "Lectures on Ethics" which was published together with reports of conversations Wittgenstein later had with F. Waismann and Rush Rhees, *Philosophical Review*, vol. LXXIV (1965) pp. 3–12, 12–36.' Wittgenstein's discussion of examples in non-ethical contexts are also influential. In addition to the papers in Winch, op. cit., Wittgensteinian approaches to ethics include: Rush Rhees, *Without Answers* (London: Routledge & Kegan Paul, 1969); D. Z. Phillips and H. O. Mounce, *Moral Practices* (London: Routledge & Kegan Paul, 1970); R. W. Beardsmore, *Moral Reasoning* (London: Routledge & Kegan Paul, 1969); Rodger Beehler, *Moral Life* (Oxford: Blackwell, 1978); various articles in *Philosophical Investigations*, including C. Diamond, 'Anything but argument?' (1982) pp.23–41; some papers in R. F. Holland, *Against Empiricism* (Oxford: Blackwell, 1980); and some in D. Z. Phillips, *Through a Darkening Glass* (Oxford: Blackwell, 1982)

24. Winch, 'Moral integrity', p. 162.

25. ibid., p. 184.

26. ibid.

27. ibid., p. 185.

28. Winch, 'Understanding a primitive society', p. 42.

29. Winch, 'Nature and convention', p. 71.

30. Alice Monro, *Something I've Been Meaning to Tell You* (Harmondsworth: Penguin Books, 1985).

31. For a fuller discussion of this example see 'Meaning what we say' in my *From Fantasy to Faith: Philosophy of Religion and Twentieth Century Literature* (London: Macmillan, forthcoming)

32. See J. P. Sartre 'Existentialism is a humanism' in *Existentialism from Dostoyevsky to Sartre*, W. Kaufmann (ed.) (Cleveland, Ohio: World Publishing, 1956).

33. See G. E. M. Anscombe, 'Modern moral philosophy', *Philosophy* (1958).

34. R.W. Beardsmore, 'Consequences and moral worth', *Analysis*, (June 1969) p. 183, fn.

35. Winch, 'Moral integrity', p. 185.

36. ibid.

37. ibid., pp. 186–7.

38. I. Kant, *The Critique of Pure Reason*, trans. N. Kemp Smith (London: Macmillan, 1961) A 132–3/B 171–2. Quoted by O'Neill on p. 8.

39. ibid., A 134/B 173.

40. Winch, 'The universalizability of moral judgments', p. 163.

41. ibid., pp. 163–4.

42. ibid., p. 170, fn. 16.

43. Winch, 'Moral integrity', p. 191.

44. I. Kant, *Logic*, trans. Robert Hartmann and Wolfgang Schwartz (Indianapolis: Bobbs Merrill, 1974) p. 48.

45. I. Kant, *The Critique of Judgement*, trans. James Meredith (Oxford: Oxford University Press, 1978) p. 293.

46. ibid., p. 294.

47. This was one of the main themes of my collection *Through a Darkening Glass*.

47. Winch, 'The universalizability of moral judgments', p. 164.

48. ibid., p. 165.

49. ibid., p. 164.

50. ibid., p. 166.

51. ibid.

Chapter Twelve

THE FORM OF THE GOOD, TRADITION AND ENQUIRY

ALASDAIR MACINTYRE

Coleridge with characteristic exaggeration and distortion insisted that the fundamental and irreconcilable division in philosophy is between Aristotelians and Platonists. In so declaring he silently took sides – and how uncharacteristic of Coleridge to do anything silently – in another large dispute, as to whether Plato and Aristotle are better understood as having elaborated systematically rival and incompatible points of view, or whether instead Aristotle is to be recognized as having first participated with Plato in, and then continued, a shared enquiry in which the contributions of each complement as well as correct those of the other. Those who hold to the Coleridgean view are apt, for example, to emphasize in their characterization of Platonic doctrine, not only the distinction between the *eidê* and the particulars which stand in relationship to them, but the radical separateness of the latter from the former; while, when they expound Aristotle, they understand the *eidos* as exemplified in, as informing particulars, and having no existence apart from them.

What is important about the way in which they draw this type of contrast is not only the content of the theses and the arguments, which they ascribe to each philosopher, but also the degree to which in so doing they – at least from the perspective afforded by the opposing viewpoint – abstract from and thereby distort a single and continuous, even if complex, history of questions and answers, such that Aristotle could not evade either Plato's problems or the standards for evaluating successful answers to them which Plato himself had formulated. And the best way of responding to particular Coleridgean claims about Aristotle's alleged fundamental rejections of Plato's central and most distinctive positions is by retelling the relevant parts of that history. This paper constitutes just such a response to Peter Winch's, on this matter at least, Coleridgean stance in his criticism of *After Virtue*.

Winch notes correctly that I do not take Plato to be offering what he calls 'a serious rival account of morality' to that advanced by Aristotle. He goes on to quote me as saying of Plato that he accepted like every Greek – 'that the concepts of virtue and goodness on the one hand and those of happiness, success and the fulfilment of desire on the other are indissolubly linked'. Winch then comments:

> Well, yes; but Plato saw the arrangement in which they are linked in a fundamentally different way from Aristotle. MacIntyre shares Aristotle's own radical misunderstanding of Plato in this respect. Aristotle criticized the Platonic form of the 'good' on the grounds that it was not the conception of something attainable, but it was never meant to be. Rather, it was a standard against which the lives of human beings were to be judged, an object of love rather than of a satisfiable desire. Aristotle's teleological conception of practical rationality rendered him incapable of seeing Plato's point; MacIntyre shares both the conception and the incapacity.[1]

Winch thus follows Coleridge, not only in offering a confirming instance of Coleridge's dictum by subsuming his philosophical disagreements with me under the more general disagreement between Platonists and Aristotelians but also in taking Platonic views of good and of desire to be deeply at odds with those expressed by Aristotle, so that between Plato's development and Aristotle's there is radical discontinuity. Against this account I shall argue first that the contrast between love and satisfiable desire to which Winch alludes is not be found in Plato; secondly that Plato's conception of the good in the Republic is complex and that in his account of the form of the good a number of different and not clearly compatible claims are being made; and thirdly, that Aristotle in arguing against one of these is doing so, partly at least, in order to sustain and develop certain of Plato's other claims.

I

If by 'love' Winch means that of which Plato says that human beings call it *'erôs'* (*Phaedrus* 252B), then love is satisfied in the achievement of the philosophical life in company with the loved person (256A–B). In that achievement three distinguishable goods are to be discerned. There is the good of the erotic soul which has been liberated, so that *aretê* is at work within it, rather than *kakia*. There is the good of the friendship in which each sustains the other in the philosophical life. And there is the perfection of the forms, only one of which is represented by its sensible counterparts in such a way as to draw human beings towards it immediately, and that is *kallos* (249E–250D). What the relationship of the *aretê* of the soul and the happiness of the life of philosophical friendship are to the perfection of the forms is not a question directly addressed in the *Phaedrus,* although it does become clear later in that dialogue that it is only by the use of dialectic to attain knowledge both of how the unity of each form stands to the multiplicity of particulars which derive their characteristics from it, and of how each form has its place in the scheme of genus and species which orders the hierarchy of forms, that knowledge of the forms in their perfection is to be achieved (265D–266A). For an account of the relationship of the different types of good to each other we have to turn back to an earlier dialogue, the *Republic,* but before doing so, it is worth considering the way in which the doctrine of *erôs* in the *Phaedrus* is an advance upon the psychology or psychologies of the *Republic*[2] and the direction in which that advance points us.

I speak of the possibility of more than one psychology in the *Republic,* because of what some, including Hackforth, have taken to be the difference between the treatment of desire in Book IV and that in Book IX. Hackforth argued that 'In Book IV desire was restricted to the lowest part of the soul . . . . But in Book IX it was recognized that each of the three parts has its own desire, so that the real distinction becomes that of the objects respectively desired . . . .'[3] Whether or not Hackforth was right to draw this contrast and I believe that he was not, it is clear that in Book IX it is the desire for the objects of philosophical enquiry, the forms, which is satisfiable, while the desires of the tyrannical soul are unsatisfiable (579E and 586A–B). In the *Phaedrus* this multiplicity of types of desire is exhibited as a unity, the unity of *erôs*, which can be directed in different and incompatible ways by different persons, so that at one extreme it fails to be sublimated and is expressed only as bodily appetite, while at the other its sublimation redirects it to the objects of philosophy, giving to bodily appetite only what is its minimal due. It is this unity in multiplicity which is described in the myth of the two horses and the charioteer (246A–147C and 253C–256E). What matters for our present purposes is that it is just that desire which in the *Republic* is characterized as satisfiable which in the *Phaedrus* is presented as that form of *erôs* which is directed towards knowledge of the forms. Hence within Plato's account there seems to be no place for anything that is what Winch calls 'an object of love rather than of a satisfiable desire'. But this is not the only respect in which Plato's account of *erôs* suggests grounds for doubting what Winch asserts about Plato's argument concerning the form of the Good.

It is in the *De Anima* (433a 9–30, 434a 12–21) that Aristotle first poses over again the psychological problems of the *Republic* and the *Phaedrus*. And his central problem is precisely that posed in mythological terms in the *Phaedrus*: How is the difference between desires rightly directed and desires not so directed to be characterized? Notice that the move from myth to philosophy is itself the Platonic movement from picture to concept. In so moving Aristotle does not use '*erôs*' to characterize desire as such without differentiation; for that he uses '*orexis*', reserving '*erôs*' for desire for a particular loved person which includes but does not consist solely in sexual desire.[4] And while Plato in the *Republic* had used '*epithumia*' of bodily appetite, Aristotle applies '*epithumia*' to desires for what is pleasant *qua* pleasant or aversion to what is painful *qua* painful (*NE* III, 111b 16–17). Aristotle's vocabulary for desires is thus indeed different from Plato's, most notably in the way in which it involves a rejection of Plato's anticipation of Freud in taking *erôs* to be fundamental. But this should not be allowed to obscure the extent to which Aristotle uses that vocabulary to provide answers to Platonic questions.

The desire characterized in the *Phaedrus*, which will be satisfied only with the ultimate achievements which are peculiar to the philosophical life, will itself have to be informed and directed by knowledge. And when it is expressed in dispositions which issue in action, those dispositions will have to be actualized by a knowledge of the good towards which that desire moves us. In what way could such knowledge become practical and so guide particular actions? The names which Aristotle gives to such knowledge-informed desire, which is equally desire-informed knowledge, are significant: call it, he says, either *orektikos nous* or *orexis dianoêtike* (*NE* VI, 1139b 5–6). '*Nous*' is used by Aristotle to name that capacity of mind which comprehends both fundamental theoretical truths and those characteristics of particular situations which make some truth about good or goods practically relevant. Desire so informed is *prohairesis* (*NE* VI, 1139b 5–6) and *prohairesis*, so Aristotle asserts, is of what we know especially to be good, in this contrasting it with *doxa*, which does not afford such knowledge (*NE* III, 1112a 7–8).

What Aristotle thus specifies is what is needed by everyone, as Plato describes the universal human condition in Book VI of the *Republic*, where goods are concerned everyone seeks what is genuinely good and disdains *doxa* (505D–E). The verbal parallels between the two passages are close enough to be suggestive and the contrast is one and the same. But even if Aristotle was not intentionally supplying a *lacuna* in the argument of the *Republic* – for it had become clear to him that the possession of *episteme* was not sufficient to direct agents towards what is genuinely good – he was in effect doing so. Plato immediately goes on to say that the *politeia* will be perfectly ordered when one who possesses knowledge of what is good and what makes what is just and what is beautiful good is its guardian (506A–B). And for Aristotle the virtue which issues in *prohairesis, phronêsis*, is the political virtue *par excellence* (*NE* VI, 1141b 23–4). That Plato in the *Republic* does require some account of how particular judgments are possible concerning what it is good to do in particular situations, is clear from what he says about the tasks which will be undertaken by those who, after being enlightened outside the cave, return to it. But to conclude that what Aristotle supplied is what Plato's account needed does of course require argument beyond what I have given here. Nonetheless, even this outline sketch of how Aristotle's thought concerning the relationship of desire to reason is best understood as a sequel to Plato's would be open to serious challenge by someone who took Winch's view. For on that view the basic question has simply been begged so far. I have, so it might be charged, been taking it for granted in my interpretation that knowledge of the good, understood as Plato understood it, could be, or at least yield, practical action-guiding knowledge. But if Winch is correct in what he asserts about the form of the good, then my argument so far necessarily fails. I therefore turn to ask what Plato's conception of the form of the good, as presented in the Republic, in fact was.

II

Good as a form first appears in the *Republic* in the latter part of Book V (476A). But it is worth noting that the expression *eidos agathou* had already been used at the beginning of Book II (357c) with its ordinary Greek meaning of 'kind of good'. One of the notable features of Plato's linguistic usage in the *Republic* is the way in which he first introduces certain expressions in their everyday Greek use, and then makes the transition to a new use within which the original meaning is still central, but clarified, or focused, or enriched in the light of some dialectical advance. The Plato of the *Republic* uses ordinary language to correct and to subvert ordinary language. It would of course be going too far to portray him as being as self-consciously anti-Wittgensteinian as Wittgenstein was self-consciously anti-Platonic; but to say so would be to parody a truth. Other examples of this transition from everyday use in the *Republic* are the successive uses of '*philosophos*' and its cognates and, most strikingly of all, of '*dikaiosunê*'. When the word '*eidos*' is used of forms therefore, the meaning of 'kind' or 'species' is still present. To possess that knowledge of the unity underlying multiplicity which the knowledge of a form confers (476A, 507B) is to be able to classify with rational justification and indeed to be able to put such classificatory knowledge to practical use (501B). And the first of the claims that Plato makes about the form of good in the *Republic* is simply that it is a form, possessing the same properties as other forms.

However it soon becomes clear in Book VI and again in Book VII that the form of the good is a higher-order form. In what way is this so? Gerasimos Santas has argued that the form of the good stands to other forms in a way analogous to that in which those other forms stand to particulars.[5] The stages in Santas's argument are as follows. First he takes Plato in the relevant contexts to be conceiving of forms (that is, other than the form of the good) not as properties, but as ideal exemplars which are also, so he argues, epistemic paradigms. Each such form is thus the best object of its kind, in virtue of possessing a set of ideal attributes. Santas next asks in virtue of what it is that each such form possesses its ideal attributes and he answers: 'It is by virtue of participating in the Form of the Good that all the other Forms are the best objects of their kind and the best objects of their kind to know.'[6]

My inability to accept Santas's interpretation springs from two distinct sources. The *only* direct evidence cited by Santas to show that other forms participate in the form of the good is his translation of 505A: 'The greatest study is the study of the Form of the Good, by participation in which just things and all the rest become useful and beneficial.' The difficulty presented by this translation is that the word 'participation' translates nothing in the Greek. Santas has of course distinguished predecessors in construing 505A in this way and most notably James Adam whose footnote says that 'It is only by *koinônia* with the Idea of Good that *dikaia, kala* etc. became good, i.e., useful and beneficial . . . .'[7] But it is interpretation, not translation, which reads the complex notion of *koinônia* into a monosyllabic relative pronoun. If it is replied that the relevant sentence cannot be translated without an interpretation which goes beyond what the Greek actually says, then the answer must be that G. M. A. Grube's minimal expansion of the Greek is preferable: 'That the Form of the Good is the greatest object of study, and that it is by their relationship to it that just actions and the other things become useful and beneficial.'[8] Santas also claims that Plato holds as 'a general proposition' that 'It is by virtue of participation in the Form F-ness or the F that anything which is F is F' and that 505A is 'simply an instance of' this.[9] But unless there is independent justification for translating 505A as Santas does, it is question-begging to understand the relationship of the form of the good to other forms as exemplifying this general proposition.

There is a second major difficulty which arises from Santas's account. Alexander Nehamas has shown that in the *Phaedo* – and I would argue, also elsewhere – Plato's statement of the theory of forms involves him in holding that while particulars derive their characteristics, or at least those characteristics of which particulars can be and are both the instantiation and the instantiation of their opposites, forms possess their characteristics underivatively.

> For exactly the difference in the way in which tall particulars and tallness are each tall is that whereas particulars are not tall in virtue of their own nature, but in virtue of something else, to which they happen to be related . . . , tallness is tall *in virtue of being what it is*.[10]

On the view cogently argued by Nehamas the theory of forms is needed in order to explain why a certain class of particulars, those to which opposite and incompatible predicates can both be applied, have the properties that they do in the way that they do. No such need arises in the case of forms. That *their* properties are what they are does not require further explanation. And to this we may add that the perfection of a form consists simply in its having whatever property that it has *in virtue of being what it is*. There is no additional property of perfection whose presence needs to be explained by appeal to a higher-order form. Each form is what *to kalon* is described as being in the *Symposium* : *auto kath' hauto* (211B).

On these grounds Santas's account of what makes the form of the good a higher order form ought to be rejected. Why then does Plato account it a higher-order form? The answer, I want to suggest, is because of its place in the scheme of rational justification, a scheme outlined in diagrammatic form in the representation of the divided line, but also exemplified in the narrative of the conversation which constitutes the *Republic*. In that conversation the movement is first from particular examples of types of just action, in the characterization of which Socrates' interlocutors entangled themselves in contradictions, to the *logos* of *dikaiosunê* in the *polis* and in the *psychê*. At this point, at the close of Book IV, those taking part in the conversation with Socrates sound as if they believed that the challenge first posed by Thrasymachus, and then reiterated and amplified by Glaucon and Adeimantus, has been met. But this is of course not so.

The challenge was to show that justice was good both in and for itself as well as in its consequences. What had been achieved by the close of Book IV was an account of what justice is. And the analogy between the relationship of health to the body and that of justice to the soul in respect of part-whole properties had been taken by Socrates' listeners to have supplied what was required. But they had yet to learn that the required demonstration was radically incomplete. For at best the analogy between health and justice, at the point at which it was introduced, could have enjoyed no more than the status of an as yet unexamined assumption. That health and justice are similar types of good and that the goodness of justice – given that we now do have an account of what justice is – is such that it is to be valued as an end and not only as a means still have to be shown, and cannot be shown without some account of what it is for anything to be good.

Moreover, if an account of what good is to complete the enquiry embarked upon in Books I and II, then it will have to provide an unconditional first premise or set of first premises and no longer rely upon dialectically untested assumptions, as Socrates' argument plainly does until Book V. So that an account of what good is will have to provide us with just that *archê anhypotheetos* (510B, 533C) which the form of the good turns out to be. The form of the good is indeed necessary for the completion of the theory of forms, but it is also necessary for the completion of the dialectical argument of the *Republic* concerning *dikaiosunê*. And it is the way in which it completes that argument which illuminates the way in which it completes the theory of forms. Yet at this point a further difficulty has to be introduced.

The *Republic* is a book of ironies and apparent paradoxes, not all of which are dissolved on further examination. Its central seeming paradox is that those who are being introduced to the theory of forms by Socrates lack the capacity to understand adequately what they are being told. For them, as for everyone at the same stage of instruction, images and diagrams have to be used to point towards realities, the forms, of which it is an essential property that they cannot be adequately understood by images and diagrams. So the diagram of the divided line is used to make statements about what cannot be expressed in a diagram (510E–511C); so also the person who cannot as yet use dialectical reasoning adequately – and this is possible only for those with sustained education in the exact sciences and further education in dialectic itself, neither of which are possessed by Socrates' companions in the *Republic* – that person 'does not, you will say, know the good or any other good, but if he lays hold of some image of it, he does so by *doxa*, not by *epistemê,* and is dreaming and sleeping away his life . . .' (534C). So Socrates' companions, who are being introduced to the good only by images are thereby informed that they are asleep, not awake; and so are we, the readers of the *Republic.* It follows that the interpretation of what Plato is asserting about the form of the good faces one peculiar difficulty. Any interpretation by *us* which is completely lucid and precise, nonmetaphorical, framed in well analysed concepts and not in images, will necessarily be in error. A certain obscurity has to be present in the kind of account that *we* can give. (One reason why this *caveat* has not been universally observed is, I suspect, that teachers of philosophy too often assume that when they read the *Republic* they are entitled to identify themselves with Socrates or even with the fully educated guardian; a wiser interpretative strategy is to take oneself to be lucky if one can identify with Adeimantus.) With the caution induced by this consideration we can nonetheless now proceed to catalogue the characteristics and functions ascribed by Plato to the form of the good.

Three have already been noticed. It is to explain the unity underlying the multiplicity of goods of every kind; it is to provide an unconditional first principle or set of first principles by appeal to which the tasks of rational justification can be brought to completion; and it is in particular to provide a justification for judging which particular actions or experiences or states of affairs are good. Were it not able to provide the last of these, the knowledge of it could not inform the judgments and actions of those who return to the cave in order to bring their philosophical knowledge to bear upon the practical affairs of the world (519D–520D; see also again 506A–B).

So no rational theoretical or practical enquiry can terminate with an account of one of the lower-order forms; and it is precisely in this respect that they are lower-order. It is only in the light afforded by the form of the good, only though arguments which first ascend through dialectical questioning to the first principles which the form of the good provides, and then move deductively downwards to reveal in respect of the lower-order form the unconditional foundation for what had originally been only hypotheses, that knowledge of the lower-order forms is vindicated as genuine knowledge and the status of these forms as possessing *ousia* is vindicated. So the form of the good is not itself to be identified with the truth or knowledge which it alone produces (509A, 517C), nor does it exist at the level of the *ousia* of which it is the source, but it itself in worth and power transcends the realm of *ousia* (509B). All the forms are intelligibles, unities underlying the multiplicity of sensibles; the form of the good is the ultimate intelligible. (Only the person who sees and recognizes the form of the good benefits from the truth and *nous* which it produces and is able to act *emphronôs* in private or in public (517C).)

So far matters are perhaps not too obscure; but while I am fully prepared to argue that Plato means and says what I have so far ascribed to him, I have also to allow that he certainly means and says more than this and more that is obscure. In elucidating the parable of the cave at 517C the form of the good is said to be the source, not only of the intelligible, but in the visible world of light and of the source of light. Moreover, although the form of the good certainly affords knowledge of that primary conception or set of first principles, which is somehow or other an aspect of the form itself, the form of the good is more and other than this, escaping definition in any final way, no matter how far our enquiries proceed. Its partial indefinability is a matter of the good not being identifiable with any range of particular types of good and the arguments against identifying the good with pleasure or with knowledge (505B–C) are surely intended to apply not only to those examples, but also to any other similar attempts at definition.

The good thus as an object of human desire as well as in itself is far more than a source of practical knowledge. And Peter Winch's strictures upon what he takes to be Aristotelian misconceptions of Plato serve a useful purpose insofar as they remind us of this. But Winch's own view of Plato's understanding of the good is as one-sided as that which he ascribes to Aristotle. For what emerges from an adequate reading of the relevant parts of the Republic, is that Plato's view is multiform; Plato asserts both what Winch denies that he asserts, but also in key part, at least, what Winch is concerned to assert that he asserts. Plato then assigns to the form of the good a number and variety of characteristics and of functions. And what Aristotle's criticisms of Plato at this point perhaps amount to is that such a variety of characteristics and functions cannot be exhibited and discharged by a form.

That Plato himself may have moved in some measure to a

position closer to that which Aristotle was to assume is suggested not only, for example, by the *Philebus,* but also by the different and more cautiously reticent way in which some of the topics of the *Republic* are treated in the *Laws.* The word '*eidos*' is used in that dialogue for the most part in its everyday sense of 'kind', although when at 963C the four kinds of virtue ('*aretês eidê*') are spoken of, it is natural to take this as an allusion to the theory of forms, particularly since the knowledge of the unity of the virtues is to be achieved by looking from the many and dissimilar to one form (*pros mian idean* 965C) where the word '*idea*' recalls the use of that word specifically for the form of the good in the *Republic.* But Plato goes on to assert of 'what we say to be one in *andreia, sôphrosunê, dikaiosunê and phronêsis*' (and in this use of *phronêsis* instead of *sophia,* as in the *Republic,* there is clearly an anticipation of Aristotle), 'which is justly called by the one name "*aretê*"', that it still has to be enquired 'whether it is one or a whole or both or how it is by nature' (965D), thus suggesting that what is presented in the *Republic* as a set of conclusions, albeit conclusions which Socrates' companions are incapable of understanding adequately, has been transformed once again into a set of questions.

III

Aristotle was careful to distinguish (i) the good which is that towards which all things, human and nonhuman alike, direct themselves, (ii) the specifically human good, which must be a mode of life fitted to the rational contemplative and political nature of human beings, (iii) the large variety of types of good which are generally discerned by human beings – good horses, good bridles, good places and times to ride, excellence in riding and so on – and (iv) the particular goods which are identified correctly or erroneously by particular agents on particular occasions. He was therefore concerned to identify both the unity underlying the multiplicity of these last two types of use of '*agathos*' and its cognates and the part which the first and second of these play in supplying that unity. These preoccupations are plain not only in the *Nichomachean Ethics* and the *Politics,* but also in the relevant parts of the *Metaphysics* and in some of the fragments from the lost works.

What is equally plain is that in the course of these preoccupations he discovered two things. The first was that, although the concept of *eidos* was indispensable and indeed could be further developed to serve a variety of purposes, Plato's theory of forms was incapable of providing the kind of resources needed for the solution of these problems. The second was that when, having dispensed with that theory, he had supplied his own wide-ranging and compelling account of the variety of human goods and of the good, integrating into it treatments of a number of problems which Plato had explored one by one, at least one central problem which Plato had failed to solve, re-emerged still unsolved.

Aristotle had sufficient reason to reject the theory of forms in the light of his new account of the sciences and of the nature and purpose of dialectic.[11] But he had also of course found specific reasons in the course of developing his account of goods and the good for judging the theory of forms not so much false as resourceless. Two of these merit special attention. The first concerns the underlying unity of the concept of good. Aristotle recognized that the kind of unity involved in the multiplicity of goods is not that of membership of one and the same species. But the unity specified by an *eidos*, as understood in the theory of forms, is just that which belongs to members of one and same species. So the theory of forms directs our attention to the wrong kind of unity (*NE* I, 1096a 23–9; 1096b 14–26). Moreover it may in fact be that the underlying unity of good is that of 'something existing separately and independently' – such as Plato envisaged the form of the good to be – but that such a good cannot by itself explain what the good is which is to be done or attained by human beings (*NE* I, 1096b 31–5). It is not therefore that the form of the good is dismissed out of hand, as Winch's remarks suggest, but rather that Aristotle held that it cannot supply within philosophical theory the kind of account of the unity of the notion of good which is needed. And this is confirmed by the way in which it reappears in a new guise, but still as 'something existing separately and independently' in Aristotle's mature metaphysical enquiries.

There is a much-discussed problem in the *Nicomachean Ethics* about the relationship between the conception of the *telos* of human life as the *eudaimonia* of a whole life in which the political virtues are achieved, advanced in Book I, and that of the *telos* of human life as the contemplation of the unchanging and divine in Book X. What Aristotle would have said in response to such discussions, so far as they concern the respective places of contemplative and of political activity within the best kind of human life, is fairly clear from the opening paragraphs of Book VII of the *Politics*. But what the relationships are between the goodness of the divine and the goodness of the contemplation of the divine which completes the goodness of the rest of human life is a problem reserved for Book Lambda of the *Metaphysics*. And what Aristotle says there (1072a 19–1072b 30 and 1075a 11–1076a 4) is so brief and so compressed that it would be clear that Aristotle still had an unsolved problem, even if he did not go on to conclude his remarks at the end of Book Lambda by emphasizing that no account so far of the basic relationships involved is satisfactory.

It was not that Aristotle had nothing of substance to say. He had already shown that the unmoved mover both is and has a final good; and he had already first elaborated and then revised a detailed account of the relationship of particular goods to what is for human beings the good and the best. In so doing he had stated more fully and adequately than Plato what has to be related to what, the good of contemplation to the goodness of the contemplated, but in respect of the characterization of what we, unlike Aristotle, are able to call the intentionality of that relationship and in respect of the causality involved, although Aristotle has indeed made an advance on Plato in what he is able to deny and to reject, he has advanced no further in what he is able to affirm. The goodness of the final object of contemplation, whether understood as the form of the good or as the unmoved mover, remains both in itself and in its effects too obscure.

IV

There are two distinct and opposed ways of responding to the discovery of large unsolved problems within a particular philosophical system. One is to regard the presence of such problems as a symptom of the defectiveness of that system. Such was the attitude shared, for example, by seventeenth- and eighteenth-century rationalists and empiricists. A quite different attitude is that which understands the generation of such problems as a virtue, rather than a vice, a virtue in that it opens up the possibility for some new systematic statement of philosophical arguments and theses, one which will both preserve from its predecessor whatever has so far withstood the objections posed by dialectical questioning, and yet also integrate with that inheritance new conceptual resources and forms of arguments in such a way that the difficulties and *lacunae* in its predecessor, which dialectical questioning had identified, are more adequately dealt with. So the earlier system generates its successor precisely by providing it with a problematic, a set of issues and difficulties in terms of which the philosophical achievement of the successor can be initially evaluated. This is the relationship in which the work of Socrates stands to that of Plato and in which in turn Plato's dialogues stand to Aristotle's treatises; and in so standing they furnish a paradigmatic example of the genesis of a philosophical tradition.

Progress within such a tradition may take a number of very different forms and by no means only that of solving hitherto unsolved or insoluble problems. The reformulation of problems can on occasion be as important in its own way as their solution, and in that restatement it can be crucial to preserve each of the various elements which jointly constitute the problem, rather than to arrive at a premature and misguided 'solution' by discarding one of those elements. So it is with the problem of the relationship of the supreme good, existing separately and independently, to the variety of goods pursued for the sake of this and that particular end which compose the good life for human beings. If, because of failure to give an account of that relationship, the problem is 'solved' by treating one or the other of these as having exclusive title in an account of goodness, the consequences are of either of two opposing kinds, both of which impoverish our understanding of goods and the good.

Suppose, for example, that we simply eliminate from our moral theory and practice the conception of there being any such a thing as the form of the good or the goodness of the unmoved mover, so that there is no one single supreme good towards which the good and best form of human life is directed, it then becomes the case that alternative conceptions of the good life, alternative directions are available, so that what any particular person takes to be best for him or her has in key part to be determined by what he or she chooses so to regard as his or her good from the range of goods set before him or her. This is a view of the place of choice in the moral life which is not unfamiliar in some contemporary writing.[12] And it reflects the way in which a good many serious, liberal-minded inhabitants of modernity live out their lives. But it is deeply incompatible of course with the views of either Plato or Aristotle. Suppose then that instead we retain a conception of good as existing absolutely and independently and bring all our other judgments of good into alignment with that conception. The good thus conceived will have been separated from all our ordinary human purposes; it will be a conception beyond the range of the psychological concepts with which we usually comprehend actions, purposes and what we have hitherto taken to be the goods achieved or not achieved by those purposes. 'The Good has nothing to do with purposes, indeed it excludes the idea of purpose. "All is vanity" is the beginning and end of ethics. The only genuine way to be good is to be "good for nothing" . . . .' So Iris Murdoch has elaborated one version of just this kind of view. [13] But although she draws upon what Plato says about the form of the good in presenting her view, she avowedly does so selectively in denying that the good can 'be experienced or represented' and even more so, I would argue, although she might well, like Winch, disagree, in denying that the form of the good is for Plato inseparable from a teleology, which is not only exemplified in purposive seeking for the good by human beings but which has a cosmic dimension.

It is notable that so many recent attempts to re-introduce Platonic or Aristotelian theses into the debates of contemporary moral philosophy have edited out from those theses their relationship to the metaphysical theologies of Plato and Aristotle; my own work in *After Virtue* exhibits this defect to a significant degree. What is equally notable is that any fundamental questioning concerning the relationship of one standpoint to another within the ancient debates, such as that which arises from Winch's remarks, discloses the impossibility of eliminating that dimension without distortion and impoverishment. At the same time it is also clear that the metaphysical theologies of both Plato and Aristotle, very different in important respects from each

257

other as they are, are no longer susceptible of belief from any of the standpoints which compose modern culture. If it is indeed the case, as I have just suggested, that the moral philosophies of Plato and Aristotle are to a greater extent than has recently been recognized, not to be detached from those metaphysical theologies without distortion, does this mean that the project of re-engaging Plato and Aristotle in contemporary debate, except in respect of particular isolable theses, is bound to fail? There are two ways of answering this question and the difference between them exemplifies two conflicting attitudes to the relationship between philosophy and the history of philosophy.

V

All philosophical enquiry has to begin somewhere; and, like all enquiry its directedness has to presuppose some end, some ideal of achievement. If our point of entry is in the ongoing discussions of contemporary philosophy, and it seems that for most people there is no alternative to so beginning, we shall be confronted with on the one hand a set of problems and issues, on the other a set of rival and alternative theses and theories. Obvious examples of such questions are: 'Can the concept of meaning be adequately replaced by that of truth-conditions?' 'Are moral judgments necessarily prescriptive and universalizable?' and indeed 'Is a true point of beginning possible for philosophy?' Each of these questions is confronted by alternative bodies of philosophical claims, those, for example, advanced by Davidson and by Wittgenstein, by Hare and by Foot, by Husserl and by Derrida. To what are we to appeal in deciding between these rival claims? Two kinds of complementary answer are commonly offered to this question.

One refers us to certain types of philosophical principle and procedure. But either these or their application have always turned out to be susceptible of more than one interpretation. So that characteristically their invocation does not settle debates, but only alters their locus. A second type of answer refers us to the data which provide the relevant problem or issue with part, at least, of its subject-matter: standard uses of linguistic expressions, moral intuitions, what is given to consciousness by introspection and so on. But these too rarely, if ever, provide a neutral, pre-theoretical given, against which philosophical hypotheses can be tested. Once again the appeal to the data characteristically does not terminate controversy, but merely shifts its locus.

The outcome, given these characteristics of contemporary philosophy, whether analytic or in the phenomenological or postphenomenological manner, is unsurprising. It is the continuing inability of philosophers to settle any major dispute – this is not to say that genuinely illuminating conceptual analyses of particular, local issues are not achieved – an inability which interestingly, and perhaps embarrassingly coexists with strong and stable convictions as to the rightness of their own basic contentions by the various philosophical protagonists in the various debates. If this account of the state of recent philosophy is correct then those convictions can only derive at most in part from the strength of the philosophical arguments deployed in their favour, and it is legitimate to enquire what psychological and social determinants are at work in the production of such convictions. Such enquiry could with profit consider the way in which the work of Plato and Aristotle is treated when it is reintroduced into contemporary philosophical discussion.

Part of that treatment is clearly no more than a reflection of the general features of the dominant modes of philosophical discussion, above all of its piecemeal character. So Plato and Aristotle are all too often treated not as the authors of philosophical systems, albeit of uncompleted, not fully worked out systems, but as contributors of a variety of independent arguments and theses on a variety of independent and isolable issues. But there is another feature of their treatment which this does not capture, namely that exclusion from philosophical attention of their metaphysical theologies more particularly in relationship to their understanding of the good, to which I have already alluded. It is insufficient to explain this merely by remarking in the way that I did earlier upon the unacceptability of those theologies. For many now universally or almost universally unacceptable concepts and theses are not thereby excluded from philosophical attention. It is rather that the compartmentalization of philosophical issues and problems has been accompanied by an unacknowledged expulsion of certain subject-matters from the realm of serious enquiry, so that metaphysical theology as such, and not merely certain theses advanced within it, is excluded from having any substantive connection with the theory of value and morality.

It is not that metaphysical theology may not be studied by those whose private tastes so direct them; it is rather that it has been reduced in rank to an optional, marginal area of enquiry and this type of reduction in rank reflects so faithfully the privatization of theological and religious issues in the larger arenas of modern culture, that it is at least worth raising the question of whether this is not one more aspect of contemporary philosophy which has little to do with philosophy itself, but instead is socially and psychologically determined. Yet that question must wait for another occasion. What has to be asked immediately is whether there is any alternative way of understanding philosophical enquiry which will allow us to reckon with the particular arguments and theses of Plato and Aristotle as parts of systematic wholes, so that in particular the connections between their metaphysical theologies and their conceptions of human good are preserved, and so that more generally we may not insist on encountering Plato and Aristotle so exclusively in terms dictated by the contemporary condition of philosophy, rather than in terms which at least leave open the possibility that it is our modes of thought which need to be put in question rather than theirs.

There is such an alternative standpoint and it is that furnished by the conception of a philosophical tradition which I sketched earlier, in arguing for a particular conception of the relationship of Aristotle's work to Plato's. From that standpoint philosophy is essentially historical in the form of its enquiry. The standards by which successful theorizing is to be judged are set by the question of whether or not we are able to carry further or to transcend the limitations of the best work of our predecessors, including the best work of our predecessors on the question of the standards by which the best work is to be so evaluated. Philosophy conceivable and conceived in this way was first generated by Plato's relationship to Socrates and to other earlier philosophers, and I remarked in an exposition of this standpoint elsewhere[14] that it was in so relating himself to pre-Socratic philosophy that Plato both constituted philosophical enquiry and set the standards by reference to which in the end all subsequent enquiry has to be judged. More particularly, it is only insofar as Aristotle both continued, and progressed beyond the limitations of, Plato's work that most of Aristotle's own theses and arguments can be adequately understood, let alone evaluated. Hence the presentation of Aristotle's relationship to Plato as one of simple opposition in respect of alternative and incompatible views on some particular subject-matter, the kind of opposition represented by Winch's remarks, has an importance that extends beyond the particular points at issue. So in this paper I have not only wanted to contend against such a presentation that any Coleridgean antithesis between Plato's understanding of the good and Aristotle's is misconceived, but also that such a misconception reinforces a more general way of understanding the relationship of Plato's work to Aristotle's which deprives both of their due place in the development of systematic philosophical enquiry.

The unsolved problems of the relationship of the human good to the goodness of that in the contemplation of which the final human *telos* is to be found does of course still inform the philosophical tradition after Aristotle. It reappears in a series of transformed versions in Plotinus, as well as in other Neoplatonist authors, and in Augustine; and it reaches Aquinas partly by that route and partly from his own reading of Aristotle. To what extent Aquinas solves the problem and to what extent it remains unsolved is another question that must be deferred. But it is worth remarking finally that it is as a contributor to this tradition, defined in key part by the continuities informing Aristotle's relationship to Plato, that Aquinas's own theses and arguments need to be evaluated; and it is scarcely surprising that in Aquinas's account of the supreme good Platonic elements re-appear alongside Aristotelian, in a way that would scarcely be possible if Aristotle and Plato were fundamentally at odds on these matters.

VI

Philosophical enquiry, understood as the development of a tradition, has no *eschaton*. Hegel, to whom this conception of enquiry owes so much was mistaken in supposing that anyone can ever have the last word. And so, in replying to Winch, I am not foolish enough to think that there is not some important rejoinder yet to be made. But even if I were not committed to believing this on philosophical grounds, the experience of arguing against and with Winch's philosophical positions for more than thirty years, and of being educated by them both into agreement and into disagreement, should long since have been sufficient to make the point.

NOTES

1. P. Winch, 'Reconstructing a "good for man"' *Times Higher Education Supplement,* 18 September 1981.

2. See R. Hackforth, *Plato's Phaedrus* (Cambridge: Cambridge University Press, 1952) pp. 75 and 107–8; for the relationship of dialectic to eros in the *Phaedrus* see especially H. L. Sinaiko, *Love, Knowledge and Discourse in Plato* (Chicago: Chicago University Press, 1965) pp. 96–8 and 107–18

3. Hackforth, op. cit., p. 75.

4. See Glossary 'Erotic passion' in *Nicomachean Ethics,* trans. T. Irwin (Indianapolis: Indiana University Press, 1985) p. 397.

5. G. Santas, 'The form of the good in Plato's *Republic'* in *Essays in Ancient Greek Philosophy,* J. P. Anton and A. Preus. (Albany: State University of New York Press, 1983) pp. 232–63.

6. ibid., p. 240.

7. J. Adam, *The Republic of Plato,* vol. II, second edition, ed. D. A. Rees (Cambridge: Cambridge University Press, 1963) p. 51.

8. G. M. A. Grube, *Plato's Republic* (Indianapolis: Indiana University Press, 1974) p. 159.

9. Santas, op. cit., p. 234.

10. A. Nehamas, 'Predication and forms of opposites in the *Phaedo',* *The Review of Metaphysics,* vol. xxvi, no. 3 (1973) p. 479.

11. See G. E. L. Owen, 'The Platonism of Aristotle' in *Collected Papers,* ed. M. Schofield and M. C. Nussbaum (Cambridge: Cambridge University Press, 1982).

12. See Bernard Williams, 'Ethical consistency' in *Problems of the Self* (Cambridge: Cambridge University Press, 1973) and 'Conflicts of values' in *Moral Luck* (Cambridge: Cambridge University Press, 1981).

13. Iris Murdoch, *The Sovereignty of Good* (London: Routledge & Kegan Paul, 1970) p. 71.

14. In 'The relationship of philosophy to its past' in *Philosophy in History,* ed. R. Rorty, J. B. Schneewind and Q. Skinner, (Cambridge: Cambridge University Press, 1984) p. 45; see also chapter 19 of *After Virtue* (Notre Dame, second edition. Ind: University of Notre Dame Press, 1985).

Chapter Thirteen

WINCH ON THE UNITY OF WITTGENSTEIN'S PHILOSOPHY

DAN RASHID

Words are whispers and whistles,
And all made out of air,
With something else hard in them,
That makes them be.

Jane Reis

Most of Peter Winch's writings have been concerned in one way or another, with the ideas of human action and activity, especially in connection with problems concerning language and reality. These ideas give a distinctive unity to Winch's philosophical work and his treatment of the issues is clearly grounded in his understanding of Wittgenstein. What I find particularly interesting is Winch's view of the unity of Wittgenstein's philosophy. After criticizing the inadequacy of the *Tractatus* conception of action and showing that Wittgenstein's ideas outside the *Tractatus* give a quite different account that is 'quite flatly and fundamentally at variance with the whole conception of the relation between language, thought and the world, which the *Tractatus* expresses',[1] Winch nonetheless went on to deny that Wittgenstein's criticism of the *Tractatus* conception amounted to a thorough rejection.[2] I shall mainly be concerned with Winch's view of what was involved in the *Tractatus* conception, but I shall begin with a brief look at some of what Winch finds in Wittgenstein's later work.

In his studies of Wittgenstein, Winch has done as much as anyone to emphasize the fundamental role of the idea: in the beginning was the deed – *'Im Anfang war die Tat'* – in Wittgenstein's later writings. We make sense, connections between language and reality, in our shared engagement in language-games which are themselves both activities and conditioned by unreflective responses in behaviour. A philosophically interesting description of a language-game 'belongs to logic' by showing the sense we make, or fail to make, as a matter of our application of words in the context of various ways of acting and reacting. One could say that sounds or marks *do* nothing of any logical interest: nothing is said unless such otherwise non-significant items are used in a sufficiently appropriate context to do something that makes some sense.

Nor is this a matter of somehow transforming sounds or marks into meaningful linguistic expressions by doing something *to* them. You don't acquire a language-game by learning to turn scratches and noises into words, even if learning to use words as we do involves a typical range of responses to the spoken voice and the way words look when written down.

To resist the notion that significant uses of language involve the production of physical items with something *added* to give them sense, we may be reduced to the truistic: 'to say something you have to *use words*'. The point being that neither meaningless items nor meaningful words have use added to them to produce significance. For we don't use noises and scratches when we use language, though we may make plenty; yet it can't be a word that has its use added to it, for how would it be a word prior to being used?

We get away from the idea of something added if we turn to human practices and ask of them how in these particular surroundings are contrasts drawn between sense and nonsense in actual life? Not only what is sense here, but also what kind of sense it is and the difficulties to be encountered in trying to make sense in unfamiliar ways. So when we ask, on encountering some form of words, whether this is an assertion, that a contradiction, those predictions, resolves, requests, prayers etc. Winch is particularly concerned with displaying the use to which the words in question are being put: he asks how they are regarded by the speaker, how treated by his fellows, how they relate to other things said and done at different times.[3] The apparent form of the words may mislead and there may be no particular interest in what happened at the time of speaking them. How they are words at all and what kinds of words they are is shown in the language to which they belong, where this is considered as an aspect of the lives of those who speak and have spoken it. The idea that words have had their meaning added to them so that thus endowed they may now belong to a language, has no place in this approach. 'What is *the* difference between a word and a mark?' need not challenge one into giving an explanatory account even if one admits that there are occasions on which one may ask whether something is a word or a mark, or indeed mistake one for the other.

The sketch I have given so far may remind us of Winch's characteristic treatment of problems concerning 'the application of logic in language to reality'.[4] When he writes that 'truth-functional relations between propositions are not just exhibited in the things we do with marks on pieces of paper. They are exhibited in the various kinds of human activity which, *given the appropriate social context,* count as "accepting a proposition as true", "inferring one proposition from another", "making a supposition", "choosing between alternatives", and so on'[5], Winch is both expressing his own view and elucidating 'the central role which the notion of a language-game, or form of life, plays in Wittgenstein's later writings'.[6] He has the problem of explaining how Wittgenstein's *earlier* thought is different and less than adequate, given its problems, while at the same time he wishes to show the continuity of Wittgenstein's concern with just those initial problems about the nature of logic and its application to the world. How satisfactory is Winch's account?

One may think that Wittgenstein continued to ask the same questions only to answer them somewhat differently as he worked out new philosophical conceptions to replace earlier ones. So the question of the given, 'what has to be accepted' first receives the answer the Objects, the substance of the world, in the *Tractatus;* later, the answer is supposed to be forms of life.[7] Again, 'the deed' now fills the role taken in the *Tractatus* by the relation of 'Name' to 'Object'.[8] Or, 'we have to look, not for what lies hidden *beneath* our normal ways of talking, but for what lies hidden *in* our normal ways of talking.'[9]

With what confidence can one claim of such questions and roles that they are the same, rather than indicating some resemblance other than a merely verbal one? Is it clear that the words 'given' and 'hidden' are being used in the same way? I should like to bring out some of the difficulties one gets into if an exaggerated sense of the unity of Wittgenstein's philosophy makes one think of 'the shift in point of view (as) quite slight but decisive. It does not involve a complete abandonment of everything that had been said in the *Tractatus,* but rather a rearrangement of it, a setting of it in a wider context.'[10]

We need not suppose that everything said in the *Tractatus* was completely abandoned, but we may wonder just what it is that Winch claims has been rearranged. After all, he is not saying that the doctrine of the *Tractatus* was preserved intact either.[11] What confuses is the clear demonstration of the problematical nature of key ideas in the *Tractatus,* alongside an attempt to present the later criticism of the *Tractatus* as performing the main tasks of that work, only in a new direction and with unforeseen consequences. Yet if the key ideas are exposed as incoherent by later criticism, then *they* won't survive to be rearranged, even if the critic should discern some continuity between what was originally hoped for and what has now been achieved. Only, this kind of unity cannot now be regarded as that of different works with some common content, for what the author of the *Tractatus* may have wanted to do cannot be identified with what is said in that work.

Consider what one may discover with hindsight about the notion of the elementary proposition in the *Tractatus.* Its elements, Names, connect with or correlate with their meanings, the Objects to which they refer: 'The Name means the Object. The Object is its meaning' (*TLP* 3.203). This is just what a Name does and we cannot ask how the correlation is made. Were we to conduct a complete analysis, the elementary propositions reached would display such correlations in the arranged Names. Winch notes that 'an elementary proposition is one in which the connection of names with each other and with their objects is immediately 'shown'.[12] He argues that there can be no such proposition since 'these connections are displayed not in the proposition itself, but in what *surrounds* it, in the grammar according to which the words in it are applied'.[13]

What is meant by 'these connections'? One may suppose that just those connections between Tractarian Names and Objects are displayed in grammar rather than in elementary propositions. But while Winch has indeed argued elsewhere that a Name's meaning an Object is a matter of its syntactical role in a symbolism, that view is put forward as the doctrine of the *Tractatus* itself.[14] As long as one does not suppose 'that a name's meaning is something other than and prior to its logico-syntactic role'[15] one may accept the *Tractatus* use of the term 'object' without taking 3.203 as the last word on a relationship between a linguistic and a non-linguistic item. At worst, talk of 'objects' might introduce some misleading imagery, but Winch's only complaint is against an exegesis that regards Objects as providing a metaphysical underpinning to language by transferring their powers of combination to their representatives, Names.

In the earlier essay, however, Winch attacks the notion of an Object: 'the Tractarian objects are quite unnecessary, an idle wheel, the intrusion of which is masking the true workings of the mechanism'.[16] It is in recognition of this that he goes on to say that 'All that is necessary for me to be able to say something is that the words I use should be applied in accordance with their grammar'.[17] And it is this *contrast* between meaning an Object and having a significant use that enables him to attack the idea of an elementary proposition. So the only connections shown by grammar will be those which give my *words* sense, whatever kinds of words they may be. There is no longer a focus on names, never mind on simple signs that stand in for simple objects. Name-Object and Name-Name connections perish with the elementary proposition.

Further, the elementary proposition 'must be one which of itself guarantees how it is to be taken, and no such proposition can be formulated'.[18] Winch remarks that this 'was not *clearly* seen in the *Tractatus*' without himself indicating where in the *Tractatus* Wittgenstein shows the slightest worry that such central conceptions are even suspect. For all his emphatic insistence on what cannot be said but only shown, Wittgenstein in the *Tractatus* could hardly have welcomed the result that elementary propositions cannot be put into words, for nothing else could then be said either by their truth-functions. His entire theory of language would have collapsed.

Some of the trouble seems to come from not being clear enough about what Objects were supposed to do and how, in providing the world with a fixed form, they were thought to guarantee the possibility of making sense through the making of pictures of facts. Unless considered as a projection, a picture itself is just an arrangement of elements, simply another fact. Only if those elements correlate with elements of reality will their arrangement represent another possible state of affairs. If we imagine the picture-elements making contact with their meanings along certain lines of projection, Winch protests that 'the *lines* of projection don't do what is required of them; they only function in the context of a *method* of projection'.[19] While Wittgenstein used the image of a ruler to explain representation, he failed to see the importance of the activity of measuring which makes it possible to consider the lines on a piece of wood as a scale and wrote as if the lines themselves did the crucial work. Winch comments that if I suppose that the lines of projection carry all the weight in establishing the correlation between name and object, then it will appear to me that I have got to have the object clearly in view before I can draw the lines. But once I see that it is the method of projection which is important, then I can say that 'the object drops out of consideration as irrelevant'.[20]

It is from this that Winch infers that Tractarian Objects are quite *unnecessary*, as if showing that the lines get their importance only in the context of a method were the same as revealing that neither they nor the objects they reach have any role whatsoever. This confuses the sound point that whether something is measured is a matter of the application of an appropriate technique, it being irrelevant to this just what length or distance is in question, with the idea that it is idle to introduce consideration of something that is being measured. I may say: measure what you like, the important thing is your being able to use the instrument. But I cannot add: there being anything to measure is unnecessary. All that would be unnecessary would be a specification of *which* lengths are to be determined. The acquisition and application of methods requires that there being things to measure be given as necessary, however awkward it may be to put the given into words.

Winch is closest to this aspect of the *Tractatus* conception of an Object when he writes:

In the Tractatus what has to be accepted, the given is the object (sic), the substance of the world, what is unchangeable and fixed. Given that objects are what they are, a certain mode of projection will be needed if we are to name one and use the name in propositions.[21]

He notes that 'in *Philosophical Investigations* the order of priorities is reversed. What sort of object pain is is determined by the way we use the word "pain": *in* that use we see the kind of relation between name and object that is here in question and there is nothing more to say about the object than we can say in our descriptions of the use of the word.'[22]

One might agree that Wittgenstein came to think that there was nothing for a philosopher to say about pain, say, that was not a grammatical remark about the word 'pain',[23] but can we ascribe this doctrine to the *Tractatus* as Winch does without further comment? If the *Tractatus* does embrace such a doctrine, how has the order of priority been reversed? How come there are no descriptions of our ordinary use of words, and what should we make of the explicit denial that there is any saying something about an Object? 'Objects I can only *name* .'[24]

To speak of 'the big difference' in the *Philosophical Investigations* as being in the kind of 'description' sought, does indeed make the shift in Wittgenstein's point of view 'quite slight' but not nearly decisive enough. Certainly, there is no longer any question of a search for elementary propositions hidden beneath our normal ways of talking, it being just those ways that are now to be described, but elementary propositions were never conceived of as 'descriptions of Objects': 'A proposition can only say *how* a thing is, not *what* it is.'[25]

There is of course the objection that one cannot use the example of pain and 'pain' to display an Object-Name relation, albeit with order of priority reversed, since, prior to analysis into elementary propositions, we are not at the level of *simple* things and signs which the *Tractatus* makes fundamental. While this is true, one can hardly be blamed for not employing actual examples of simple elements of reality and language since Wittgenstein himself could not find a single convincing example. A more serious criticism is that Winch confuses matters in his discussion of whether and how 'pain' is 'the name of an object' by introducing the *Tractatus* notion of a simple, unalterable element of reality and then suggesting we see the kind of relation between name and object revealed in the use of the *word* 'pain'. Yet, not only does our pain-language involve all sorts of other words, why should we suppose that an examination of the word 'pain' itself shows anything about the *name* of an object even in some non-

Tractarian, non-technical sense? It is as if we were to say: 'pain' may not be a Name deputizing for an Object, but let the use teach us how the name does relate to its object. Which leaves it unclear when we are to count a use of the word as the use of a name and what would be added by calling it a, or the, name of an object.[26]

Should one reply that whether we (sometimes) call 'pain' a name or not is of little philosophical interest so long as our pain-language is clear to us, particularly in its resistance to that model of Object and Name which turns out to leave no role for an indescribable object,[27] then the *Tractatus* model comes in for decisive rejection and the unity that Winch attempts to establish is as elusive as before. And if the rejection is on the grounds, not that the model of Name and Object cannot be extended to cases like pain, but that it lacks any application since Objects would be idle wheels whether thought of as 'private' *or* 'public', any case for the view that *Tractatus* doctrine in this area survives with modifications in a wider setting, becomes considerably weakened. It remains puzzling how Winch could have allowed the idea of a 'method of projection' first to convince him that Tractarian Objects are unnecessary, since sense is a matter of applying words in accordance with grammatical rules, and then to reintroduce them, with the illustration of pain, apparently with some role to play, only not now that of 'what has to be accepted, the given', the utterly simple, and so on.

A complication arises from the occurrence of the expression 'method of projection' in the *Tractatus* itself where at 3.11 we are told that the perceptible propositional sign, spoken or written, is used as a projection of a possible state of affairs by the proposition's sense being thought.[28] Until it projects a state of affairs by having that sense thought through it, the propositional sign has no sense to show and it says nothing either. Even the sign as projection, the proposition, does not yet *contain* its sense though it is already a possible expression of that sense. But it is also a possible expression of any other sense of the same form, so the definite sense that it does show, more or less clearly, has to enter it from elsewhere. Its sense is the sense it is filled with by a particular thought, the thought being that particular one by virtue of the state of affairs it is a thought of. The possibility of a standing in relation R to b is contained in the thought that aRb, and whatever contains that sense is necessarily just that thought.

Further, the objects of the thought, a and b, appear quite transparently in it, however disguised they may be when the thought is expressed in a sign of the form xRy but which also possesses extraneous features and might anyway have been used as a projection of c being R to d. When the proposition expressing the thought is itself made transparent by removing everything except those sign-elements that correspond to the objects of the thought, then and only then would one have arrived at Names arranged in elementary, completely analysed, propositions.[29] Yet prior to the undertaking of any such analysis and a condition of its possibility, is the definite sense contained unambiguously in one's thought, where simple Objects are simply meant by simple thought-elements.[30]

The paraphrase and expansion offered here of the Tractarian sections concerning thoughts may not explain how a propositional sign can be used as a projection of a possible state of affairs, but I have tried to show how vitally important Wittgenstein seems to have considered thinking a determinate sense as the only method of projection by which language is made possible: unless I *mean* just this configuration of these objects in my thought, I cannot *use* a sensibly perceptible sign to represent just *this* state of affairs. So the sign-elements must have added to them both elements of reality and thought-elements which are intrinsically related before the signs can be used to represent in some particular way. For unless the thought element 'a' in the thought that aRb just meant the Object a, one could ask what one meant by *'a' in that thought,* which is absurd since there is no intelligible alternative for 'a' in aRb to mean. In contrast, it may be intelligibly asked of a sign both what it means, if anything, and how it is used in a symbolism that may be more or less perspicuous.[31]

While there is a contrast between arrangements of signs which have sense and others that do not, the former expressing thoughts and the latter not, one cannot distinguish thoughts that make sense *from those that do not*: 'we cannot think anything unlogical'.[32] A piece of nonsense may be saved by giving a meaning to a sign so that a thought is now expressed; there is no such thing as saving a thought by giving an element a meaning. Neither thoughts nor their elements are given meanings, we neither construct them nor use them. The idea seems to be that unless we just *have* thoughts, the language in which we use signs to make pictures of possible states of affairs would itself not be possible. Once language is possible so is analysis, for 'the possibility of propositions is based upon the principle of the representation of objects by signs'.[33] But elementary propositions are less basic than the thoughts they may express and the simple signs it is possible to reach at the end of analysis are parasitic upon the elements of thought and reality between which the fundamental representing relations already hold. If no thoughts were ever expressed they would still be logical pictures; even if none were thought, Objects would still form the substance of any possible world.

It may be mistaken then to place the emphasis Winch does on elementary propositions and their constituent Names, though it is surely right to give the idea of 'the last interpretation' a fundamental role in the *Tractatus* even if, on the account I have presented, it is in the thought and only secondarily in the elementary proposition that the relations between Objects and their representatives are absolutely '*fest*'.[34] The reason one cannot suppose the order of priority between Objects and Names to be reversed is that Objects are supposed to be unconditionally given for any world, including one in which thought and language are mere possibilities, while Names may remain possible end-products of analysis even when thought and language exist. Reversing the order of priority abolishes the indestructible Objects to leave only 'objects of comparison': 'What looks as if it *must* exist belongs to language.' There is nothing metaphysical about an instrument of our language, such paradigms can come and go.[35] Their names become signs actually used in some particular language-game(s) rather than theoretical elements of any symbolism.

One can also agree with Winch's reference to the idea of an 'inner process': 'we are constantly under the temptation to think that there *must* be such a process if there is ever to be such a thing as thinking about something, or saying that something is the case. And this temptation is the very same temptation as that which led Wittgenstein to talk about "elementary propositions" in the *Tractatus*.[36] Yet just because thinking that p and saying that p are treated so differently in the *Tractatus,* it is not the elementary proposition whose 'existence guarantees that something definite has been said'. What stands alone and shows its sense through the immediate correlation of its constituents with objects is again the thought which confers derivative sense on any elementary proposition in which it may be expressed.

With this qualification Winch's point is strengthened for, as he has himself pointed out,[37] logical analysis does not move in the direction of the inner, or the mental; it is supposed to result in propositions, which have so far been hidden, but not in something hidden beneath or within any proposition. In producing elementary propositions, analysis reveals the *form* of the thought which the original unanalysed proposition disguised. But the best candidate for the hidden 'inner process' is the occurrence of the thought itself which gives analysis its point by revealing its form in elementary propositions presented in an adequate symbolism.

Winch ends his essay by quoting *Zettel* 211:

> In philosophy one is in constant danger of producing a myth of symbolism, or a myth of mental processes. Instead of simply saying what anyone knows and must admit.

My reservations about the idea that there is a unity to Wittgenstein's philosophy along the lines that Winch emphasizes come from what I take to be a failure to consider Objects and Thoughts in a way that brings out how deeply embedded and entwined together such myths are in the *Tractatus* attempt to show what must be presupposed and added if our words are to make sense.

NOTES

1. 'Wittgenstein's treatment of the will' in *Ethics and Action* (London: Routledge & Kegan Paul, 1972) p. 110.

2. See Winch's introductory essay 'The unity of Wittgenstein's philosophy' in P. Winch (ed.) *Studies in the Philosophy of Wittgenstein* (London: Routledge & Kegan Paul, 1969).

3. See for example, 'Im Anfang war die Tat', 'Darwin, Genesis and contradiction', and 'Meaning and religious language' in his collection *Trying to Make Sense* (New York: Blackwell, 1987).

4. 'The unity of Wittgenstein's philosophy' p. 2.

5. ibid., pp. 8, 9.

6. ibid., p. 8.

7. ibid., p. 19.

8. 'Im Anfang war die Tat' in *Trying to Make Sense*, p. 53

9. 'The unity of Wittgenstein's philosophy' p. 19.

10. ibid.

11. ibid., p. 17. Winch's remarks on there being 'differences between what stating a fact amounts to in one sort of example and what it amounts to in other cases' distinguish him sharply from a view such as Kenny's according to which *Philosophical Investigations* contains the *Tractatus* picture theory.

12. ibid., p. 14.

13. ibid.

14. See 'Language, thought and world in *Tractatus*' in *Trying to Make Sense*.

15. ibid., p. 10. Winch does not distinguish the signs that are actually used in a symbolism from the simple signs with which the former could be replaced in logical analysis. Prior to analysis we do not have Names to use and if we should ever find any it is not clear what using them would be. Any Name is 'used' as a deputy for an Object, but that is not what Winch requires with his notion that Names have syntactical roles the description of which reveals the Objects meant.

16. 'The unity of Wittgenstein's philosophy' p. 13.

17. ibid., pp. 13, 14.

18. ibid., p. 15.

19. ibid., p. 13.

20. ibid., p. 13.

21. ibid., p. 19.

22. ibid., p. 19.

23. L. Wittgenstein, *Philosophical Investigations;* 281 shows that such an agreement would be overhasty; 281 is about pain but not the word 'pain'.

24. L. Wittgenstein, *Tractatus Logico-Philosophicus*, 3.221.

25. ibid., 3.221.

26. 'The unity of Wittgenstein's philosophy' includes the remark: 'What we have to recognize is that there is *no* language-game the philosophically puzzling aspects of which will be illuminated simply by saying that it involves the use of a name to refer to an object' (p. 18). I find it strange that Winch should then have proceeded to speak of pain and 'pain' in terms of object and name.

27. *Philosophical Investigations* 293 makes it clear that Wittgenstein is rejecting that model, where all the 'Object' has is its 'Name', rather than modifying it to fit cases of the expression of sensations.

28. 'Language, thought and world in *Tractatus*' shows that Winch reads 3.11 quite differently as if the phrase 'method of projection' were introduced to explain what thinking is. I am not at all clear how it would do so but in any case Wittgenstein does not need to give an explanation of thinking the sense here since he has already done so in 3 (The logical picture of the facts is the thought). It is the idea of projection, first mentioned in 3.11, that needs explanation. Winch is arguing that the term 'thought' is a logical one, which is true, for Wittgenstein has not drawn it from empirical psychology and is attempting to give the logic of

representation. But one can be interested in the logical relations between
the appropriate mental processes, which look as if they have to do what
words alone could never do, and the words that enable thoughts to be
perceived by the senses, without ceasing to think of thought-processes as
mental. 'The idea of an uncorporeal occurrence which lends life and
sense to speaking' (*Philosophical Investigations,* 339) is a philosophical one,
as is the idea of the mental which is essentially related to its object: 'This
queer thing, thought' is supposed to enable the use of mere signs as
projections of states of affairs because it, somehow, 'deals with the very
object *itself*' (*Philosophical Investigations* 428).

I see no reason for supposing, as Winch does, that Wittgenstein's reply
to Russell's query concerning the constituents of a thought applies only to
unexpressed thoughts. Though Wittgenstein's 'explanation' is not terribly
helpful, it does clearly show his philosophical conception of thoughts as
mental structures. The empirical details do not interest the logician, what
matters is there having to be such phenomena constituting a special sort of
language if language in the usual sense is to be possible, so the mental
what-nots are supposed to be *like* words and yet without them ordinary
words would signify nothing. See *Notebooks: 1914–16,* p. 130.

29. *Tractatus* 3.2.

30. So thought-elements cannot ever be identical with words, however
word-like they may be. It is striking that Wittgenstein never speaks of
undertaking the analysis of thought into 'elementary-thoughts' consisting
entirely of arranged simple thought-elements. With thought, the
elements are already there simply meaning their objects. Unless this is
presupposed, there can be no such thing as the completely analysed
proposition in which there would be just as many signs as the Objects
meant by the thought-elements. Thoughts require no 'analysis' since
their elements already must be as simple as any simple signs analysis of
propositions might provide. One might, however, speak of 'the inner
process of analysis' presupposed by the *Tractatus* view of understanding
language. For a thorough treatment of these matters see Norman
Malcolm's *Nothing is Hidden* (Oxford: Blackwell, 1986).

31. On my reading this would not apply to simple signs.' On Winch's,
the use of Names can be described just as much as the use of any other
signs in a symbolism for he takes 'having a meaning' as equivalent to
having a use or syntactical role. Yet a logical constant would have a role in
a calculus, only not that of standing in for a *Bedeutung* as a Name does.

32. See the Preface to the *Tractatus* which envisages a boundary to the
expression of thoughts in words, with nonsensical combinations of words
as the other side of the boundary, but cannot apply the idea to thoughts
themselves.

33. *Tractatus* 4.0312.

34. 'The unity of Wittgenstein's philosophy' p. 10.

35. See *Philosophical Investigations.* 55–9.

36. 'The unity of Wittgenstein's philosophy', p. 11.

37. 'Language, thought and world in *Tractatus*', pp. 15–16.

MAIN PUBLICATIONS

OF PETER WINCH

(Those publications marked with an asterisk are reprinted in *Ethics and Action,* London: Routledge & Kegan Paul, 1972.)

1952 'The notion of "suggestion" in Thomas Reid's theory of perception', *Philosophical Quarterly* .

1955 'Contemporary British philosophy and its critics', *Universities Quarterly* .

— 'Necessary and contingent truths', *Analysis.*

1956 'Social science', *British Journal of Sociology* .

1957 'The universities and the state', *Universities Quarterly.*

1958 *The Idea of a Social Science and its Relation to Philosophy* (London and New York: Routledge & Kegan Paul). Translations published in Portuguese, German, Italian, Spanish, Finnish, Icelandic, Japanese, Danish, and Dutch.

1959 'Authority', *Proceedings of the Aristotelian Society* (Supplementary volume). Reprinted in A. Quinton (ed.) *Political Philosophy* (Oxford: Oxford University Press).

* 1960 'Nature and convention', *Proceedings of the Aristotelian Society.*

1962 'The logic of social inquiry', *History and Theory.*

1964 'Mr. Louch's idea of social science', *Inquiry.*

*— 'Understanding a primitive society', *American Philosophical Quarterly.* Reprinted in D. Z. Phillips (ed.) *Religion and Understanding;* in B. R. Wilson (ed.) *Rationality* (Oxford: Blackwell, 1970).

* 1965 'The universalizability of moral judgments', *The Monist.*

* 1966 'Can a good man be harmed?', *Proceedings of the Aristotelian Society.*

* 1968 'Moral integrity', Inaugural Lecture, University of London, King's College (Oxford: Blackwell).

* 1969 'Wittgenstein's treatment of the will', (*Wittgenstein Über* *den Willen*), *Ratio*. Reprinted in T. Honderich (ed.) *Philosophy Through its Past* (Harmondsworth: Penguin Books, 1984).

— *Studies in the Philosophy of Wittgenstein*, ed. and Introduction 'The unity of Wittgenstein's philosophy' (London: Routledge & Kegan Paul). Translated into Spanish.

1970 'Psychiatry' in *Morals and Medicine* (London: BBC Publications).

— 'Understanding and explanation in sociology and social anthropology' in R. Borger and F. Cioffi (eds) *Explanation in the Behavioural Sciences* (Cambridge: Cambridge University Press). Translated into German.

*— 'Human nature' in *The Proper Study* (London: Macmillan).

* 1971 'Ethical reward and punishment', *The Human World*.

— Ihminen ja Yhteiskunta Hobbesin ja Rosseaun Mukaan', *Sosilogia*.

*— 'Trying and attempting', *Proceedings of the Aristotelian Society* (Supplementary volume).

1972 *Ethics and Action* (London: Routledge & Kegan Paul).

— 'Authority and rationality', *The Human World*.

1974 'Popper and scientific method in the social sciences' in A. Schipp (ed.) *The Philosophy of Karl Popper* (New York: Open Court).

1975 'Teleological explanation' in S. Korner (ed.) *Explanation* (Oxford: Blackwell).

1976 'Language, belief and relativism' in H. D. Lewis (ed.) *Contemporary British Philosophy*, Fourth Series (London: Allen & Unwin).

1977 'Meaning and religious language' in S. Brown (ed.) *Reason and Religion*, (Ithaca, New York: Cornell University Press). Reprinted in *Trying To Make Sense* (Oxford, and New York: Blackwell, 1987).

— 'Causality and action' in R. Tuomela (ed.) *Essays on Explanation and Understanding* (Dordrecht and New York: Reidel).

1978 Introduction to H. Price (ed.) *Simone Weil: Lectures on Philosophy*, (Cambridge: Cambridge University Press).

— Translation of Wittgenstein's 'Cause and effect: intuitive awareness', *Philosophia* (vol. 6, nos 3–4).

—   'Le Nécessaire et Le Bien' in G. Kahn (ed.) *Simone Weil Philosophe, Historienne et Mystique* (Paris: Aubier Montaigne).

1979 'Apel's transcendental pragmatics' in S. Brown (ed.) *Philosophical Disputes in the Social Sciences* (Brighton: Harvester Press).

1980 *Culture and Value* (Translation of Wittgenstein's *Vermischte Bemerkungen*) (Oxford: Blackwell).

1980 'Eine Einstellung zur Seele', Presidential address to Aristotelian Society. Reprinted in *Trying To Make Sense* (Oxford and New York: Blackwell, 1987).

1981 'Im Anfang war die Tat' in I. Block (ed.) *Perspectives on the Philosophy of Wittgenstein* (Oxford: Blackwell). Reprinted in *Trying To Make Sense* (Oxford and New York: Blackwell, 1987).

1982 'Ceasing to exist', Lecture to the British Academy (Oxford: Oxford University Press). Reprinted in *Trying To Make Sense* (Oxford and New York: Blackwell, 1987).

—   'Text and context', *Philosophical Investigations.* (January). Reprinted in *Trying To Make Sense* (Oxford and New York: Blackwell, 1987).

1985 'True or false', *Inquiry* (vol. 31).

1989 *Simone Weil: The Just Balance* (Cambridge: Cambridge University Press).

INDEX